★ ★ ★ ★ ★ ★ ★

WITHIN ARM'S LENGTH

DAN EMMETT

★ ★ ★ ★ ★ ★ ★

WITHIN ARM'S LENGTH

A Secret Service Agent's Definitive Inside Account of Protecting the President

ST. MARTIN'S PRESS NEW YORK

 Printed in the United States of America. For information, address St. Martin's Press, 175 Fifth Avenue, New York, N.Y. 10010.

www.stmartins.com

Library of Congress Cataloging-in-Publication Data

Emmett, Dan, 1955–
Within arm's length : a secret service agent's definitive inside account of protecting the president / Dan Emmett.
pp cm
ISBN 978-1-250-04471-6 (hardcover)
ISBN 978-1-4668-4317-2 (e-book)
1. Emmett, Dan, 1955– 2. United States. Secret Service—Officials and employees—Biography. 3. Presidents—Protection—United States. I. Title.
HV7911.E46A3 2014
363.28'3092—dc23
[B]

2013046361

St. Martin's Press books may be purchased for educational, business, or promotional use. For information on bulk purchases, please contact Macmillan Corporate and Premium Sales Department at 1-800-221-7945, extension 5442, or write specialmarkets@macmillan.com.

First Edition: June 2014

10 9 8 7 6 5 4 3 2 1

★

This book is dedicated to the 29 men and women of the United States Secret Service killed in the line of duty, and to the men and women of the Central Intelligence Agency killed in action, represented by 107 stars on the wall at Langley.

★

Contents

★

The Man in the Arena

It is not the critic who counts; not the man who points out how the strong man stumbles, or where the doer of deeds could have done them better. The credit belongs to the man who is actually in the arena, whose face is marred by dust and sweat and blood; who strives valiantly; who errs, who comes short again and again, because there is no effort without error and shortcoming; but who does actually strive to do the deeds; who knows great enthusiasms, the great devotions; who spends himself in a worthy cause; who at the best knows in the end the triumph of high achievement, and who at the worst, if he fails, at least fails while daring greatly, so that his place shall never be with those cold and timid souls who neither know victory nor defeat.

—*President Theodore Roosevelt*

★

Preface

When the staff of St. Martin's Press offered me the opportunity to write a revised edition of *Within Arm's Length,* I was thrilled. Not only would I have the opportunity to write for a prestigious publishing house, but I would also have the chance to take the many comments from readers about my first book and incorporate them into a more detailed, expansive work about my life and career in the Secret Service and the Central Intelligence Agency (CIA).

One constant question from readers has been: What does the title of the book actually mean? The answer is simple. "Within arm's length" is the Secret Servcie doctrine that proclaims that, for an agent to properly protect the president, he must be literally within arm's length of that president. Any greater distance between president and agent will render the agent incapable of effectively responding to an attack. During my career, I had the honor of being within arm's length of three sitting presidents. I felt this title to be the most appropriate of all those considered.

Those who read the first edition of *Within Arm's Length* will find that the stories within have been greatly expanded here, with much new material included. I believe that those interested in the Secret Service and the CIA and in what life is like inside these agencies will find that this edition is in essence a new book, not merely a rehash of an earlier work.

I ended the previous version with my retirement from the Secret

Service and my entry into the CIA. In the last chapter, I wrote that my CIA experience would be a story for another time. That time is now.

In these pages I have included much information about my entry into the CIA subsequent to my Secret Service retirement and how that experience came to pass. Unfortunately, due to the nature and details of my work at the CIA, not as much can be written as I would like—but that is the intelligence business. For the majority of my time at the CIA, I was a member of the National Clandestine Service, formerly the Directorate of Operations. As such, the most interesting details of my work there remain classified.

Still, I have included stories from my six years with the CIA that will perhaps provide the reader with a snapshot into a world where relatively few have been. Given these limitations, this book is primarily about the life of a Secret Service agent and the events that led to my being selected as a member of America's most elite law enforcement agency.

Due to the complexities of both the culture and the mission of the Secret Service, presenting an account of a Secret Service agent's life and career is a daunting task. In these pages you will share in the long and frustrating process of applying to be an agent; the excitement of executing search and arrest warrants in the worst sections of New York City; the feeling of apprehension I experienced while running alongside the president of the United States through downtown Washington, DC, during morning rush hour, when an assassination would have been quite easy. I will take you to some of the most dangerous places in the world, such as the demilitarized zone between North and South Korea, as the president stands on a bridge separating the two countries, in plain view of unpredictable, heavily armed North Korean soldiers. You will share in the unique experience of flying aboard Air Force One and feel the awesome responsibility of driving the president of the United States in an armored limousine. There are also some humorous moments, as being a Secret Service agent is far from all work and no play.

No former agent has ever written about most of these topics in any detail, although non-agents have published things that perhaps should not have been made public. Few of these books include any new material regarding what it really means to be a Secret Service agent; none captures the unique culture of the organization.

Some recent books about the Secret Service are so-called tell-all works that do nothing more than rehash boring old stories about the people protected by the Secret Service. Others potentially place a strain on the trust that is essential between agent and president. Any president of the United States should feel confident that private matters will be kept in confidence forever, even after the president's death. Betrayal of this confidence can turn to danger if the president feels he cannot trust the Secret Service to be discreet. A president then begins to create too large a buffer between himself and the Service, thus making himself more difficult to protect.

The first word in "Secret Service" is, of course, "Secret." What you will not read about in this book are the detailed methods and tactics utilized by the Secret Service to protect the president. There is no classified or "for official use only" (FOUO) information regarding the White House security procedures or weapons and training such as has been broadcast in television specials over the years. While some individuals I protected during my career will be mentioned in the context of general anecdotes, I have told no out-of-school stories. This book is about the Secret Service as my colleagues and I viewed it from the trenches and about some of the experiences of a working-level Secret Service agent who held several positions in the organization.

I have not attempted to portray the Service or its agents larger or brighter than they actually are; nor have I attempted to vilify the Service or anyone in it. The picture presented here is authentic and accurate. Regardless of what literary critics may say, I believe my writing will be judged as factual and fair by the ultimate critics: those who served with me and knew the Service as I did during the period from 1983 through the George W. Bush presidency.

★ ★ ★ ★ ★ ★ ★

WITHIN ARM'S LENGTH

★

Prologue

All Secret Service agents, and especially those assigned to the Presidential Protective Division, constantly live with the reality that their lives can be exchanged at any time for that of the president. That reality permanently resides in the back of an agent's mind, where it is not dwelled upon, yet is always present. In every Secret Service agent's career, however, there are incidents that bring this reality home. These incidents remind agents that their lives are never truly their own but belongs to the United States and the office of the presidency. In short, Secret Service agents are expendable in all matters related to protecting the president.

During one such incident, as with many others during my twenty-one-year career, I was reminded of this reality. My assignment was to prepost in a room with President Bill Clinton, where he was to meet with Syrian dictator Hafez al-Assad. My express purpose for being in the room was not to cover and evacuate the president in the event of an attack but rather to neutralize any threat to POTUS (the president of the United States) regardless of who posed the threat. Literally translated, that meant kill the Syrian bodyguards if they drew their weapons for any reason. I suppose I should have been flattered to be chosen for such an assignment, but I realized that if I did have to shoot the Syrians, like them, I would in all liklihood be experiencing the last day of my life.

Prior to entering the room with President Clinton and Assad, I took a few seconds to think of my wife and family. I said a quick prayer to the effect that, if called upon to kill the Syrians, I would do it with maximum efficiency and President Clinton would survive even if I did not. As my prayer ended, I was filled with a single-minded resolve bordering on calm rage. No matter what, I would carry out my assignment to the utmost of my abilities, and, true to my former training as a marine, I would accomplish the mission at all cost. Then it was game time.

As directed, I preposted in the conference room, and as President Clinton and Assad entered, so did their security details. I made eye contact with the Secret Service shift leader and we exchanged looks of understanding that the situation was one that was being controlled by the Secret Service, not the Syrians.

As I slowly moved behind Assad's men to gain the best possible firing position, I noticed from the imprint of their tight-fitting suit coats that these men were carrying Skorpion machine pistols. I knew the Skorpion well and had fired it during terrorist weapons familiarization training. As a result of this excellent training, I not only knew what type of weapon the Syrians were carrying but what it was capable of. In a bind, I could also use one to good effect. The Skorpion was a .32-caliber weapon with a ten- or twenty-round curved magazine that fired fully automatically, giving it little accuracy in any situation, especially in a packed room. If fired in such a venue many would be shot, including, perhaps, the president of the United States. That, of course, could not be permitted.

As I stood behind my potential targets, I began running scenarios through my head, playing the "what if" game. There really was only one "what if" in this case. If the Syrians drew their Skorpions, I would per my training shoot each of them twice with my Sig Sauer pistol until the threat was neutralized, I had expended all ammunition, or I was out of the game.

I repositioned myself a bit in order to ensure that President Clinton and Assad would not be in my line of fire in the event I was forced to shoot and actually missed at such close range. As bad as a shootout in this small room would be, it would be catastrophic beyond imagination if a Secret Service bullet from my pistol struck either POTUS or Assad.

Obviously and thankfully the Syrians did not draw their Skorpions and I was not forced to kill them, nor they me. It could have easily happened, however, and the incident was a cold reminder of what is expected of Secret Service agents throughout their careers.

Who are these men and women that protect the president of the United States, and where does America find such people willing to not merely face danger but to sacrifice themselves if necessary for the office of the presidency? The answer begins with the search for men and women who are worthy of trust and confidence.

WORTHY OF TRUST AND CONFIDENCE

Almost every organization has a motto. The motto of the Marine Corps is "*Semper Fidelis*," or "Always Faithful"; the FBI motto is "Bravery, Fidelity, and Integrity." For the United States Secret Service, the motto is "Worthy of Trust and Confidence."

All Secret Service agents carry with them a walletlike object known as a commission book; when opened, it reveals a badge and a photo ID and contains an inscription proclaiming agents' authority under federal law to carry firearms, make arrest for offenses against the United States, and provide protection to the president of the United States. It also states that the bearer is "Worthy of Trust and Confidence." The United States of America can trust the bearer of the commission book in all matters of national security.

These Secret Service agents deemed worthy of trust and confidence are frequently depicted as menacing, large-biceped bodyguards with no sense of humor hiding steely eyes behind dark glasses. This image is not reality but only urban legend.

On the surface, to the casual observer, Secret Service agents are in many respects like anyone else. They are fathers, mothers, sons, and daughters. They are your neighbors, friends, relatives, coaches,

PTA members, and fellow citizens. Under the surface, however, they are quite different from the average citizen. The difference lies in their unique profession and in what each is prepared to do in order to preserve our form of government and way of life. The men and women who carry the commission book proclaiming them to be worthy of trust and confidence are willing and have been trained to forfeit their lives without hesitation for the office of the presidency. Their willingness to do this is without question, their outstanding and continuous training assures it. This primary mission of keeping the president alive at any cost distinguishes both the Secret Service agent and the Secret Service itself from all other government agents and agencies.

My career was not unique. By substituting others' names for mine, this book could be about any one of several hundred, if not several thousands, of agents who since 1902 have been found worthy of trust and confidence and afforded the honor of protecting the president of the United States with their own lives. This book, then, is a typical agent's story, but it is one that has seldom, if ever, been told in such detail.

★ CHAPTER 1 ★

The Death of a President and the Birth of a Career

From May 16, 1983, until May 16, 2004, I served as a special agent in the United States Secret Service. There I was afforded both the honor and the tremendous responsibility of protecting three sitting presidents.

In the span of that career, I learned above all else that there is no such thing as a routine day in the Secret Service. Anything was possible, from the boredom of answering telephones in the office to flying on board Air Force One or perhaps going for a morning run with the president of the United States. On some days I was afforded the chance to do all of these things.

Through the years, many people have asked how and why I chose the Secret Service as a career. The answer is complex but lies in the inescapable fact that children are highly impressionable creatures. When I was only eight years old, the murder of President John F. Kennedy and the global changes it brought about created impressions that would transform my life forever.

Over the course of that fateful weekend in November 1963, an idealistic third grader named Dan Emmett made the decision that one of his career goals was to become a Secret Service agent, one of the men who protected the president of the United States. Two decades later that was precisely what I did. This is the story of that career, first imagined as a child. Through a great deal of hard work and a bit of good fortune, my dream flourished into reality.

BEGINNINGS

Secret Service agents, like most men and women in armed law enforcement, tend to come from the middle class and upper middle class. My upbringing was very similar to that of thousands of others who chose the same career path I did, with the only differences being specific dates and the names of towns and relatives. If you wish to truly understand the mind-set of people in this profession and why they chose their respective career paths, you need to examine their formative years.

The third of three sons, I was born in 1955 at the end of the baby boom in the small town of Gainesville, Georgia, located about fifty miles northeast of Atlanta. My brothers and I were each born six years apart; no two of us were in college at the same time. That is how carefully my parents planned things. In their lives nothing happened by chance, and this is one of the most important lessons I learned from them. Always plan ahead and have both a backup plan and a backup to the backup. From the time I could understand language, I often heard Dad remind my brothers and me, "Prior planning prevents piss-poor performance." As with most things he said during the forty-four years I was privileged to be around him, I have found this to be sound advice.

While neither of my parents progressed in formal education beyond the high school level, both were determined that my two brothers and I would all graduate from college. They made sacrifices characteristic of their generation, and we all did.

My father and mother were born in 1919 and 1920, respectively, and were products of the Great Depression. Both had grown up in families with little money, but through hard work and good financial planning, they accomplished amazing things together in their fifty-nine years of marriage. That partnership ended only after Dad passed away in 1999, with Mother following him in 2013.

My father was a very serious, self-made man who never really had a childhood. The son of a cotton mill worker who was also a Baptist minister, Dad was forced to drop out of high school at the age of sixteen in order to help support his family of two brothers and four sisters by working in the mill.

Partial to dark suits with white shirts and dark, thin ties, he greatly resembled former Secretary of Defense Robert McNamara, complete with wire-rimmed glasses and swept-back dark hair. A World War II veteran of the Pacific theater of operations, he was extremely patriotic and was an active member of both the American Legion and the Veterans of Foreign Wars. Dad loved God first, his family second, and baseball third, although the order could vary at times depending on what teams were in the World Series.

After marrying my mother in 1940, Dad discovered, largely as the result of her promptings, that he possessed a talent for business, and he escaped his dead-end career as a millworker by becoming a furniture salesman. In 1950, Dad started his own furniture business, appropriately named Emmett Furniture Company, which he owned for over sixteen years prior to moving on to other successful business ventures.

My mother was the quintessential mom of the late 1950s and early 1960s. Always perfectly attired, she vacuumed and cleaned our immaculate home while dressed somewhat like June Cleaver. In spite of her hectic schedule, she always had dinner on the table each evening promptly at six o'clock when my father arrived home from work.

As a child, I spent a lot of time at Dad's furniture store—"the store," as we referred to it. Most days during the school year, Dad dispatched one of his two deliverymen, Robert or Reeves, to pick me up from school and transport me to the store, where I would do homework, play in the large area of the rug department, or watch the newest Philco black-and-white TVs until it was time to go home. I remember one of the best parts of being at the store was the drink machine, which, for a dime, provided to me by Dad from the cash drawer, would produce the coldest Cokes and 7Ups in the world in wonderful glass bottles.

The old building that housed Emmett Furniture was built in the 1920s and smelled of new furniture and fresh floor wax. There were always a lot of interesting people coming and going, including policemen, local politicians, businessmen, and just about anyone you could think of. Dad was a friend of Congressman Phil Landrum from our Ninth Congressional District, and one day as I sat watching cartoons, he appeared. This was during the early 1960s. Unlike today, constituents generally held congressmen in high esteem, and I recall feeling very special as this important man sat and talked with me for a few minutes.

Other days one of Dad's deliverymen would drop me off after school at the public library, where my mother worked part-time. There I would do homework and immerse myself in books about World War II or anything else I could find related to the military or guns. Considered cute at the time, I was fussed over by Mom's coworkers, who loved to give me dinner-spoiling treats and seemed to delight in patting me on my blond crew-cut head.

I attended Enota Elementary School within the Gainesville, Georgia, city school system. The quality education found within this system has over the years produced two astronauts and many doctors, lawyers, and engineers, as well as a couple of Secret Service agents. It was a time in America when, due to lack of government interference, many public schools provided a quality education found only today in private schools. Corporal punishment was still alive and well within the public schools, and disciplinary transgressions were met with a ruler impacting the palm of the hand or the principal's pledge paddle across the backside.

Each day we diligently studied reading, writing, arithmetic, and American history as it actually occurred, with no one lecturing, for example, that Pearl Harbor was the fault of the United States. The Supreme Court had yet to order religion removed from public schools, so we recited the Lord's Prayer during morning devotional, along with Bible verses and the Pledge of Allegiance. No one refused to join in any of these activities, and there were no complaints from any parent about the curriculum of hard academics, God, and patriotism.

At recess, we cultivated healthy competitive spirit by playing a variety of violent and sometimes injury-causing games, including tackle football with no pads and dodge ball, now banned in many schools. While almost everyone received a bloody nose and got scraped up from time to time, not everyone received trophies for every sporting activity. Those who lost in dodge ball or other sports did not seem to suffer permanent physical injury from the bloody noses or a lack of self-esteem.

Political correctness and a phobia of anything gun-related had yet to seize the country, and I recall one very interesting show-and-tell day in the sixth grade. One of my classmates brought to school a fully automatic .30-caliber M2 carbine provided to him by his father, a police captain. The captain had procured the weapon from the armory of the Gainesville Police Department for his son's show-and-tell. The school was not put on lockdown, and everyone, including the teacher, enjoyed the presentation on the history and functioning of the weapon. At the end of the day many pedestrians and people in vehicles watched unconcerned as my eleven-year-old friend walked across the school grounds with his carbine slung over his shoulder on his way home.

In addition to the challenging academic curriculum, we also trained for the likelihood of nuclear war.

During the early 1960s, especially after the Cuban missile crisis, everyone, including the school systems of America, was concerned about a seemingly inevitable thermonuclear war with Russia. Unlike many schools in the early 1960s, my grammar school did not practice the insane act of "duck and cover," which had students hiding from thermonuclear destruction under their desks. Desks provided no more cover from a nuclear explosion than they would a falling light fixture. Instead we practiced evacuation drills.

The idea was that if we were all to be vaporized, maybe some of us could at least make it home and die with our families or in our own homes and yards. Traveling the great circle route, it would take an ICBM about twenty minutes to travel from the Soviet Union to its designated detonation area over the United States. That at least gave us some time. Better to be on the move and die rather than huddled like rats under a desk. I vividly recall that on at least one occasion, upon the given signal, all students formed up into groups and walked home. It was a useless exercise but a lot more exciting than duck and cover, and we got most of the day off from school.

Guns played a large role in my upbringing, and I always seemed to have an affinity for understanding their function as well as a natural talent for using them. My father advised me very early in life to "never point a gun at anything you do not intend to shoot." Later the marines would modify that lesson to "never point a weapon at anything you do not intend to kill or destroy." At the age of eight, with my Daisy BB gun in hand, I roamed our neighborhood with other gunslingers for hours on end. We tested our skills by pushing our Daisys' maximum effective range to their utmost limits. It was not unusual to see a group of boys walking down the street in our neighborhood with their BB guns, and on some days we sported actual firearms, usually .22 rifles. Other than the bird population being thinned a bit, no damage was done as a result of our possessing these weapons, and no one shot out an eye. It was during this time that I learned about adjusting sights for windage and elevation, as well as the basic fundamentals of shooting. By the time I entered the Marine Corps some years later, I was already self-trained to the point that firing expertly with the M16 rifle and M1911 pistol came easily.

Many of my relatives were military veterans from World War II or Korea. Dad's World War II service had included helping to liberate the Philippines from the Japanese. Like many World War II veterans, he spoke little of his military exploits, but when he did, I listened, completely fascinated. Uncle Olan had been an army tank platoon commander who was captured by Rommel's forces in North Africa, and he spent the remainder of the war confined to a POW camp in Eastern Germany. The Germans were brutal hosts, and he nearly froze and starved to death on several occasions, emerging from captivity a broken man. He received a medical discharge. Uncles Fletcher and Bud had served in the European theater of operations and barely survived the experience. As far as the new generation, one of my cousins had just received his commission in the air force and would one day fly missions over Hanoi in an F-4E Phantom. His brother became a naval officer on board a nuclear attack submarine while another cousin was living in Germany, married to an army infantry officer.

Due to the constant exposure of being around military veterans, combined with a sense of adventure and patriotism that seemed built-in at birth, I always felt it was my duty, my destiny, in fact, to serve America, as had my father, cousins, and uncles. It was simply assumed by most of my relatives that, when my time came, I, too, would contribute. At the time, my future contribution was naturally assumed to be military service, and one day that would come to pass—I became a Marine Corps officer. But my contribution also turned out to include a great deal more.

A DEFINING MOMENT

On Friday, November 22, 1963, I had just emerged from school looking very Opie Taylor–like after another brutal week of third grade. I was walking down the sidewalk when someone said that President Kennedy had been shot and was dead. I was puzzled but discounted it as a hoax, as such a thing could not possibly happen.

On that day, Robert, one of Dad's deliverymen, was designated to pick me up from school and deliver me to the store for another afternoon of homework and playtime. I approached the green pickup truck with "Emmett Furniture" on the side and climbed up into the cab, laboring under the weight of my books, which I carried in an official military haversack. Inside the truck, I found Robert wearing, as usual, his aviator sunglasses and smoking his usual Phillies cheroot.

Normally reserved in a confident way, today Robert's demeanor was different. He was obviously disturbed about something. "What's wrong, Robert?" I asked. With some degree of difficulty, he answered, "President Kennedy has been assassinated." I was not familiar with the word *assassinated* and asked for further explanation, which he provided. So it was true: President Kennedy was dead. Not only had the world just changed, but without my realizing it, so, too, had my future.

Robert drove the 1962 Ford pickup to the store, a five-minute trip. We rode in silence, listening to the news on WDUN-AM radio. Upon arriving, I joined many of Dad's customers gathered around the three or four televisions in the TV department and watched Walter Cronkite go over what details were known about the assassination, which had occurred in Dallas, Texas.

Oblivious of my presence, Dad's customers talked about possible Russian or Cuban involvement. They probably did not think such a young boy could comprehend any of it. The mention of Russians concerned me, as I remembered the year before, when America and the world came to the brink of nuclear annihilation during the Cuban missile crisis, prompting our school evacuation drills. If the Russians had killed our president, there would certainly be war, according to those gathered around the television sets.

Over the weekend I watched live TV as Kennedy's coffin arrived at Andrews Air Force Base (AAFB) in Maryland. It was a place I would come to know intimately twenty-seven years later. I recall seeing the president's blood still on the First Lady's legs and dress. I also recall with great clarity Lyndon B. Johnson's first address to the nation and how I did not like him, as he was completely different from John F. Kennedy, whom I liked a great deal.

Later, on Sunday, November 24, my family and I watched as the accused presidential assassin, Lee Harvey Oswald, was gunned down in Dallas police headquarters, also on live television. Having yet to learn about the concepts of due process and guilt beyond a reasonable doubt, I remember feeling that justice had been done now that the man everyone seemed to believe had killed the president was also dead.

Up until that point in the weekend, I—along with everyone else in America—was in shock over the assassination, attempting to grasp the fact that John Kennedy was no longer the president of the United States. Since I had no memory of President Dwight D. Eisenhower, it seemed Kennedy had been president my entire life. Now he was gone. As depressing as the entire situation was, a moment was about to occur that would ultimately change my life forever.

Somewhere during the confusing and emotional events of that weekend, I viewed a photo made moments after the fatal shot to Kennedy's head. The photo depicted Secret Service agent Clint Hill on the back of the presidential limousine attempting to protect Mrs. Kennedy and the president by shielding them with his own body. I asked my father who the man was and why he was on the president's car. My father explained that the man was a Secret Service agent and that he was trying to protect the president by blocking the assassin's bullets. He explained that it was his job to take the bullet meant for the president. I remember not quite comprehending the concept that a man's job was to place himself in front of a bullet meant for the president. While I knew nothing much about anything at the age of eight, I knew enough to know that being a Secret Service agent sounded incredibly important and dangerous.

This dramatic image, which personified not only Agent Hill's unquestionable courage and devotion to duty but also the importance of the Secret Service as an organization, was without doubt the chief factor in my decision to become a Secret Service agent. Children are indeed impressionable.

★ CHAPTER 2 ★

College, the Marine Corps, and Ronald Reagan

As the years passed, so did many career ambitions, everything from astronaut to surgeon. In the end, however, two always returned. In addition to one day pursuing a career in the Secret Service, I had to no one's surprise set the intermediate goal of becoming a commissioned officer in the US military. I viewed the military not only as my patriotic duty but also as a place where I could exercise my spirit of adventure.

I had been an extremely adventurous child, prone to risk taking, and I liked things that were just dangerous enough to produce some adrenaline. I could be seen many afternoons riding my homemade skateboard down our street, going as fast as possible with no helmet or protective pads of any kind. As I grew older the machines became more dangerous and my love for them more intense. That love was somewhat dampened on a summer day in 1971 when I crashed my Mustang Mach 1 into a tree. In two weeks the Mustang was repaired, with a new front end, and I continued on my way, delighted to once again be in control of a 351-cubic-inch V8 engine, albeit more cautious.

I graduated from high school in 1973 and enrolled at North Georgia College, in Dahlonega, Georgia, twenty miles from my hometown. A military college known for its academic excellence, North Georgia seemed like a good college for me to attend, since my first goal upon graduating was to serve my country in the military. All males living on campus were required to participate in ROTC, which meant wearing uniforms and learning the customs of the US Army.

The commandant of cadets was a West Point graduate who had served in the Korean War. He was one of the finest men I have ever known. Most of the army officer cadre on campus wore their hair long, even by army standards, and most sported sideburns. Some were a bit portly, although no one was hugely out of shape; but it was apparent that physical training was not a priority for most of them. Their appearance was in a sense a representation of the army itself during the early 1970s. Enrollment at North Georgia College was down due to the unpopularity of the yet to be ended Vietnam War, and the laid-back attitude of the cadre was probably meant to attract and retain more cadets.

With the end of the conscript army and the beginning of the all-volunteer army, recruiting commercials invited young men and women to "join the people who joined the army" and offered, "Today's army wants to join you." Conversely, I had seen marine recruiting commercials and posters with men sporting very little hair that boasted of keeping its standards high and its ranks small, wanting a few good men and not promising a rose garden. The hard-nosed Marine Corps approach to recruitment designed to attract unique, extreme individuals intrigued me, but I had never met a marine officer and there were none at North Georgia College.

After some discussion with other like-minded cadets I was informed that recruiters from the marines were allowed to search for suitable applicants for their officer programs on campus. They would usually set up a place in the student center one or two days out of each quarter for interested students to come by and talk; they would also set up a time and place for students to take the Marine Corps officers' written exam. One day a marine recruiting team led by Captain Kenneth L. Christy was on campus, I decided to see what the marines had to offer. As it turned out, what they offered was an attitude and a challenge.

My first meeting with Captain Christy occurred at a motel just outside the campus where he and his recruiting team were staying. As I pulled into the motel parking lot on a beautiful autumn afternoon, Captain Christy stepped out of his vehicle, and I immediately realized that I was looking at what a military officer was supposed to look like. He was a little over six feet tall, with large biceps, resembling a shorter version of actor Clint Walker. With a large chest created by thousands of bench press repetitions and a small waist honed from thousands of miles of running combined with hundreds of thousands of sit-ups, he looked more like a model wearing a marine uniform than an actual marine. In addition to his imposing physique, he wore aviator-style prescription glasses and intentionally sported extremely short hair. His perfectly tailored uniform was made complete with the addition of silver parachute wings and three rows of combat ribbons, which included a bronze star and two purple hearts from his tour in Vietnam during 1967. His highest award was the Bronze Star, with combat *V* for valor. Years later, at no request of his own, it was upgraded to the Navy Cross, the nation's second highest award for valor after the Congressional Medal of Honor.

After we'd introduced ourselves to each other, Captain Christy invited me inside the motel lobby, where we talked about the marines. While the purpose of my visit was to take the marine officers' exam, it soon became apparent that this was actually an interview to determine if I would even be afforded the chance to take the written exam.

Sizing me up, Captain Christy all but stated that, from the looks of me, I probably could never make it through marine training, and that another branch of the military might be a better choice for me. Whether he was serious about my appearance or whether his words were meant as a challenge designed to attract those seeking a challenge, I was sold on the marines at that point. Captain Christy smiled a bit and summoned his equally impressive gunnery sergeant, directing him to administer the officers' written test to me. If I passed, it would signal the beginning of my journey into armed military service by way of the Marine Corps Platoon Leaders Class (PLC) program.

The PLC program trains college students as officer candidates during the summer at Marine Corps Base Quantico, in Virginia. Then, after receiving their degrees, successful candidates are awarded commissions as second lieutenants in the US Marine Corps. It sounded easy, but it was a program that had proven fatal for some and had permanently damaged others.

The gunnery sergeant sat me down at a small desk and handed me the test booklet for marine officers. Four hours later I completed and passed the written exam to attend Marine Corps Officer Candidates School (OCS). Rebellious and undisciplined since adolescence, with a resentment of authority in almost all forms, I had for some inexplicable reason just joined the most disciplined branch of the military services.

Perhaps I somehow knew that I needed the type of discipline that could only be found in the marines. As the great football coach Vince Lombardi once said, "There is something in all good men that yearns for discipline." I apparently yearned for discipline and would soon learn it under the most trying of conditions.

As the day for me to depart for OCS grew nearer, the reality became more sobering. It was one thing to take a written exam to qualify for OCS and quite another to graduate or even to get on the airplane to go. Later, I was reminded of a Troy Donahue movie in which his character makes the comment, "How can I lead other men, I don't even know where I am going." At the time that pretty well summed up my leadership skills.

HELL UNDER THE VIRGINIA SUN

Marine Corps Platoon Leaders Class summer camp is a physically and psychologically brutal rite of passage designed to produce commissioned officers and leaders for the US Marine Corps. This period of my life was crucial in forming the person I was to become, as well as the type of Secret Service agent into which I would one day evolve.

Almost from the moment I arrived in Quantico, on June 1, 1975, every waking moment became a challenge to survive. On most of the days that followed, my platoon mates and I would have taken odds that none of us would live through the summer, much less graduate from the program.

Over the next several weeks, in the humid Virginia heat that never seemed to subside and with our heads shaved to the skin, we ran five miles each morning wearing leather combat boots, that seemed to eat skin while constantly being physically and verbally harassed by the staff. On my summer construction jobs in high school, many of my coworkers were ex-convicts, and a few were convicted murderers. I had been around profanity but now realized that the Marine Corps drill instructors (DIs) took profanity to a level approaching art. Their ability to weave meaningful profanity into every sentence spoken was almost awe-inspiring.

Each day presented its own difficulties. On Saturday mornings, after three hours of physical training, we would stand motionless on the asphalt parade deck under the oppressive summer sun undergoing equipment and personnel inspections, during which candidate after candidate collapsed from heat exhaustion. The staff was essentially free to do practically anything short of killing a candidate in order to determine the candidate's suitability to become a Marine Corps officer, and over the years there have been occasional fatalities. Each day began at 0430, or 4:30 a.m., with physical training that has killed strong men, hospitalized many, and caused others to quit the program. The day ended at 9:00 p.m. with lights out, at which time we all slept like the dead until the lights went on again at 4:30 a.m.

Staff Sergeant McLean, one of several DIs assigned to our company, and our primary tormentor, threatened every day that if I and my fellow candidates did not get ourselves "unf—ked," he would personally kill us all, or, worse than killing us, he would send us home well before graduation.

Staff Sergeant McLean was twenty-eight years old, six feet five inches tall, and carried no unnecessary body fat. With piercing blue eyes and a voice that could be heard probably for miles, he was one of the last marines to leave Vietnam and was a veteran of several years as a DI at Parris Island, where he trained enlisted marines. He was the Hollywood poster image of what a marine DI should look like, and I knew from the moment I saw him that my platoon mates and I could expect from him the best and most severe training allowable under the Uniform Code of Military Justice. He did not disappoint us, ever.

There were other DIs besides Staff Sergeant McLean. Gunnery Sergeant Gilpin, who chose to shave his entire head each morning, loved to repeatedly inform candidates that if any of us actually believed we were going to be allowed to serve as officers in his Marine Corps, we were all crazier than a "shit-house rat." The statement might be addressed to the platoon as a whole or to an individual, and while no one really had any idea what a shit-house rat was, we knew it must be in some way worse than the standard rat.

Gunny Gilpin was a master of head games and he could play them at the most inopportune times. One morning before physical training I was seated in the head—the bathroom—with my red USMC shorts at my ankles when the Gunny appeared and sat down on the toilet next to mine. This was in the "old Corps," when there were no patricians separating the porcelain thrones. Although the head was empty except for me and the Gunny, rather than him choosing any one of twenty other possibilities, he felt it necessary to conduct his business next to me. Now comfortably seated and reading the newspaper, the Gunny carried on normal small talk with me as if we were old friends. This is when I began to catch on that our DIs were actually human beings and in all likelihood pretty decent sorts. On the physical training (PT) field ten minutes later however, the Gunny was once again the inhumane maniac we all loved and admired.

The main curriculum consisted of Marine Corps history, drill, weapons, leadership, and tactics classes, combined with a never-ending physical training regimen—all conducted under the critical gaze of battle-hardened officers and enlisted instructors.

These men continually evaluated us for leadership potential. The Marine Corps philosophy of leadership dictates that, above all, before a man can lead and give orders, he must first learn to follow orders. As a result of this philosophy, failure to immediately carry out orders to the letter could result in one of many possible forms of punishment being inflicted on a candidate. It was a form of operant conditioning, Marine Corps–style, and it worked.

One such corrective measure required a man to run the perimeter of the quarter-mile asphalt parade deck while holding an M14 rifle (weighing 10.32 pounds) above his head until collapsing in the summer heat, or until the DI felt that a point of instruction had been learned. If no rifles were available, a foot locker would suffice. These punishments could be doled out for something as small as failure to recall upon demand one of ten general orders, having a dirty rifle, or anything the DIs felt important; and everything was important to them. The point was to teach not only instant obedience but also attention to detail, all designed to save lives in combat. The program was also, as much as anything, a test of who could think and function effectively when pushed to the end of human endurance and who truly wanted to become Marine Corps officers.

Every other week, we participated in forced marches of up to twenty miles with only two quarts of water per man in 95-degree temperatures with 100 percent humidity while carrying full field packs, helmets, and rifles. Those who fell back or were too slow were pushed and dragged along by the DIs, all the while enduring the worst verbal humiliation imaginable. The scores of unfortunate souls who dropped due to heat exhaustion, heat cramps, or heat stroke were placed in the back of a deuce and a half truck, where a navy hospital corpsman who unceremoniously inserted a rectal thermometer to monitor their temperature packed them in ice. For me, death would have been preferable to this humiliating life-saving measure. If a man fell back too far, he was deemed unqualified to continue training and then simply placed in one of the safety vehicles, never to be seen again.

One of the most important things we were taught was to overcome the natural human tendency to quit a task when physical discomfort becomes too great. Quitting was never an option in this world of real and would-be warriors, and practically anything or anyone could be used as an example.

One morning during a three-mile run a platoon mate had to throw up, which was not uncommon. The problem as seen by the DIs was that my friend stepped out of formation and stopped running in order to disgorge his morning chow. Upon return to the platoon area, we showered and dressed for the remainder of the day's training and then stood at attention in front of our racks (beds). It was then that we noticed that there was one man missing: the one who had dropped out to throw up. About that time, the ancient screen door of our Quonset hut, which had seen officer candidates come and go since 1942, flew open. Our missing platoon mate was propelled down the center of the squad bay by a host of DIs. He was scarcely recognizable as our comrade or even as a human being due to the fact his white T-shirt and red PT shorts were, along with the rest of him, now mud-brown from low crawling through various mud pits and culverts around the base. This seemingly cruel and demeaning treatment was designed to instill in each of us the awareness that if a marine quits in combat, much worse things can happen than being dragged through mud. Each of us from that day forward learned to throw up while running.

In order to build aggressiveness and fighting spirit we were each schooled in the art of bayonet fighting. With each candidate armed with an M14 rifle and bayonet attached, Staff Sergeant McLean taught us the basic moves of the thrust, smash, slash, and horizontal butt stroke, designed to place cold steel in an enemy's guts or smash his face and head into pulp. For hours and hours we practiced these moves until the rifle felt as if it weighed twenty pounds instead of ten and each movement became embedded in our muscle memory. Then it was time to practice on each other—with pugil sticks.

A pugil stick is roughly the size and weight of a rifle. It resembles a giant Q-Tip and is padded on both ends. Each man who is to fight dons a football helmet and groin cup and is then paired up with an opponent. At the DI's whistle, each man does his best to knock his opponent down or render what would be a lethal impact or blow with his simulated rifle. After about two seconds into the match, all formally taught moves go out the window and each man is essentially using his pugil stick as a club.

The real purpose of the exercise is to instill aggressiveness and fighting spirit as much as to teach bayonet fighting. The DIs had a great time watching their respective men fight one another like modern-day gladiators, and betting among DIs was not uncommon. If a man did not exhibit the proper amount of aggressiveness he was paired against two opponents and fought until he could no longer hold his weapon or had satisfied the DIs that he possessed sufficient killer spirit to be a marine officer. These drills were usually conducted in a secluded area, away from civilians and with a conspicuous absence of officers. The reward for doing well was a canteen cup of lukewarm iced tea and being left alone by the DIs for an hour.

In order to teach merciless killing, a match was not considered to be over until the DI blew his whistle. Even if one man was on the ground, the victor was to continue pounding the vanquished until the sound of the whistle could be heard. I suppose it could be said that this was literally the school of hard knocks.

I had two bouts. In the first I soundly defeated my opponent, while in the second I woke up staring at the clouds in the blue Virginia sky through the grill of my football helmet. While it may be great in baseball, batting 500 in bayonet fighting is not considered successful. The biggest lesson I learned from this training was that before I tried to engage a man with a bayonet at the end of a rifle, I would first have to be out of ammunition.

With a total attrition rate of around 50 percent, the seemingly merciless nature of the program was partly designed to convince as many candidates as possible to drop on request (DOR) or quit. The philosophy was that if a man would quit on a run or a march, he would probably quit in combat, and these types of men had to be identified and weeded out. While many from other platoons quit, none from my own platoon dropped out. Nor did anyone from the ten platoons run by Staff Sergeant McLean during his tenure as an OCS DI (1974–1978). This was a record that no other DI could match, and it was not the only record our DI held during this assignment. No officer candidate or staff personnel ever bested his three-mile run time of less than seventeen minutes.

As bad as things were at times, the thought of quitting never entered my mind. Of all the things learned about myself that summer, perhaps this character trait was the greatest, and it would serve me well as a Secret Service agent, when challenges tested both my nerves and my stamina.

Days and weeks passed, and the DIs never let up their relentless pressure. We were constantly reminded that being dropped from training, even on the last day, with our families sitting in the graduation audience, was always a possibility. There was, of course, a method to the seemingly total madness of the DIs. Those of us who graduated would become Marine Corps officers and in the future might command our enlisted instructors. Each of these instructors wanted to be certain that we were competent to one day lead them under the worst of conditions, and they went to great lengths to make certain we were up to the task.

As the training became more vicious with each passing day, and with our ranks within the battalion continuing to dwindle, one thing was always clear to everyone: No matter what the undertaking, whether it was a twenty-mile hike or a five-mile run in boots, Staff Sergeant McLean and our other DIs and officers always participated in these events. They led from the front. None ever commanded us to do anything they could not or would not do themselves. This type of leadership, known as "leadership by example," was one of the main lessons hammered into our very souls during that hard summer by our seemingly callous mentors. I would take such lessons with me throughout life, and my Secret Service career.

The night before graduation, I sat on the cool cement floor in our dark squad bay with three of my best friends drinking vodka and grape Kool-Aid from a metal canteen cup stamped "1944" on the bottom. That cup somehow made it home with me rather than being turned in with the rest of my equipment and now serves as a pencil/pen holder on my desk.

On graduation day the ordeal finally ended, and those of us who had survived stood on the same parade deck where we had endured so much misery. We hardly believed we had made it. We had begun with over 600 candidates and finished with 321. I came in at 118. Final class rankings were based on three main areas: physical fitness, academics, and leadership. While my final ranking was not numerically superior, even the man who finished last, at 321, had much to be proud of.

At the graduation ceremony, Staff Sergeant McLean shook hands with me and then smiled one of the few smiles I had ever seen on his face as he congratulated me on finally getting myself "unf—ked." It was a day never to be forgotten, and I have not.

Marine Corps Officer Candidates School was my first experience in a world where a man was expected to do his job and do it well, and yet there would be no accolades given. Graduation was the reward, and doing one's job was simply expected. With the hell that was Marine Corps Officer Candidates School now behind me, I headed back to air-conditioning, cold beer, civilization, and the remainder of college.

I completed college with a degree in criminal justice, and on August 19, 1977, I realized the long-sought-after goal of being commissioned as a second lieutenant in the US Marine Corps. As I stood in my summer service alpha uniform, taking the oath of office of a commissioned officer, I could scarcely believe it. The entire day was a blur, and after working for so many years to attain this seemingly impossible goal, I felt it was all happening to someone else while I merely observed.

The celebratory festivities of my commissioning lasted well into the evening and then moved into the following morning. When I awoke sometime around noon and saw my uniform strewn about, the realization began to set in that I was now a Marine Corps officer and no longer a civilian. It was a great feeling that helped abate the hangover.

After completing the Basic School and the Infantry Officer Course, I proudly served four years of active duty, most of it with Second Battalion, Ninth Marine Regiment, at Camp Pendleton, California, and was honorably discharged with the rank of captain.

During my service, I was placed in command of from 38 to 180 enlisted marines. I put into use all the traits and leadership skills taught by my drill instructors and officers at OCS. As a leader I was certainly a work in progress, but I had learned above all else that the principle of leadership by example was the most important of all. If a man leads from the front, others will invariably follow. This was to become a critical part of my leadership inventory in the years to come as a Secret Service agent. Eventually, I would train new agents and lead other agents while protecting the president of the United States.

RONALD REAGAN

During most of my active-duty obligation, including in the final months, I was stationed at Camp Pendleton, California. While I had enjoyed my marine experience, I had decided to leave the marines when my expiration of active service rolled around in November 1981. That decision was confirmed on March 30, 1981. I had just come in from a five-mile run with my marines when the news on the radio in our company office announced that President Reagan had been shot outside the Washington Hilton.

With the attempt on President Reagan's life, and with my military service coming to a close, I became focused once again on my never-forgotten childhood ambition of becoming a Secret Service agent. The only problem was that I had absolutely no idea how to go about it. But I was a marine officer, and, even after I put my uniforms away and my hair grew to normal length, I would be a marine officer for the remainder of my life. As always, I would not give up and would somehow find a way to achieve my goal.

★ CHAPTER 3 ★

Never Give Up Unless You Are Dead

November 19, 1981, found me at the wheel of my 1978 Camaro leaving Camp Pendleton, bound for Georgia at the highest rate of speed I could manage without being arrested or killed. My luck ran out in Mississippi, when a young trooper who showed no mercy stopped me and was not the least impressed that I was a marine officer returning home from four years of active duty. He was polite and professional as he handed me the ticket.

Upon arriving back in my hometown and establishing temporary residence at my parents' home, I began the quest of applying for the position of special agent, United States Secret Service, with absolutely zero success. This enterprise of becoming a Secret Service agent was becoming a great deal more difficult than I had originally thought, and for months no one in the Secret Service Atlanta field office would return my calls.

Then one slow day in the summer of 1982 between my primary activities of working out, assisting in the teaching of a scuba course, and taking flying lessons, I called the Atlanta Secret Service office for the fourth or fifth time in as many months and asked to speak to an agent. The secretary, as usual, asked what it was in reference to. Having learned from my mistake of actually declaring that I was interested in applying for the position of special agent, I stated that I would only discuss the matter with an agent. Fearful I was a psycho who might want to hurt the president or do some other thing she could get into trouble for, she connected me with the duty agent. After learning of my motive for calling, he hurriedly tried to dismiss me by saying that the Secret Service was not hiring and probably would not be for some time.

Rather than saying, "Thank you for your time, sir," I continued to keep the hapless duty agent on the phone, wearing him down with questions about the Secret Service until he finally gave up and said he would send me an application, which he did. This was far too important an issue, and I would not take no for an answer. The Marine Corps had taught me, among many other things, that when an objective cannot be taken one way, find another, but never give up unless you are dead.

I completed the paperwork, sent it in, and waited while continuing to pursue my varied interests. After several weeks, the office manager called and informed me that the special agent in charge (SAIC) wished to interview me for an agent's position. My persistence had paid off. I was at least going to be afforded an interview, and it was now up to me to capitalize on this opportunity, which was apparently offered to very few.

At the appointed time and date, I appeared in the Atlanta office for my interview with Special Agent in Charge Jerry Kivett. As I sat in the waiting area of the field office, I realized that this was without doubt one of the most important days in my life and that I had best not botch it.

I was escorted into Mr. Kivett's office by the office manager and sweated in my seat after trying to give the firmest handshake I could muster. I then quickly offered a silent prayer that I did not stumble over words or make a poor impression on this man, who now held my future and the dreams of my youth in his hands.

Mr. Kivett was something of a Secret Service legend. With only a short amount of time in the organization, he had been assigned to Vice President Lyndon B. Johnson, soon to be President Johnson, on November 22, 1963, and was aboard Air Force One when LBJ took the oath of office to become the president of the United States.

Mr. Kivett came directly to the point, which was no surprise to me. While burning holes in me with his stare, he asked, "So, Dan, why do you want to become a Secret Service agent?" I gave the best answer I could muster, beginning with the childhood memory of Clint Hill on President Kennedy's limo in Dallas and how the image had created a lasting impression. From there I continued to speak, but I have no recollection of what I said. After continuing to stare at me for what seemed like minutes, he asked if I had seen the footage of President Reagan being shot, along with the Secret Service agent who was protecting him. "Yes, sir," I answered. He then asked if I thought I could do what the agent did when he placed himself in the path of the bullet meant for President Reagan.

I recall thinking for a moment and then saying something to this effect: "The Secret Service must have a great training program. From my past experience in the marines, I know I respond well to training. While I hope I will never be placed in the position of the agent who was shot, I am confident I would respond according to training."

Mr. Kivett's face assumed a slightly pleasant expression, and he said, "That is a very good answer." I was seated before a man who had been in President Kennedy's motorcade in Dallas on November 22, 1963, a man who had been under fire during the assassination of a president, a man who understood better than almost anyone what being a Secret Service agent really meant. Had I incorrectly answered his question—had I given almost any response other than the one I did—there is no doubt that he would have simply sent me to the door leading out of the office. Instead, he sent me to the office next door to be interviewed by Mr. Robert F. Coates, assistant special agent in charge (ASAIC) of the Atlanta field office, for round two.

Attired in a three-piece suit minus the jacket, Mr. Coates was in his late forties, balding, and just as intimidating as Mr. Kivett, but less formal. After practically ordering me to sit, he continued the quest to determine my true motives for wanting to become a Secret Service agent.

It became readily apparent to me that these men did not like to waste time. Mr. Coates, like Mr. Kivett, quickly came to the point and asked, "Are you looking for a job?" I replied, "No, sir, I am looking for a career in federal law enforcement."

Both men's questions were designed to weed out grossly unfit candidates. Mr. Kivett's were aimed at spotting the head case who wanted to die as a martyr protecting the president or the person who possessed no stomach for this type of work. Mr. Coates's question was designed to identify the person just looking for a neat-sounding job, with no serious thoughts of what being a Secret Service agent really meant. There were other questions from Mr. Coates regarding my background and some designed to test my knowledge of the Secret Service. Then the initial interviews with these hard men from the "old school" ended, and I was on my way home, where I would wait for the next phase in the selection process, assuming there was to be another phase. While I felt I had done the best I could, I had no idea if my best had been good enough.

A couple of weeks later, I was called again by the office manager in the Atlanta office and was told that Mr. Kivett had selected me to take the written exam for the position of special agent. The test was known as the Treasury Enforcement Agent Exam. It was difficult—designed to test vocabulary, reading comprehension skills, observation skills, and, for some unknown reason, the ability to do what I considered very complicated math word problems. I took the test with four other applicants and was informed later that I was the only one who passed, scoring a 73 out of a possible 100, with 70 being the passing grade. For the first time since my application, I became optimistic about my prospects for joining the Secret Service.

The test I squeaked through was the same one that had been given for at least three decades, when the Service only hired a handful of agents each year. It was designed to be difficult. My test booklet was so old it practically was falling apart. Prior to 1983 most new agents were only hired when older ones retired. The mandated number of agents never really changed unless there was a crisis or incident, and even then it did not increase significantly at once. When JFK was killed there were fewer than four hundred agents in the entire Secret Service, with less than forty on the president's detail. As a result of his death there was a hiring increase in 1964. The numbers again increased in 1968 after Robert F. Kennedy was killed. Prior to his death, the Secret Service did not protect major presidential candidates but the Service was immediately mandated to begin protecting these candidates after his death. In 1976 President Gerald Ford was the target of two assassination attempts, by Sara Jane Moore and Lynette "Squeaky" Fromme. More agents were hired. With the attempt on President Reagan's life, the number of agents was increased from sixteen hundred, where it had been for years, to two thousand. These slots had to be filled as quickly as possible.

Months passed with no word from the Atlanta office. Then one day, with no warning, I was requested by telephone to appear back in Atlanta for the panel interview phase of the selection process. The panel was one of the last major hurdles to be cleared in the selection process and consisted of three senior agents, each of whom asked a long series of questions over an extended period of time.

When I arrived for the interview, I was escorted to the office of Robert F. Coates, now the special agent in charge, having replaced Jerry Kivett after his recent retirement after over twenty years of dedicated service to America.

After introductions to the members of the panel, Mr. Coates began the panel interview by asking the same question as he had in the initial interview months earlier: "Are you out looking for a job?" My answer was the same as before. "No, sir, I am looking for a career in federal law enforcement." He then passed the questioning over to the other two agents, who spent the next several hours asking questions dealing with my Marine Corps service, experience with weapons, contact sports I had played in school, my workout routine, any illegal activities I might have been involved in, and my willingness to relocate if hired. They also posed a myriad of hypothetical situations, seeking my opinion as well as a recommended course of action.

After returning home that evening, I thought I was doing the right thing by writing Mr. Coates a note thanking him for his time and for the interview. A book I had recently read concerning job interview etiquette had plainly stated it was considered appropriate and expected for a person to send a thank-you note to anyone who had afforded him or her an interview. I learned that this was not necessarily the case in the US government.

Days later, I was at my parents' house when the phone rang, and I answered it. The voice on the other end said, "This is Bobby Coates from the Secret Service. May I speak to Dan Emmett, please?" I replied, "This is Dan Emmett, sir." Mr. Coates said, "I got your thank-you note, and we don't go in for that sort of thing at the Secret Service." He continued on to say that he was thanked by the government twice a month, meaning each time he was paid. At that point, I felt my chances of becoming a Secret Service agent were zero, and I thought his next words would be that I was no longer under consideration. After a pause for effect, he said, "Come on down to the office and pick up your background information forms," and then the line went dead. I traveled back to Atlanta that day, picked up the papers as directed, completed them in record time, and returned them to the Atlanta field office. Then the wait began in earnest.

THE RELUCTANT BANKER

In order to pay the bills while waiting for my dream job at the Secret Service to come through, I worked as a management trainee at First Atlanta Bank. While I knew nothing of banking, a headhunting agency I had signed up with sent me to the bank for an interview. The bank was looking for former junior military officers who supposedly knew about responsibility and leadership and could be taught the banking business. It sounded good in theory and they offered me the job. I was broke, so I accepted.

For a man who loved adventure and challenge, this was the worst job imaginable, combining boredom and monotony with an incredible feeling of total hopelessness. I had little in common with my coworkers, and carrying on even the simplest small talk was difficult. Most of my colleagues knew that I possessed no banking experience and had fallen into the job because of my military experience. Many did not like it and were not bashful about showing it. Each morning as I willed myself out of bed, my future seemed as dark as the cold Atlanta mornings I had to face each day.

One day in April 1983 I had just been chastised by my supervisor for taking fifteen minutes for my afternoon break instead of the allotted ten. This was during a time when smoking was permitted in most buildings and employees took regular smoke breaks in addition to their allotted breaks. I reminded my boss that I did not smoke; therefore even with the extra five minutes of break time I was still taking about an hour less time each day for myself than the smokers. He, of course, was a smoker.

Later that day, as I was sitting at my desk contemplating things in general, none having to do with banking, the phone rang. I stared at the annoying black object for a bit before picking up the receiver. I heard a voice say, "This is Bobby Coates, Secret Service." I think I uttered something creative like, "Yes, sir." He continued, "I have a job for you, a GS-5 in Charlotte, base salary 13K per year if you want it. Take a few minutes and call me back with an answer." I stammered out something to the effect that I did not need a few minutes and would gladly accept the position. He stated that he would like to have me in Atlanta but that there were no openings and that GS-5 was the only pay grade available. I did not care in the least where the job was or even what the pay was. Given the state of mind I was in, I would have accepted the Mars field office if that had been the offer.

Mr. Coates gave me three possible report dates and informed me that I would have to pay for my own move to Charlotte, North Carolina. In that I owned virtually nothing this presented no problem. I took the first available report date, May 16, 1983. We hung up, and I sat at my desk in a total daze. After eighteen months of trying I had made it. Barring any unforeseen catastrophe, I was going to be a Secret Service agent.

★ CHAPTER 4 ★

The Charlotte Field Office

On Monday, May 16, 1983, I appeared at the front door of the Charlotte field office, United States Secret Service, for my first day as a special agent. I wore a gray pinstripe suit recently purchased from J. C. Penney and presented as a gift from my parents. As one might expect, I had slept little the night before. It was almost 8:30 a.m., and no one answered when I pushed the buzzer at a door located at the end of a short hallway. Unlike the large offices, such as New York, which have a 24/7 presence, small offices such as Charlotte operate regular business hours, usually 8:30 a.m. to 5:00 p.m. There is a duty agent who locks up at night and sets the alarms. He then fields any duty calls that occur during non-duty hours forwarded to him by an answering service.

Finally, at 8:35 a.m., a short, compact man who resembled the actor Robert Conrad, dressed in a blue sports jacket and gray slacks, appeared from the elevator bank just outside the office. He looked at me and asked if he could help as he placed a strange-looking key in the door of the office. I said, "Hi, I am Dan Emmett, first day on the job." The seasoned-looking agent offered his hand, introduced himself as Paul and invited me in, directing me to take a seat.

Other agents began filing in with their coffee and stopped to introduce themselves as well as get a look at the new guy. Another agent named Ron and I were the first hired in Charlotte since the late 1970s, and everyone wanted a look at the new meat. I rose as each of my new colleagues and mentors came by to say hello.

The office manager arrived. She was matronly and friendly, at the same time possessing a hard appearance, giving the impression she took no static from anyone. She had worked for the Secret Service since the 1950s and knew everything there was to know about administration within the organization. She had also seen every new agent to walk through the door at Charlotte for the past thirty years. In terms of the Secret Service, she had seen it all.

She escorted me across the hall to the office of the special agent in charge, who directed me to remain standing and hold up my right hand in order that I might be sworn in as an employee and special agent of the Secret Service. In those days new hires were sworn in as agents on the very first day, not at the end of all training, as they are now. I was familiar with the words of the oath, as it was the exact same oath of office I had taken as a marine officer seven years earlier: "I do solemnly swear that I will support and defend the Constitution of the United States of America against all enemies, foreign and domestic; that I will bear true faith and allegiance to the same; and that I take this obligation freely, without any mental reservation or purpose of evasion; and that I will well and faithfully discharge the duties of the office on which I am about to enter, so help me God."

After my swearing in, which lasted less than a minute, the SAIC, as expected, briefed me on things in general, including his philosophy of good agent work ethic. As I sat in his office I continued to sneak peeks at the walls for photos of him with politicians. There were none. He then lectured me on an unexpected theme that I discovered later was of universal concern throughout the Secret Service.

BOOZE, BROADS, AND BUICKS

The SAIC stared at me for a moment and then proceeded to tell me that the fastest way for an agent to get into trouble was by abusing the three Bs: booze, broads, and Buicks. Roughly translated, this meant combining infractions involving alcohol, women, and misuse of the government car.

Each Secret Service agent in a field office was given a government car to use, not only while working but also at night. It could be taken home. This benefit of the job was known as "home to work," and the Secret Service was one of the few agencies that offered it. Home to work was a tremendous privilege, and the rules were clear: No use of the car was authorized other than for official business, which included going directly from home to work and work to home. No one was allowed to ride in the car other than on official business—no children, no wife. There was to be no stopping at the grocery store, dry cleaners, or bars—especially bars. The SAIC tied it all together by saying that, while circumstances sometimes necessitated the bending of these rules, I was never, ever to combine all three of the Bs in one event. By this he meant going out for drinks and then driving the government car with an unauthorized passenger, such as a woman. He ended the briefing by stating that any misuse of the government car, or the "G-ride," as it was known, meant an automatic thirty-day suspension without pay. Warning received.

After my swearing in and lecture on the evils of alcohol, cars, and women, I was handed off to an agent who took me to the part of the office where suspects were fingerprinted and photographed. He took what would be my official Secret Service photo. It would appear in my coveted commission book and would be kept on file at HQ. I still have a copy of it. I had another taken at the twenty-year mark. Side by side, the photos scarcely resemble the same person, although I still had most of my hair twenty years on.

The next morning, after being introduced to the daily ritual of morning coffee in the downstairs coffee shop, run by a very nice old man named George, I was introduced to Frank, one of the firearms instructors in the office and one of the oldest agents still on the job. His protection experience went back to the Eisenhower days, when

Frank walked the links of Burning Tree Country Club with Ike while carrying a Thompson submachine gun in a golf bag. On this day in 1983, Frank's job was to qualify me with the Smith & Wesson standard issue revolver, if possible, and help get me ready for upcoming agent training.

The course of fire a new agent was required to pass in order to carry a weapon was not a combat course but rather a bull's-eye-type course called the SQC, or Standard Qualification Course. It was fired all single-action, meaning the hammer had to be pulled to the rear and cocked in order to fire each round. It was only a thirty-round course and designed to teach the fundamentals of shooting.

Frank and I drove to the Charlotte Police Academy range in his G-ride. Upon arriving, he explained the course of fire. After allowing me to dry-fire the weapon, meaning cycle it with no ammunition to get the feel of the revolver, Frank produced live ammunition and allowed me to try my luck.

I qualified on my first attempt, with a score of 290 out of a possible 300. Frank was very pleased with me and with himself. I did not reveal the fact that I had been firing handguns since the age of thirteen and was the top shooter with the .45 pistol in my marine unit. I liked Frank and had no problem with letting him believe it was his instruction that had carried the day. All organizations need men like Frank, and all new guys should listen to them.

Satisfied I was competent to at least carry a gun, Frank handed me the weapon along with twelve rounds of .38 special +P+ ammunition, a holster, and one speedloader, which carried an additional six cartridges. I was now armed and dangerous, although probably more so to myself than anyone else. While obviously proficient in the use of a weapon, I had yet to receive any instruction on the legalities of when I could and could not use it. This was standard procedure in the old days but was changed sometime in the 1990s. Today, agents do not carry weapons until they graduate from agent training.

The following week, the entire Charlotte field office and the smaller satellite offices of Wilmington and Raleigh converged on the same police academy range. The purpose of this gathering was for the mandatory quarterly firearms requalification for all agents in the state of North Carolina.

At the end of the training day and after qualifying with the revolver, Uzi submachine gun, and Remington 870 shotgun, I met with Paul, the agent I had met on my first day, and we headed for his road district of western North Carolina for some basic criminal investigative work. It was a part of on-the-job training, where a new agent was passed around from senior agent to senior agent to learn how things worked.

We checked into our respective hotel rooms, where we would live for the next three days, and then met at the bar to plan the evening's activities, which included my introduction to the covert world of how to bend the three Bs a bit without repercussions.

THE NOT SO GLAMOROUS WORLD OF CHECK FORGERY INVESTIGATIONS

When a government check is stolen, the thief usually forges the payee's signature and cashes the check. This becomes a federal violation investigated by the Secret Service. Today these investigations are largely unneeded, due to direct deposit, but in 1983 they made up the majority of investigations conducted by the Secret Service.

Check investigations were truly at the dull end of the Secret Service mission spectrum. At the other end was the all-important protection of the president, which took a very special person to accomplish. Any junior detective could succeed at check investigations. Until 2002 the Secret Service fell under the Department of the Treasury, and because all government checks are drawn on the US Treasury, investigations were assigned to the Secret Service.

While the Secret Service still has jurisdiction over these cases, today there are few compared to the 1980s. Today's Secret Service, in addition to the staple investigation of counterfeit currency, also investigates credit card and bank fraud. Even though check forgery cases are rare, these new types of investigations keep every field agent more than occupied. In a sense it is a shame that the check forgery cases have all but gone extinct: They were how every new agent was broken in, and they offered what amounted to basic training in the field of investigations. The new Secret Service agent of today will never know the down-in-the-gutter experience of working them.

The danger these cases presented to the agent far outweighed the importance of the cases themselves. Investigating federal crimes in rural America was as dangerous as working in a large city, and it was easy to imagine that an agent could be made to disappear in this setting.

In the mountains of North Carolina, for example, you frequently worked alone. Many of the people who lived in extreme rural North Carolina existed in their own world and did not recognize federal law or the legitimacy of an agent's authority. While an agent had complete legal authority to be on a person's property in order to ask for cooperation in an investigation, many of those who needed to be interviewed believed that agents were trespassing.

To ensure his own safety, the wise agent would befriend a local deputy to accompany him on these cases. Each deputy knew almost everyone in the county, and the chances of being shot by a check forgery suspect were far less with the deputy along. This sometimes backfired—a deputy who was related to or friends with the suspect would call ahead and warn of the agent's visit. It seemed that almost everyone in the extreme rural areas of North Carolina was related either by blood or marriage. It was almost the norm rather than the exception to arrive at the residence of a suspect to find no one home, even though the suspect was unemployed.

On my first day of working these cases, Paul and I interviewed one or two payees and obtained some handwriting samples. Most of these individuals were living in deplorable conditions that smelled of stale urine, and each seemed to have an army of mongrel dogs that guarded the mobile home or shack he resided in. I learned the lesson of the rural dog the hard way.

Paul and I had pulled up in front of a mobile home off a dirt road with a typical narrow dirt driveway. The first advice Paul offered was always to back the car in rather than to park nose first—for an expedient getaway if things went wrong. The second was to dress appropriately for such assignments. I was dressed in a three-piece pinstriped suit I incorrectly thought appropriate for criminal investigations, while Paul was dressed in a sports jacket with wash-and-wear pants. It was on this day that I discovered an agent needed two different sets of work attire: one for dress-up events such as protection, the other for days when getting dirty is a distinct possibility.

As we exited Paul's car I heard distant barking and saw the fast approach of a large, mud-caked mongrel. The owner who had seen our arrival stood in the doorway of his aluminum castle and told us not to worry: "The dog don't bite." He did not say anything about not jumping on a rookie Secret Service agent. As the dog ran toward us, he decided that I would be the best person to soil. He happily jumped on me, his front paws leaving a bounty of mud and who knows what else on my starched white shirt and suit and tie. Having now had his fun, the owner called the dog back. Paul was having a bit of fun, too, holding back laugher over my predicament.

Paul identified us, stated our business, and said that we needed some handwriting samples. The dog's owner agreed to provide them. Inside, at the kitchen table, as I slid a form in front of the man to complete, a large drop of tobacco juice dripped from his mouth, staining the handwriting form. Seeing my quiet but noticeable disgust, Paul could barely contain himself. When we got back into his car he burst out laughing until tears ran from his eyes. Between gasps of air he said, "Welcome to the glamorous world of the Secret Service." In every profession there is a period of paying one's dues, and these cases amounted to that for a new agent.

As much as I disliked these investigations, I soon realized that check cases were the main activity in a small office like Charlotte. If I was ever to get to the presidential detail, I had to do them and do them well. But agent school was coming soon, and I would be, at least for the time being, delivered from these less than glamorous investigations.

★ CHAPTER 5 ★

Special Agent Training

The key to success of any law enforcement organization is the selection and hiring of the best people available, followed by intensive, exhaustive, never-ending training. Arguably, few personnel in law enforcement are trained to the level of an agent of the United States Secret Service. I don't believe there is any organization in the law enforcement arena that places as much importance on continued training throughout an agent's career as does the Secret Service. This is especially true in the areas of firearms and executive protection. This training begins the day a new agent is hired, when he or she is assigned a mentor, and it continues until retirement through frequent refresher training.

In addition to never-ending on-the-job training, each new hire has six months of initial formal training. This training is divided into two phases—criminal investigations followed by protective training—and it is conducted at two separate facilities.

The first school a newly hired agent trainee attends is the Criminal Investigative Training Program (CITP), located in Brunswick, Georgia, at the Federal Law Enforcement Training Center (FLETC). There, a new agent learns the basics common to all agents in federal law enforcement agencies. This school is not specific to the Secret Service but is a generic course designed to certify each student in the 1811 series, or criminal investigator category. The curriculum includes basic firearms training, physical fitness, defensive measures, and how to conduct a criminal investigation from the beginning through judicial adjudication. Each class is comprised of forty-eight students, with twenty-four being Secret Service agent trainees and the other twenty-four from various other agencies within the federal government.

After graduation from CITP, the Secret Service agent trainee attends the second phase of his or her training at the Secret Service Special Agent Training Course (SATC), held at the James J. Rowley Training Center (JJRTC) in Laurel, Maryland, sometimes referred to as Beltsville. This school belongs exclusively to the Secret Service, and it is here that the new agent learns how to provide executive protection for the president, as well as conduct investigations specific to the Secret Service, such as investigations of counterfeit and financial fraud. Firearms proficiency with all issued weapons specific to an agent of the Secret Service is ensured by many hours of range time with the issued Sig Sauer pistol, Remington shotgun, and Heckler & Koch MP5 submachine gun.

In addition to this training, each new agent is certified as a first responder in order to save lives in medical emergencies. This training, conducted by qualified EMTs and others from the medical community, gives each new agent the knowledge and tools necessary to respond to any medical emergency, from a heart attack to delivering a baby. It has saved many lives over the years.

Each new agent receives a significant amount of water survival training conducted in the state-of-the-art training tank (a large swimming pool) at Beltsville. In addition, the Secret Service trains its own water rescue swimmers, whose skills rival those of military combat swimmers. There is also an almost daily regimen of aggressive defensive tactics and challenging physical training.

Upon graduation from all required training, new Secret Service agents are prepared for any situation they might encounter over the course of their careers, everything from a gunfight, to subduing a resisting suspect, to stopping arterial bleeding, to the all-important covering the president and evacuating him in the event of an attack.

Graduation, however, does not signal the end of training for an agent. Quite the contrary. Over the course of a career, each agent returns to Beltsville many times to receive refresher training in protection, firearms, and computers, and to hear the latest about investigative techniques and capabilities. Each is also briefed on the latest Supreme Court decisions relevant to the Secret Service.

Even after reporting to one of the two major protective details, PPD and the Vice Presidential Protective Division (VPPD), each agent undergoes two weeks of training every eight weeks. Known as protective detail training (PDT), it keeps each agent who is on the presidential and vice presidential detail sharp in all related skills. During this two-week period, agents requalify with their service pistol, submachine gun, and shotgun and are given the physical fitness test, consisting of push-ups, pull-ups, abdominal crunches, and 1.5-mile runs for time. A refresher in medical emergencies likely to be encountered by an agent is also given. The final day of PDT is spent engaged in attack on a principal (AOP) exercise, where agents are subjected to several mock attacks simulating assaults on their protectee. These attacks could include responding to a lone gunman on the rope line or a long-distance shooter, a medical emergency, and perhaps a water emergency such as exiting a crashed helicopter. In this scenario, several agents are seated blindfolded in a device submerged in water that simulates a helicopter fuselage. The fuselage is then rolled and inverted, and the agents must swim out of the simulated helicopter on one breath of air while fighting panic and with no visual reference. The problems are a bit different each time, so no one can really know what will come next. All agents, including supervisors, participate. It is without doubt the finest protective training in the world. It is also the major reason the Secret Service has been so successful in protecting the nation's leaders over the decades.

Like most police agencies, the Secret Service through the years has had its share of changes in training doctrine and philosophy for new agents. The emphasis varies with each new director. Some have believed that the school should be somewhat of a gentleman's course, while others have implemented measures that resemble those used in state police academies or military boot camp. It is for this reason that agents trained during different time frames will often offer different recollections of their training.

MY TRAINING BEGINS

In compliance with my orders to report to FLETC in June 1983, I departed Charlotte and drove first to my parents' home, in Gainesville, Georgia, where I spent a weekend visiting the family and some old friends.

The next day found me a little sleep-deprived en route to my first training stint at FLETC. I arrived at the base, checked in, and headed for my room, where I found my roommate, Mike, and several men from my class. Mike was an outgoing, likable fellow who seemed to collect people of all types wherever he went. He also on this day had a cooler of cold beer, which always helps make new friends.

All of us hit if off right away and had a lot in common. Almost everyone was about the same age, twenty-eight. Almost everyone had a work history that was focused on either law enforcement or the military, and almost none of us were married. Later that day, when the beer in Mike's cooler ran out, most of us went to nearby St. Simons Island for dinner.

The next morning we attended our first day of training, punching one another in the ribs to keep one another awake. I am surprised that none in my class over the course of the next few weeks suffered any permanent rib damage.

It was a long eight weeks, living with Mike in a small concrete block room just large enough for two people, but, as with thousands of other students over the years, we made do. Each day, we attended class, practiced our future trade, and generally had a pretty good time of it.

The saving grace of this experience was that our class was convened during the summer. As a result we could be found every Saturday and Sunday enjoying the beaches of St. Simons Island. Even on weekends, we began each day at the beach with a brisk three-mile run through the surf, then settled into our places while enjoying refreshments, the ocean, and the gracious hospitality of both tourists and locals alike.

Eventually we each grew a bit weary of the routine, the prison-style uniforms, and the food. Our elation was almost unbridled when it came time to graduate. Due to a lively graduation party the night before that was held on base so no one had to drive, almost everyone the next day was a little worse for wear, although functional. Someone gave an unmemorable speech and then we were handed our diplomas, and off we went, back to our home offices to await the next SATC class and the next round of the best training in the world with some of the best friends and comrades a man could wish for.

Soon after returning to Charlotte in August 1983, I received orders to report to the final phase of agent training at the JJRTC for SATC 84. Our class was to run from September through October 1983, and it would be here that I would learn the part of being a Secret Service agent that interested me the most: protection.

Our new home would be the General Scott Hotel, in a very bad neighborhood of Washington, DC, on Rhode Island Avenue, not far from our main classroom building, which was located during those days at 1310 L Street. Over the years, this area has been cleaned up, and it is scarcely recognizable today as the same place. In those days, if you walked out of the hotel and turned left you would live to see another day, but if you turned right you could be murdered in seconds. This was during a time when new agents reported for training with the issued revolver, so at least we had protection.

Unlike at FLETC, where two agents shared a small room, at the Scott we had no roommate. The rooms at General Scott were old but comfortable, and quite large, with two double beds. There was also a parking garage below the hotel where you could park at no cost.

The Scott was a three-dollar cab ride to Georgetown, which had the richest social environment for young men to be found anywhere in the United States, as far as we were concerned. Everyone could see that this was going to be a great deal more enjoyable than the spartan digs we had endured at FLETC. And we were given a stipend to pay for our hotel and living expenses, unlike at FLETC, where we lived on base, with everything provided.

Most of our instructors were fresh from the field or a protective detail. They all had a laid-back demeanor, and few, if any, were in any kind of decent physical shape. There were one or two instructors who conducted fitness classes, and they were it as far as PT instructors went. My two special agent class coordinators were both new from the detail and never worked out with us. We saw one of them in the morning, then again in the evening before we swooped out of the building and into Georgetown, usually to a bar known as The Sign of the Whale, where we would relax from a long day of training.

Still, management let it be known that any of us could be sent home at any time with absolutely no warning or explanation, and that we were under constant evaluation. Given the amount of rope reeled out by the service, some students did come dangerously close to hanging themselves at times, and that was part of the plan. An agent frequently works alone as well as with a team, and each must be trustworthy enough to work within the lines of conduct established by the Secret Service. In many cases there is no one to monitor agents on the road, and they are simply expected to do their work in a professional, unobtrusive manner. Hence the philosophy of laissez-faire training. If a man tripped up in training, he would most certainly trip up in the world. If he did foul up conduct-wise in training, he would be dismissed, and some in other classes were.

The most intense part of our training, mandatory for employment, was firearms. Almost every day we fired hundreds of rounds of ammunition so that by the end of the week, each man could scarcely hold a gun. Shoulders grew sore and faces swollen from the recoil of 12-gauge shotguns with sharp metal folding stocks. But as a result of this training we were all becoming very proficient with these lethal tools of our trade. All in my class were super-competitive alpha males, and there was no such thing as a relaxed day of shooting. In any course of fire, whether it was with the revolver, submachine gun, or shotgun, we all tried our best to outdo each other, with the loser buying the beer at our next social outing, which usually occurred that evening.

Secret Service Uniformed Division firearms instructors provide this firearms training. They are arguably the finest firearms instructors in the world. Each is an expert in the use of all weapons utilized by the Secret Service, as well as possessing the ability to convey this expertise to others. In some cases, this is no small feat, as some new trainees have never fired a weapon, while others possess so many bad traits and habits that they almost have to be trained from scratch.

As training progressed we all came to know and understand each other's strengths and weaknesses and became like a family that worked, played, and occasionally fought together, but we were a family nonetheless. We might argue among ourselves, but woe to the poor soul who trifled with any man from my class. To push one of us was to push all.

I recall one late Saturday evening in a Georgetown bar when a young, somewhat intoxicated professional of some sort tried to start an altercation with a classmate. Had our classmate obliged, it would have been certain catastrophe for the drunken hero. This young man, emboldened from too much alcohol, was unhappy with the fact that his female companion was paying more attention to one of my friends than to him. He had apparently spent a great deal of time and money on this young woman, and he became a bit annoyed when she elected to leave with my friend instead of him. There were several of us sprinkled about the establishment. After making the unwise decision to push my friend to prove his bravery in front of this woman, the pseudo-tough guy found himself opening the door to the bar with his head while carried in a horizontal position by several perfectly attired Secret Service agents. It was all in good fun with nothing bruised other than perhaps the offender's head and deflated ego. Although the bouncer found the situation amusing, he suggested we find another place to finish out the evening, but he invited us to come back soon. We gladly complied with both of his requests.

INSTRUCTORS MADE OF IRON AND INSTRUCTORS WHO THREW IRON

A number of instructors were tasked with shaping us into agents, and each had his own area of expertise and approach to teaching. Our primary hand-to-hand combat instructor was into competitive martial arts, and he was a very unusual guy. During competitions and training sessions he had broken most of his fingers. Two or three digits still pointed at odd angles, and he delighted in being the object of a demonstration. He seemed to love pain.

One such demonstration included having another instructor kick him full force in the groin; he would display zero emotion and no change in facial expression. As a result of his unique talent for ignoring pain, we referred to him as "Iron Balls," but of course never where he could hear us.

Most, but not all, of these instructors were fun people who enjoyed their work, including the somewhat seemingly demented hand-to-hand instructor. One instructor, who did not seem to fall into the category of even approachable, did, however, seem to enjoy throwing cast-iron training handguns at the head of any student he did not feel was paying attention to the lesson. These dummy weapons were designed for official training purposes, although they could also be used unofficially to deliver a point, as a classmate discovered.

One day, a student was not paying attention, and this instructor let fly with the training weapon, striking the student squarely in the head drawing considerable blood and nearly knocking him unconscious. The instructor looked at my bleeding classmate, who was beginning to resemble a case from the ER, and spelled his name for the student in case he wanted to file a complaint. We looked at each other and looked down at our colleague, each of us with an "oh, shit" look on our faces, and then helped him to the emergency medicine office, where he was tended to and promptly returned to class. Even if my friend had required stitches and hospitalization, which, fortunately, he did not, there would have been no complaint filed.

This particular instructor became one of our best friends after graduation. He was from the old school, and simply believed that hard lessons were the ones best remembered. Being a graduate of the Marine Corps school of pain presided over by Staff Sergeant McLean, I had no problem with this sort of thing and understood his methods. Then again, I was never struck in the head by a flying cast-iron handgun.

ELEVATORS AND DISLOCATED JOINTS

As with most who serve in the military and law enforcement, everyone in my class enjoyed life a great deal, and there was always something fun going on, usually at someone's expense. One morning, that someone was me.

On this day, the class was sitting around the mat room and practicing various holds on each other while waiting for our sadomasochistic instructor to arrive. Without warning, I was seized by three of my classmates, who handcuffed my ankles together and my hands behind me. We had been practicing handcuffing, and I was duped into believing it was practice until I was carried like a freshly slain deer toward the elevator banks. Upon reaching the elevator, my classmates lowered my PT shorts to my knees and threw me into the elevator after pushing the buttons for all floors. Keep in mind that this was a main Secret Service building, where many people worked and rode the elevators each morning. Just before the door closed, my pals picked me up again, and this time delivered me to the women's locker room, where I was unceremoniously deposited on the floor amid several female Secret Service employees in various stages of undress. Hearing screams of disapproval, my classmates returned to retrieve me, at which time I was delivered to the mat room and then released in time for class as if nothing had occurred. If this type of incident occurred today it would probably trigger a congressional investigation. In those days, this was considered good, clean fun, and as usual, no complaints were lodged.

During the same session, while practicing a counter to a rear chokehold, I dislocated the elbow of my partner and good friend, who happened to have been one of my morning assailants. There was an audible pop heard by all in the mat room, he went pale, and his elbow was not in the place where it should have been. He was taken to George Washington Hospital, where his elbow was relocated to its normal place, and then he returned to training. Even today controversy about the issue still swirls, and I am asked whether or not I intentionally popped my friend's elbow.

THE FORMAL FOLLOW-UP

A great deal of our training was both practical and fun. An example of this was training in how to operate out of the formal follow-up.

The vehicle behind the presidential limousine is called the follow-up, and each agent in the Secret Service is a virtuoso at jumping in and out of it while the vehicle is moving. In today's super-modern Secret Service, this vehicle is an armored Chevrolet Suburban and does a fantastic job in its role of carrying the working shift and all of their equipment. In the 1980s, before the advent of giant all-wheel-drive SUVs, the Secret Service employed what were known as formal follow-ups. These were Cadillac sedans heavily modified with running boards, handrails, and convertible tops. Up until about 1990, almost all formal follow-ups were a version of this, and the shift usually rode with the top down if weather permitted.

Upon slowing down and preparing for arrival, the shift would climb out onto the running boards while holding onto the handrails for a fast jump to the ground, where they could quickly surround the limo. It was the most impressive-looking thing the Presidential Protective Division did publicly, and new agents could not wait to try it.

Prior to the state-of-the-art drivers' training now done at Rowley, all vehicle training was conducted at a nearby abandoned airstrip used by the Office of Strategic Services (OSS), predecessor to the CIA during World War II. This was the setting for our formal follow-up training. The strip was a paved runway about thirty-five hundred feet long. It had not been used in decades for the intended purpose but provided a perfect place to run cars at full speed for thirty seconds or so.

Richard was our instructor for the day, had recently come to training from PPD, and was a bit of a wild man, a fact we were about to discover. The exercise began with Richard demonstrating to the class on a stationary follow-up how to mount the running boards, which foot went up first, and how to hold onto the handrails. He then demonstrated how to get off the boards safely while the vehicle was moving. After a few more demonstrations, it was time for us to give it a try.

We assumed that Richard was going to simply drive up and down the old runway at a slow speed a few times just to give us an idea of what the whole experience was like and to provide a basic familiarization. This was not the case.

With Richard behind the wheel, the car first moved out slowly, with four agents walking next to the follow-up and some inside for the ride. As the car gained speed, the agents walking alongside jumped on the boards in the prescribed manner and held on as Richard put the accelerator to the floor until he easily hit sixty miles per hour.

Approaching the end of the landing strip, Richard began to slow down in order to make a 180-degree turn and speed to the other end. As he turned left with tires squealing, the agents on the right-hand side were holding onto the rails with all their strength as Richard accelerated and the centrifugal force pushed to the outside of the turn. Then Richard sped flat-out to the other end of the runway, where he decelerated and turned, this time to the other side, nearly flinging off the students on the left side of the car, who were holding on white-knuckled, hoping not to lose their grip. Richard gave each car full of students several runs up and down the strip until he was convinced every agent knew how to work the formal follow-up. Like most of SATC, the exercise was a tremendous amount of fun, but we were all glad to be alive at the end of the day. We felt confident that we could certainly work the formal if called upon.

After eight weeks, graduation day finally arrived. The ceremony was held in a small room at 1310 L Street, Washington, DC, which barely accommodated the class of twenty-four and the small audience. Graduations from SATC are now gigantic productions accommodating over two hundred people and go on for an hour or so. In 1983 the proceedings lasted about fifteen minutes. I recall that the deputy director of the Secret Service made the commencement speech, but I do not recall anything more, as our class, much like FLETC, had enjoyed a vigorous graduation party the night before. With the presenting of diplomas, it was time to bid farewell to my friends and think about heading back to Charlotte, where I would begin my career in earnest.

★ CHAPTER 6 ★

Back to Charlotte

On Halloween night, 1983, I returned from Washington, DC, to my apartment in Charlotte, North Carolina, having completed all required training to be a full-fledged agent. I was both exhausted and thrilled. During the six-hour drive home, I reflected on all that had happened in the six short months since I had been offered the job of Secret Service agent. In spite of the fact that training had been highly enjoyable, I was looking forward to some time alone to reflect a bit and sleep, which I did for most of the weekend. I was also looking forward to whatever assignments might come my way, even check investigations.

The following Monday, I reported to the office ready to go to work. One of the first things that happened upon my return was that my friend Mike and I, along with another agent, Ron, all of us rookies, were sent to Atlanta, Georgia, to work at an event for President Reagan. Atlanta was always a good town to visit, and with this being our first protective assignment since graduation, we were very enthusiastic. Even though we knew it would only be standing post at some obscure location in the general vicinity of President Reagan, it was still protection.

We arrived in Atlanta and checked into our hotel, where all out-of-district agents were staying, and immediately began to run into old friends from SATC. The first official activity was to attend the agent briefing. This is a gathering, usually in a hotel ballroom or conference room, at which the advance team from the presidential detail briefs all agents assigned to help with the visit. Each member of the advance team is introduced, and the itinerary of POTUS (the president of the United States) is read. Each agent is given general instructions regarding the event, including where and when to report the next day.

After the agent briefing, which lasted about an hour, most of the new agents on this trip proceeded to the hotel bar, where we began to mentally prepare for our next day's assignments and compare stories about our respective field offices. Mr. Coates, the SAIC of Atlanta, was there, and I said hello to him, careful not to thank him for hiring me. I fondly remembered the verbal beating I had received a year earlier for my thank-you note. He asked me how the job was going, and I told him that it was going very well. It was also on this trip to Atlanta that I saw what would change my immediate career goal from getting to PPD as soon as possible to another assignment instead.

My assignment for the visit was standing post at the motorcade arrival and departure area to ensure that no one placed an explosive charge. While there, I saw five very fit-looking agents sitting in a Mercury station wagon with M16 rifles and semiautomatic pistols. This was a Secret Service Counter Assault Team (CAT).

CAT is one of the special, or tactical, teams of the Secret Service, and it is comprised of agents whose mission it is to respond with speed, surprise, and violence of action against organized attacks against the president. I had heard about CAT but knew little about the program, as it was fairly new and was practically classified at the time.

I walked over to the Mercury for a better look and started a conversation with the agent in the rear of the station wagon. He was also a former marine, and after I talked to him for a few minutes, I was so impressed I decided that CAT was where I wanted to go next in my career after my assignment in Charlotte ended. The CAT agent handed me a piece of paper that was like an application, of sorts, for the program, and told me to fill it out when I got back to Charlotte and send it back to him.

While talking to the CAT agent in Atlanta, it did not come up in conversation that an agent had to be at least a civil service grade GS-9 before applying to the program. I was a GS-5 and would not attain the grade of GS-9 for two more years. CAT would have to wait for the time being, but it was without doubt the next thing on my career scope.

CAMPAIGN 1984 AND TEMPORARY PROTECTION ASSIGNMENTS: SENATOR TED KENNEDY

The president of the United States may assign Secret Service protection to anyone he wishes. An example of someone who did not rate protection by law but received it by presidential directive was Senator Ted Kennedy. This type of detail is comprised of agents from various field offices like Charlotte. These small details that last for a few days to a few weeks are where junior agents learn the protection business. It is also where, for each young, idealistic agent, the reality hits that, contrary to popular belief, protection is anything but glamorous. Instead, it is very demanding work that requires a great deal of stamina and vigilance.

During the final thirty days of the 1984 presidential campaign, Kennedy went on the campaign trail for Democratic nominee Walter Mondale, who was washed away in a landslide victory by Ronald Reagan. Since Ted was the last of Joseph and Rose Kennedy's sons still living, two having met their fates as the result of assassins' bullets and one blown into vapor during World War II, President Reagan signed an order in October 1984 granting Kennedy Secret Service protection until the end of the campaign.

Just over a year out of agent school and still assigned to the Charlotte office, I volunteered for this temporary detail and was happy to be on the road for what turned out to be a very interesting thirty days with the senator. Of the fifteen agents selected for this assignment, almost everyone was similar to me, probably by design. We were all young, male, single, and did not care how many days the assignment lasted.

This assignment was considered very high-profile due to our protectee. Prior to assuming our duties with the senator, the entire detail spent a day at the Secret Service training center in Beltsville conducting protective detail training.

The assignment with Senator Kennedy was a tough routine that only the young could have endured, working thirty straight days with no days off and sometimes visiting several cities a day. It was my first experience waking up in a dark hotel room with zero idea of what city or state I was in and with the feeling of total sensory deprivation. It was as if a large part of my memory had been totally erased. This phenomenon would occur many times over the next twenty years as I woke up in hundreds of hotel rooms around the world, having to force myself to remember where I was and, more importantly, what time I had to be ready for work.

My shift started out on midnights, and I watched over the senator until 8:00 a.m. He was traveling to a new city each day. We were relieved early around 6:00 a.m. by the day shift, at which point we would stagger into a cab and travel to an airport for a flight to the next city the senator would visit. After arriving, we would drone on to our hotel, where we would normally find our rooms not yet available and proceed to sleep in the lobby until they were ready. In some cases this was not until 3:00 in the afternoon. After getting three or four hours of sleep, it would be time to wake up and, in a haze, prepare for the next midnight at the new location. This was probably as close to feeling like a ninety-year-old at the age of twenty-nine as you could get. This went on for ten days before we moved to a shift that ran from 4:00 p.m. to midnight.

It was on this assignment that I learned, among other things, that friendly crowds are in some cases more dangerous to a protectee than hostile crowds, and that sometimes the most innocuous-appearing individuals could present the biggest problems. Hostile crowds tend to at least understand the fact that they can only get so close to a protectee and that any intrusion over a certain barrier will result in arrest. Friendly crowds tend to move forward toward a popular protectee like a human wave, which cannot always be stopped by something as temporary as a rope line or five agents.

In 1984 the Kennedy family was still royalty in the state of Massachusetts. Everywhere we went in that state, enormous crowds would appear to hear the senator speak and to try to get as close to him as possible. While we always had rope lines surrounding the stage, some paid little attention to them, with most of these menaces to security being ancient blue-haired ladies. As the senator would come down from the stage after his speech and work the crowd, we would always be overwhelmed by what appeared to be hundreds, if not thousands, of women in their seventies and eighties, each wanting to touch Senator Kennedy and with no regard for the flimsy barrier or our presence. On one such occasion, as the senator was moving down a rope line shaking hands, a woman of about eighty-five unfastened the rope from a stanchion in order to be next to him. I politely escorted her back into the crowd and refastened the rope, but others slipped through and closed in on Senator Kennedy. Due to the gender and age of our interlopers, we were not permitted to employ our usual tactics in such situations. We had to simply form a human shield around the senator, hoping none of these constituents poked him in the eye with a pen while demanding an autograph.

Patrick, Senator Kennedy's youngest son, accompanied his father on some of these stops and was practically mauled by the geriatric set. On one occasion Patrick was wearing one of his uncle Jack's PT-109 tie clasps. These items were given away by President Kennedy during his brief time in office and were quite valuable—not to mention the sentimental value they held for Patrick. After one rope line encounter Patrick ended up with his hair tousled so badly by these women that he looked as if he had just gotten out of bed. He also had his tie almost ripped from his neck, and his precious heirloom went missing. I felt badly about Patrick's having lost his PT-109 tie clasp, but we were only five agents against hundreds of elderly groupies.

Senator Ted Kennedy was an excellent protectee. He understood how we worked and what his responsibilities as a protectee were. He always told us what he intended to do before he did it, making our job of protecting him much easier. He had been around the Secret Service since 1960, when JFK was elected president, and had been assigned a Secret Service detail of his own in 1980, when he unsuccessfully ran against incumbent Jimmy Carter for the Democratic nomination for president. He knew what we would and would not do on his behalf, and an example of this understanding occurred early in the assignment.

One evening the entire entourage had just arrived at the home of a former senator in Malibu, California, where Ted would remain overnight with several associates. It was getting dark, and people were milling about, trying to find luggage and so forth, when a young, attractive woman turned to me and directed, not asked, that I carry her suitcase into the house. This was not going to happen under any set of circumstances. Secret Service agents never carry luggage for anyone, and to be not asked but ordered by her to do so was, from an agent's perspective, totally vulgar. The security doctrine behind this response is that an agent must not have anything in his hands; he must be available to respond to a threat. Luggage handling is also a function of paid staff, not people who are there to protect the principal. During my twenty-one-year career I made an exception to this on one occasion and of my own volition.

I was temporarily assigned to the Secretary of the Treasury detail on a trip to several countries. It was one of those details that was more of a courtesy than anything else, because the Secretary of the Treasury was our ultimate boss. We had arrived at the hotel where the Secretary and his wife would be staying and picked up our post, which consisted of one agent standing in front of the Secretary's door. The luggage had been delivered to the suite door and left there. As I stood in front of the door to the suite the Secretary's wife appeared and began to wrestle with the large, heavy items. There was no one around and certainly no threat, so I moved the luggage into the room for her. One reason I elected to help was that she did not ask. Had she asked, I probably would have done it anyway, but I was impressed by the fact that she did not use her position as the wife of our boss to utilize the Secret Service for duties not intended.

In Malibu, as I stood in the driveway silently staring at Senator Kennedy's young friend, formulating a response that would not result in my being sent home from the assignment, Ted intervened. In the classic Kennedy dialect, he said to her, "Err, ah, the agents don't carry bags." Someone who was actually paid to do such things appeared, and the source of my annoyance disappeared along with her bags. The agents don't carry bags. Damned right. We will die for our protectees if necessary, but don't ask us to carry bags. It was reassuring to see that Ted knew and respected this.

HOLLYWOOD NIGHTS

On this assignment, we spent several days in Los Angeles and Hollywood, where Senator Kennedy campaigned for Walter Mondale by day and by night attended a never-ending series of parties hosted by the Hollywood elite.

Some of these functions lasted well into the early-morning hours, and one had to be impressed by the stamina displayed by these icons of the screen. I recall thinking that Warren Beatty was obviously not working at the time, because he seemed to be at every function the senator attended and delighted in being as close to Kennedy as possible.

As famous and wealthy as these people were, many found it more interesting to sip their martini and talk to an agent than to associate with their fellow actors. Sometimes their interest in the Secret Service made it difficult for us to do our work of keeping an eye on the senator, as we stood surrounded by a group of actors, each taking turns asking questions. Almost all had a Secret Service anecdote each felt compelled to share with us, some going back to the JFK era.

Character actor Richard Anderson, who played Oscar Goldman on *The Six Million Dollar Man,* always seemed to get a kick out of offering to make all of us bionic. Robert Wagner, or RJ, never talked to us but would nod and throw a cool, knowing look our way as he passed by. RJ was always the epitome of Hollywood cool as he held the obligatory drink and cigarette of a senior movie star. Sinatra was more outgoing and at one event actually referred to us as "those Secret Service cats." One somewhat obscure actor was preparing to appear in a film as a Secret Service agent and asked for some pointers. Each of us, when the moment presented itself, took turns coaching this young actor in how to be more realistic in his role. He was very appreciative and wanted to know if there was anything he could do for us. We answered yes and asked that he tell his producer and director that, contrary to most Hollywood efforts, real Secret Service agents do not wear sunglasses indoors.

One evening I was standing post outside the senator's hotel room door with strict orders to allow no one to enter when actor Gregory Peck appeared. There was to be a party in the senator's suite, and Mr. Peck was an invited guest, although he was early. He was tall, and his persona was identical to the one portrayed on the screen. As he looked at me, saying nothing while smiling pleasantly, I felt as if I were standing before General MacArthur, or perhaps Captain Ahab. I said, "Good evening, Mr. Peck," and knocked on the door to the suite, allowing him to enter. I was not going to make General MacArthur wait to see Ted Kennedy.

FEAR OF FLYING

Because many of the towns we visited were small, we flew almost everywhere on compact, twin-engine aircraft. I had earned a pilot's license in 1982 and had also flown a great deal in the marines—

mostly with my men in the back of helicopters that practically defied the laws of aerodynamics they were so old and worn-out. Many were a testament to an old saying: "If you put a powerful enough engine on a brick, it will fly." These little planes that Ted and his Secret Service detail flew in did not scare me, although they did raise some apprehension from time to time; it always gave me a feeling of great adventure to be in one. You just never knew what would happen.

At twenty-nine, I had not yet experienced the epiphany of mortality. Ted, on the other hand, had personally seen the light in 1964, when a small plane in which he was a passenger crashed, killing several on board and breaking his back. Ted was in traction and rehabilitation for months and as a result hated flying, at least in small airplanes. It seemed to be a continuation of the "Kennedy curse"—one of his sisters, Kathleen, had been killed in a crash in 1948, as had his brother Joe in World War II as a naval aviator.

On one memorable occasion, we had the great experience of flying in a DC-3 operated by Provincetown-Boston Airlines from Boston to Hyannis, Massachusetts. The DC-3 was an aviation classic—the last one having been built in 1946—and one of the greatest airplanes ever flown. It was the mainstay of all commercial airlines from the late 1930s until the late 1940s, and it was quite a thrill to fly in one of these historical old beauties. Despite their age, several hundred still fly today at locations around the world.

On this day, the weather was terrible, with low clouds, rain, and a lot of turbulence. It was too rough a ride for cabin service. As we flew onward in our intrepid DC-3 through black clouds heavy with rain that streamed down the windows in tracks, I noticed from my left side window that, in addition to rain, there was a steady stream of oil running down the cowling of the old radial engine. I was not alarmed, as I knew all of these old engines leaked something but were still safe. It was when they stopped leaking that you had to worry, because it meant the engine was out of whatever fluid was being swept into the slipstream. The weather conditions continued to deteriorate, to the point that I almost expected to see a gremlin on the wing at any moment.

Realizing how much Senator Kennedy hated flying, and especially in this type of weather, I turned and observed him seated two rows behind me, staring at the seat in front of him with his normal reddish complexion now a ghostly shade of pale. He looked up at me and I gave him a reassuring smile he did not return, at which time he resumed his staring contest with the seat.

After descending through solid dark gray cloud cover and then breaking out over Hyannis at about a thousand feet, the pilot put us in the landing pattern and expertly squeaked the tires on the Hyannis runway. When the engines were shut down, the door with ladder included was lowered, and before any of us could unstrap, Ted was moving down the aisle and off the airplane. We quickly moved after him, wondering why he was in such a great hurry and where he was headed without his Secret Service detail.

As we entered the tiny terminal, we saw his destination. Soon, fortified after his latest flying adventure, he moved to the waiting cars. The senator had also been sitting on the left side of the plane and had no doubt seen the stream of oil being blown back across the cowling, in addition to the evil-looking weather. It was in similar weather that he had crashed twenty years earlier and was nearly killed.

One of our most memorable aviation mishaps occurred while we were on the ground. Our shift of four agents, the senator, and Patrick Kennedy had boarded a twin Cessna. We had just strapped our seatbelts when the nose of the aircraft began to pitch up ever so slowly, as if we were already in the air. With a discomforting metallic thud, the tail settled on the tarmac like a model plane missing its clay counterweight in the nose. We were still sitting stationary on the ground, with the engines stopped. Everyone could not help but laugh—everyone, that is, except the senator, who found no humor in our predicament.

The two pilots, not yet in the plane, stuck their heads in and politely asked that the heaviest of us move to the front of the aircraft. Ted was by far the heaviest, but he liked the rear seat and no one was going to tell him to unstrap and move forward. We four agents changed seating, and with the added weight of the pilot and copilot, the airplane began to pitch downward until the nose gear once again found its proper place on the ground. With the balance of the airplane now corrected, we took off without incident.

WALKING THROUGH A TIME WARP

The last few days of the assignment were spent at the Kennedy family compound in Hyannis Port. When we arrived at the residence, I was impressed by its majestic New England elegance. The main compound included the home formerly owned by the patriarch of the family, Ambassador Joseph P. Kennedy, along with another house across the driveway that had been owned by the late Robert F. Kennedy. By 1984, ownership of the ambassador's home had been relinquished to Senator Kennedy, and Ethel Kennedy still lived periodically in her and Bobby's home.

Nearby sat another house, which faced one of three streets bordering the compound. Located at 111 Irving Avenue, it was a large Cape Cod, with gray shingle siding, and had once been owned by the late President John F. Kennedy.

I saw the house every day and was aware it had once belonged to President Kennedy but knew little more about it. I had assumed it was simply an empty or nearly empty house that was at one time the summer home of the thirty-fifth president of the United States.

On the thirtieth and final day of our assignment, Senator Kennedy hosted a party for the Secret Service agents who for the past month had been willing to trade their lives for his if necessary. The senator appeared at the festivities dressed in a blue denim shirt with a black warm-up jacket and displayed a shock of disheveled, graying hair that had not seen a stylist in several weeks. This was a drastic departure from his usual appearance over the past month—his daily attire was a perfectly tailored Brooks Brothers suit.

While cordial, the senator was always somewhat reserved around his Secret Service detail, but with the assignment now over, he became the perfect host as he encouraged each of us to have more lobster and beer. Most of us needed no encouragement, even though we were dead tired and everyone was looking forward to getting home.

Late in the afternoon, as the festivities began to taper off and almost everyone had departed for the airport and home, Kennedy moved among the few agents who remained and asked if anyone would like to tour his brother's house, meaning the home of the late President John F. Kennedy. As I was helping myself to another beer, I heard the senator ask, in the unmistakable dialect that seemed unique to the Kennedy family alone, "How about you, Dan?" I looked up from the beer keg, nodded, and replied, "Yes, sir, thank you, I would enjoy seeing the president's home."

After obtaining keys to the home from the estate's caretaker, who greatly resembled Spencer Tracy in *The Old Man and the Sea*, the senator escorted three of us on the short walk to the back entrance of President Kennedy's house. The senator casually explained that the house was largely in the same condition as when JFK had sometimes lived there. I thought he was referring to the furniture and drapes. While this was partially the case, I soon realized that the senator was referring to a great deal more.

I expected him to provide a brief escort through the home, but instead he handed me the key and said, "Here, Dan, please lock it up when you are done." And then he left. Although only fifty-two years old, the senator moved back toward the main house with the posture and gait of a much older man. It was clear that the passing of the years since the assassinations of his brothers, President Kennedy and Bobby Kennedy, had done little to relieve his pain. He was still grieving. During my time with him, he also seemed a man tormented by the other tragedies that had occurred in his life. Secret

Service agents are often with their protectees in settings far from the media and crowds. They observe politicians in a light not seen by anyone outside their families. Sometimes the view is tragic.

It took only moments after entering the house for me to realize that it had not received the news of President Kennedy's death. Frozen in time, it seemed to be waiting for its windows to again vibrate, announcing the arrival of a helicopter delivering the president and his family for another weekend or holiday at Hyannis Port with friends and a multitude of relatives. It had now been waiting in silence for twenty-one years.

At first glance, the president's home seemed much like any other and was furnished as expected, with furniture and décor that ranged from antique through early 1960s, complemented by an abundant supply of *Life* magazines and newspapers. The subtle clue that this home was perhaps not like others began with the discovery that these reading materials were all printed in 1963 or earlier.

The other two agents and I began to explore the old house, laced with a hint of dampness from the late New England autumn. Soon, however, my colleagues each declared he had to leave for the airport or miss his flight. As we bade farewell, I realized I should probably have gone with them, but I was not yet ready to end this once-in-a-lifetime opportunity.

Now alone, I moved through the house and slowly began to discover a museum's worth of President Kennedy's personal belongings. As I allowed this more-than-unique experience to sink in, a revelation occurred: I was walking through a time capsule, an inner sanctum that probably few outside the Kennedy family had seen since 1963.

Some of the priceless items that now surrounded me included framed photographs of President Kennedy and his family, both on the walls and resting on various tables and shelves. Other items I stood before included business suits in President Kennedy's closet, which upon closer examination revealed his name sewn inside by someone possessing great skill in such matters. Arranged neatly on wooden hangers, each seemed to be waiting for President Kennedy to return and wear it once again.

As I continued to explore, apprehension began to set in, making me feel I had inadvertently surpassed the boundaries Senator Kennedy had intended when offering access to the home. The stillness and quiet became deafening and I knew it was time to leave.

Alone in President Kennedy's bedroom, which darkened by the minute in the fading afternoon light, I felt for the house key in my pocket and prepared to conclude my self-guided tour. As I was about to depart the bedroom and the house that time had forgotten, two items on the bureau suddenly caught my attention. Curious, I moved closer for a more detailed examination—and found a pair of gold cuff links. The cuff links seemed to be waiting, like the house itself, for their owner to return. But who was their owner? Standing in the cold bedroom of the late president, surrounded by the fading light of Election Day 1984, I read the initials engraved on the face of each accessory and realized to whom they had once belonged. The owner of these mysterious lone cuff links had been President John F. Kennedy.

Although any number of possibilities existed as to how and why these artifacts were lying on President Kennedy's dresser in 1984, it did not seem an unreasonable assumption, given the undisturbed state of other items in the house, that these heirlooms had perhaps been resting on the dresser since 1963. That possibility alone was a bit unnerving, as was the presence of the cuff links themselves.

As I started to pick one up for closer examination, my hand abruptly halted, as if grasped by an unseen force. These cuff links were perhaps last touched by President Kennedy himself; I did not feel I should be the next to touch them. In addition to entrusting the Secret Service with his life, Senator Kennedy had also trusted each of us to merely tour the home, not touch items probably considered sacred to him. The handling of these treasures would have been totally unprofessional. I was not a tourist left to run amok in the president's home but a Secret Service agent trained from the first day of my career to respect the personal lives and property of those I protected. As with all other objects I encountered in the home of President Kennedy, these two items were left undisturbed where they lay.

As I stared at the objects, a draft of cold air moving through the quiet stillness of the house reminded me yet again that it was time to go. Leaving the cuff links in their resting place while thinking of how much trust the senator must have had in us, I exited the house using the same door through which I had entered, locking it on the way out per the senator's instructions. After a brief search for the senator to return the key, I discovered him walking along the beach in front of the compound.

When I handed him the key, he said, "Thank you, Dan, I appreciate your work and that of the Secret Service very much."

"Thank you, Senator, for allowing us the honor of viewing the president's home," I replied.

We talked for a few minutes. He politely asked me where I was from and how long I had been a Secret Service agent. Feeling more comfortable with the senator and with the assignment now over, I almost asked about the cuff links. Not certain, however, if he would appreciate the range of liberty I had taken with the tour, I elected not to raise the subject. After a pause in the conversation, I sensed that he wanted to be alone. We shook hands, and I left him standing on the beach staring out at the ocean, seemingly looking for something or someone. It had been a long thirty days for him also. I then walked to the command post, formerly the home of Bobby Kennedy, gathered my gear, and called a cab, which would take me to the airport, where I would board an airplane for the trip home.

AN UNEXPECTED CHANGE OF DIRECTION

It was now 1986. After three years as an agent in Charlotte, with my desire to transfer to the Counter Assault Team well known, the SAIC brought me into his office one day and delivered some excellent news. "Dan," he said, "it looks like you are going to be in the first CAT class in 1987."

"Thank you, sir," I said and left his office, my feet barely touching the ground. CAT was growing and needed agents—preferably military veterans, and at the time there were very few of us. It was time to now put investigations behind me and move on to the most important mission of the Secret Service, which is to protect the president of the United States. Unknown to me at the time, however, there were forces at work that would alter these plans.

One morning in the late spring of 1986, I had just arrived at work and was sitting at my desk planning the day's activities, which included report writing, lunch, and running a few miles, followed by an hour in the weight room. CAT school was a very physical course and I wanted to ensure that I was ready for the challenge. Something seemed different today, however. Everyone seemed distant—as if they knew something I did not. Something was up, and I sensed it had to do with me.

As I sat at my desk looking over a check forgery case, the SAIC came in and said he wanted to see me in his office. I knew this was either very good or very bad, as SAICs do not normally seek out GS-9s and invite them into their office.

Upon entering his office, I sat down in the same chair I had sat in three years earlier on my first day as a Secret Service agent. The SAIC sat behind his desk, appearing almost to take cover there, and wasted no time in stating his purpose. He said, "Dan, you are being transferred, but it is unfortunately not to CAT." He looked down at his desk with his hands folded, seemingly unable or unwilling to look me in the eye.

I asked, "Okay, where to, then?"

Without looking up, he said, "The New York field office."

Being transferred to New York was the ultimate nightmare come true for any agent, young or old, and it took a few seconds for the words to sink in. I was well aware, from previous trips to New York on temporary assignments, that it was a large, dirty, noisy, and above all highly expensive place to live. This did not play into my career plans, and I had absolutely no interest in being transferred there.

My first visit to New York had been in 1984, when I had been assigned to Indian head of state Rajiv Gandhi. His mother, the former prime minister of India, had recently been assassinated and he had subsequently been targeted. In 1992 he would meet the same fate. I was on the midnight shift and we were required to wear our ballistic vests, which was very uncommon. We worked with Indian security but did not dare turn our backs on them and trusted none of them. We were working and staying in the Waldorf Astoria, a hotel that would play a part in my life many times over the next twenty-five years. After getting off one morning I ventured out into the streets of New York for the first time. I was there for no more than five minutes before beating a retreat back to the hotel. I had never witnessed such chaos, with people moving in great insectlike swarms to God knows where. The assignment ended in a couple of days and I headed back to Charlotte with the intent to never visit again.

After regaining my internal composure in the SAIC's office, I asked, "What has changed so dramatically that I am being pulled from CAT and sent to New York?"

Without really answering the question, he stated that Secret Service headquarters had selected me for the assignment, and that while it was not what I wanted, it would be good for my career. As he finished delivering his news, he looked up at me, seeming to expect a response of some sort, and asked if I had any questions. I asked if being assigned to a large office had helped his career. He stated that he had never actually served in a large office but that career paths were different today and again asked if I had any questions.

I answered no and asked if that would be all. He said it was for now, and as I stood to leave, I said, "It might be a good idea to get someone else on deck; I am not at all certain I will take the transfer." I saw the confusion and near panic on his face. I suppose he expected me to respond to the news in any number of ways, but not to threaten resignation.

An agent had balked at orders recently. Mike, my best friend in the Service and old FLETC roommate, had been given the same treatment a few weeks earlier. His fate was to be Los Angeles, but, to the horror of the SAIC, Mike, rather than take the transfer, resigned. For another agent to resign from Charlotte over a transfer would not be good for the SAIC. As with all SAICs, his headquarters image was all-important to him. For two young agents to walk off the job would suggest weak leadership. It would be assumed that the SAIC had in some way failed to properly motivate and indoctrinate the youth in his office to happily accept transfers to large offices.

I walked into the hallway, which was lined with coworkers looking at me as if I had been on death row and was walking toward the gas chamber. I almost expected someone to say, "Dead man walking." All the faces of my peer group were filled with survivor's guilt and fear. Each was sorry I was going to New York, but all were glad it was not them, and all were now terrified it would be them next time around. For more than one colleague, it would be.

For better or for worse, I was a career agent, and, while I never had any intention of resigning, I put off signing my paperwork as long as possible, since it would officially launch me to the New York office. I suppose the deliberate avoidance of signing my orders was a quiet rebellion on my part, although a bit immature and certainly futile. Each day, my first-level supervisor would call me into his office, where my transfer papers sat on the desk awaiting my signature. Each day, I told him I had not yet decided whether I was going or not and then left his office without signing.

All of the other agents in the office were becoming more and more uncomfortable over the whole thing, including the SAIC. Everyone was nervous because if I did not go, someone else would have to.

Finally, on the last day possible before being threatened with disciplinary action, I signed the papers, an act that began the countdown for my transfer to the office of investigations, New York. As I signed the piece of paper acknowledging my receipt of orders, I did not realize that while the New York experience would do absolutely nothing for my career, contrary to the assertions of the SAIC, it would become one of the many defining points in my life.

★ CHAPTER 7 ★

The New York Field Office

New York Field Office: a bottomless black hole of despair that knows no limits.

—AUTHOR UNKNOWN

Upon receiving a T-number, or transfer number, an agent who has been selected to relocate to another assignment in a different geographical area is entitled to a ten-day house-hunting trip to the new region.

After overcoming the initial shock of receiving orders to New York rather than CAT, I began to get my affairs in order, including planning my house-hunting trip. The Charlotte assistant to the special agent in charge, who had served on PPD, was very clear about it. He said to me one day, "Dan, they screwed you, so screw them back." What he meant was that I should do whatever I wanted to do in preparation for my move and not worry about my casework. I was not so interested in screwing the Secret Service but was in a bit of a panic about where I was going to live in the New York area on my salary.

Therein lay the worst part of an agent's being transferred to New York. It wasn't so much the city and the surroundings but rather the cost of living. If the government had paid agents enough to live in New York proper, things would have been much better. As it was, most agents were forced to live in New Jersey or even Pennsylvania. This made for one of the worst commutes in America.

One June day in 1986, I boarded an airplane bound for Newark, New Jersey, and my house-hunting trip, where I would search for an apartment to live in for the foreseeable future. Upon landing in Newark, I picked up my rental car and headed south to the town of Plainsboro, New Jersey, where I knew other agents lived.

Upon arriving in Plainsboro I selected an apartment on the top floor of a building overlooking the first fairway of a golf course, paid my first month's and last month's rent as a deposit, and went on my way. I decided that the following morning I would, just for fun, drive into New York to try to find the field office. Having never driven into New York City, I was expecting an exciting adventure and was not disappointed.

After arriving in New York I spent the day touring the field office and exploring the vast World Trade Center complex. It was like a city within a city, much of it underground. There were restaurants, banks, bars, stores, and PATH tubes—subwaylike trains that ran under the Hudson River and came out on the other side in Jersey City.

The following day I returned to Charlotte from my New York adventure, cleaned up my remaining cases, and, on a molten hot day in August 1986, climbed into my Porsche 911 and headed north to my New Jersey apartment and my new life.

A few days later I checked into the New York field office for my first day of work. One of the first things I saw upon entering the office that morning was a sign taped to an agent's desk. It read: "New York Field Office: a bottomless black hole of despair that knows no limits."

I thought to myself, this is still a Secret Service office. Everything should be standardized, and, therefore, the adjustment to the work itself should not be very hard. I would soon find out that the culture of the Secret Service was not universal. Large offices had their own way of doing things, and New York was the largest of them all.

CHECKS AGAIN

Even though I had over three years of experience as an agent and had worked all types of cases assigned to the Secret Service, all the recent transferees and I began our New York careers working forged checks.

The contrast between working these cases in North Carolina and working them in Manhattan and the Bronx was off the scale. In North Carolina we had to deal with a certain type of criminal and his or her rural surroundings. In New York, both the landscape and the criminals were different. Instead of mobile homes and falling-down shacks, in New York we had to enter the most horrid tenement slums in America. It was not unusual to have to step over human feces in the hallways as well as unconscious humans with needle tracks in their arms. There were no mud-caked dogs to greet one, but upon entry into these apartments we encountered another menace: the American cockroach.

In some of these apartments the walls were alive with these insects, and the cupboards and kitchens were infested. One did not dare lean against a wall or even touch anything if it could be avoided. In addition to dropping on you, these little menaces would crawl up your leg and take refuge. After returning home in the evening, the first thing an agent who had been in this environment did was to completely undress down to his skivvies and leave all clothes and shoes on the front step or hallway of his residence. On more than one occasion after I had done this and had shaken out my clothes, a roach that had managed to steal a ride would drop to the ground and then be murdered on sight by me. I could not blame the roach for wanting to get out of the slums of New York and move to the suburbs of New Jersey.

I learned that the answer to this problem was to get as many of these people as possible to come down to the field office for questioning. It was preferable to entering their world, which was both unpleasant and dangerous. Many people who were harboring friends and relatives from the police lived in these apartments, which made working a two hundred–dollar check case a great deal more dangerous than it should have been.

INVESTIGATIONS VS. PROTECTION

When I checked into the New York office I soon realized to my amazement that many agents did not want to do any type of protection but rather only liked investigations. I found this to be puzzling on many levels. Not that a person would like investigations—I just found it strange that people who wanted to be strictly criminal investigators would join an agency that spends half its time protecting politicians. For those people, there were many other options that did not include being in the Secret Service. Many sought those options and left for police departments and other federal agencies, while others stayed and bitched about having to do protection.

The Service has traditionally had a low attrition rate other than through retirement. Many of the agents who do leave prior to retirement leave within the first three years on the job. They leave because they discover that protection is not what they want to do, and if they stay with the service they will always be pulled away from their investigations to protect someone. They want to chase bad guys all the time and be full-time investigators, not part-time. People have to do what makes them happy, but I never understood why these types even bothered applying to begin with.

Secret Service investigations generally center around financial crimes—there is no physical victim, although perhaps someone's credit card has been stolen and used, or a person is stuck with the loss of receiving a counterfeit twenty-dollar bill. The case can, therefore, be put into a drawer and left unattended for twenty-one days, which is the usual maximum time a field agent will spend on the road doing temporary protection, let's say on a presidential candidate. For example, an agent could be working the biggest credit card fraud case in the history of his office but is also on a presidential candidate detail that requires him to go out on a twenty-one-day rotation. What happens to the big caper for those twenty-one days? In many cases it goes into a drawer, where it sits until the agent returns and picks it up again. For obvious reasons, this could not be done with murder cases, kidnappings, extortion, bank robberies, and such.

Much to the annoyance of the agents who would rather chase counterfeiters, credit card thieves, and check forgers than protect politicians, protection—not investigations—is king and always trumps investigations in importance in the Secret Service. The New York office lived in a world of its own, however, in that many agents there believed the primary job of the Service was investigation, not protection. This myth was regularly shattered when POTUS visited New York, or when it was UN General Assembly time, which occurred every fall.

During UN General Assembly time, virtually all investigative work in New York came to a halt due to the huge number of visiting foreign heads of state who by law are protected by the Secret Service. Every agent from the office was used in some way to support the protective mission, and during such times, it became glaringly obvious that protection was the number-one priority. The investigative-oriented agents, however, continued to insist that they were real cops, that investigations were the main purpose of the Secret Service, and that agents who liked protection were mindless pretty boys.

Some of these agents liked to dress à la Don Johnson from the *Miami Vice* TV show, which was popular at the time, complete with no socks in warm weather. Having a scruffy beard, longer than normal hair, and a complete wardrobe of go-to-hell clothes was considered by these men one way of thumbing their noses at protection. Although they did this under the guise of blending in with the people on the street, another reason was that the grungier they became, the less likely it was that they would be pulled for a protective assignment.

As far as blending in, most looked like what they were: Secret Service agents dressed in messy clothes trying to look like the man on the street.

Still, an agent in New York had to produce investigative results, and as long as an agent did, no one bothered him. The bosses realized we all worked very hard, as well as enduring the unendurable beast that was the five boroughs of New York, so our taking a little personal time every now and then, including coming into work a bit late on occasion, did not bother them. In such a pressure-filled environment as New York, it had to be that way. If the bosses cracked down too hard, there would be a quiet mutiny. No arrests would be made, so a balance had to be struck between work and relaxation. Most of the bosses in New York had started there and had a solid understanding of what it meant to be a manager in such a challenging place.

Not much in New York was standard-issue, including the regular investigations engaged in by the Secret Service. In addition to counterfeit and credit card investigations, somehow the NYFO had also received jurisdiction over a form of telephone service theft known as "blue boxes."

Blue boxes were Texas Instrument calculators that had been reconfigured to produce telephone tones. A person attached the instrument to his or her phone line, and then, using the tones that emitted the same sound as regular telephone buttons being pushed, made long-distance calls anywhere in the world for no charge—in effect, stealing service from the phone company. This was in the day when few had cell phones, and most of these criminals who were blue-box artists were from other countries. This was in some way a federal violation, and we only investigated them for the easy arrest and conviction stats they generated.

We did a lot of these cases, and they were relatively simple. A warrant was not required, since a federal officer may make an arrest without a warrant for a felony in progress. The telephone company monitored the line, and when it became active, they contacted the waiting search team, and in they went, seizing the blue box and placing the owner under arrest. Again, the offense in and of itself was not one of the biggest, but the entry into areas where blue boxes flourished was dangerous. In 1984, going to a corner deli in New York could be dangerous.

Criminals involved in stolen credit cards or counterfeit money and even blue boxes were usually involved in other things a lot more serious. While a person might not be willing to go to war over phony money, he might over drugs or a lot of genuine cash he had from ill-gotten gains. You never took anything for granted on any execution of a warrant, and we served a lot of warrants in New York.

A warrant execution team is broken down into sections, the first being the entry team. The entry team is usually comprised of the strongest agent, with a battering ram made of a large-diameter piece of storm pipe with handles welded on, and an agent armed with a short shotgun. The remainder of the team, approximately six agents, then follows.

Upon entry, the shotgun agent and the agent with the battering ram clear the rooms one by one, searching for anyone who might pose a threat. Upon finding anyone, they pass him or her back to the rest of the team, where he or she is handcuffed and detained in a central area, such as the living room. After the premises have been secured, the people taken into custody are sorted out as to who needs to be kept and who can be released. Anyone on the premises is thoroughly searched, for agent safety, and an agent is posted at the door to ensure that no newcomers show up while a search is in progress. After the scene has been secured, the entry team helps the search team look for the items to be seized. The fun of the entry is usually over in less than two minutes, but it is pure adrenaline. You never know what potential threat is waiting on the other side of the door.

The Supreme Court had ruled that before knocking down a door when executing a search warrant, the police had to announce their identity and purpose, and then wait a reasonable amount of time for the person residing at the residence to answer the door. The law could have been a hindrance to law enforcement were it not for the fact that the Supreme Court never defined what constituted a reasonable amount of time. As a result, we knocked and yelled, "Police, search warrant," and before the "t" in warrant was enunciated, the door was down and we were in. To wait any longer gave the bad guys time to get rid of any evidence they might have or, more importantly, grab a gun and kill you.

The execution of warrants in New York never seemed to end, and the process was dangerous not only to the agents serving the warrants but to the people on the other side of the door. Whenever law enforcement executes any type of warrant, there is usually a lot of confusion at the target location, depending on how many persons are there. Sometimes events can come close to spinning out of control even with the most highly disciplined teams. On one occasion, an innocent was almost killed.

The entry of the day was another blue-box case. Over time I had come to dislike these cases immensely—the violation didn't amount to anything, and people could get hurt. The target this day was, as had come to be the norm, a bad section of the Bronx.

The team formed up close to the target location, but not close enough to be detected by any possible countersurveillance, and waited for the phone company to call, telling us the line was up. Finally the call came, and we moved out to the target location. We stacked outside the door, and on the signal from the team leader, the door was breached and in we went.

I was on point with the shotgun, as had become the norm. Being one of the few single agents in New York, I usually volunteered for the shotgun assignment because of the hazards associated with being among the first two agents through the door. My volunteering had nothing to do with bravery but rather logic and expendability. Single agents were considered more expendable than married agents with children, and many of the husbands and dads were more than happy to let me have the assignment. If I got blown away there would be no widow or orphans, just two grieving parents who wished that their son had played it safe and become a banker.

We had become pretty smooth with these entries, as we had done so many; we were quickly moving from room to room, clearing the area and finding surprised people who were totally taken off guard by our presence. We had almost finished clearing the small apartment when we came to a room with a locked door.

The battering-ram agent and I smashed the lock and made our entry. A boy of about sixteen lay in bed with his right hand under a pillow. I pointed my Remington 12-gauge shotgun at his head and chambered a round, safety off, while I shouted the standard command "police, don't move," followed by "show me your hands." He did not look the least bit frightened, but just stared with a blank expression. As I repeated the command for the young man to show me his hands, he began to move his right hand as if edging it toward something, but he did not bring it out from under the pillow. As I held the most dangerous weapon in the world for close combat at this boy's head, I could feel my right index finger move inside the trigger guard. Action is quicker than reaction, and if this boy came out with a gun—which at this point I had to assume he was about to—there would be no time to do anything other than kill him.

Maintaining my scan to avoid tunnel vision while simultaneously watching the boy, I was now conscious of my breaching partner next to me, pointing his revolver at this young man who seemed determined to die on this particular day. Propped up on his left elbow, the boy began to slowly move his hand out from under the pillow. I pulled the stock tighter into my shoulder and prepared to fire. I remember moving my point of aim from his head down to his chest. For some reason, I thought that there would be less gore if I hit him center of mass rather than in the head.

Then the hand came out. There was nothing in it and nothing under the pillow. As I lowered my shotgun, I exclaimed an expletive and let out a heavy sigh of relief. The young man had been asleep when we entered, with his hand under the pillow. When we breached the door, he was frozen stiff with fear, he later said to one of our Spanish-speaking agents. As it turned out, the kid was from a South American slum and spoke no English. He had no idea what I was saying, only that two Americans were pointing large guns at him, and he was too terrified to move.

We finished securing the apartment and began the search, where we found two blue boxes—one that was up and running and another one hidden. This incident reminded me of what I already knew: these chicken shit blue-box seizures were not worth a person's life, including that of the boy I had come within a delicate trigger pull of killing. My breaching partner said to me later that he nearly pulled the trigger on his revolver, which he had cocked into single-action mode. I don't know what became of this kid. I just know that he came within a gnat's ass of dying that day.

I went home and had a few beers, thinking of how I had come as close as a person can come to killing another human being without its having happened, and then I put it behind me and moved on. It was just another day in New York, where anything could happen at any time; and in the world of law enforcement, this incident was nothing special. What made it unique was that while uniformed street cops run into this type of thing almost daily, Secret Service agents run into such situations just frequently enough to scare the total hell out of them.

Other than the drive to and from work, not every day in NYFO was full of stress. It was actually quite the opposite. NYFO was in all probability the mecca of Secret Service practical jokers, and, like all things in New York, these jokes were huge, some on such a grand scale they would rival anything concocted by the best comedy writers in Hollywood. These practical jokes were viewed as a necessity given the environment of the city and of the office. They could be benign and subtle, carried out by one person, or in some cases grand productions that required a cast of many.

For example, years earlier the NYFO had an SAIC who always

wore a hat. In the mornings after arriving, he would remove it and hang it on a hat rack just outside his office door. One day an agent replaced the SAIC's hat on the rack with an identical yet smaller-sized hat. The following day this bold agent who obviously cared nothing about his evaluation, replaced that hat with one too large. The next day he would replace it with the original hat. For quite some time the SAIC could not understand why his hat never fit the same two days in a row. This type of subtle humor was designed to help break the stress that was always present in New York, and although the boss may have been aware of the harmless prank, he never let on.

One day I became the object of such a joke, and at the end of it I stood in awe of the pranksters. Not long after arriving in New York I was assigned a case that involved an arrest warrant for a man named Juan Ferrer. I decided that I would try to find and arrest Mr. Ferrer with the help of the rest of the forgery squad. I dutifully prepared briefing sheets that provided all known information on him, including all known residences or other likely places he might be. I divided the squad up into two-man teams and assigned each an address.

At 6:00 a.m. the following morning we all hit our locations searching for Ferrer. No Juan. We all left our business cards with telephone numbers at the various locations and instructed the recipients, all of whom we had awakened, that it would be better for Ferrer to turn himself in than for us to have to keep looking for him. We always said that at search locations, but seldom did anyone call or turn himself or herself in.

One day not long after, I had just returned from lunch when I noticed on the message board under my name a note that said that Ferrer had called and wanted to talk to me. Juan had left a number, and I dutifully performed a cross-check linking it to an address in midtown Manhattan. Once again I gathered the boys together and briefed them.

Everyone in the squad came along, including the boss. It was all by the book as we parked the cars away from Ferrer's apartment and then moved to the building and up the steps. Another agent and I banged on the door while I identified myself in my best Fernando Lamas accent as "Servicio de Secreto and open el puerto." From the other side there came Spanish gibberish that sounded something like Bill Dana doing his José Jiménez routine. "Sorry, señor, no hablo ingles." I banged on the door again and it opened just enough for a face to appear. The face belonged not to Juan Ferrer but to an agent and friend, who slammed the door. It took at least three seconds for me to realize that the whole thing had been a setup and that the apartment belonged to several agents in the office who lived together. Behind me were about ten agents, my boss included, laughing so hard some were rolling in the hallway. One produced an SS-issued Polaroid camera to record the event and my expression. The door opened again with my friend on the other side beet-red from laughing and from oxygen starvation, gasping, "Servicio de Secreto??????!!!!!." He was laughing so hard he could not breathe.

This was a practical joke, New York–style and it was done with such planning, preparation, and precision one could not help be impressed. I often thought that if only we had spent as much time devoted to our actual jobs as we did with practical jokes, we could have cleaned the entire city of New York of all crime, even those cases not assigned to us.

In spite of the working conditions in New York, we always managed to make the best of things. One very hot summer day I was relegated to the surveillance of a residence in the Bronx from the inside of a surveillance van. This van was essentially the responsibility of the office support technician (OST) who was in charge of all electronic and vehicular surveillance equipment assigned to the office. Joe, our OST, was in his fifties and a native of China but had been a US citizen and a native of New York for many decades. Joe was compact in stature, and, while one of the nicest men I had ever known, he was a genuine badass, with about a million black belts in various martial arts. If he so wished, Joe could kill a man in seconds using nothing but his hands and feet. In addition to working for the Secret Service, Joe was also part owner of the best Chinese restaurant in New York.

With Joe driving the van and me in the back and the curtain behind Joe drawn, he skillfully parked the van across the street from the target location. He exited the van, locked the doors, and walked down the street so as not to draw attention to himself or the van while I watched the house in question through a side porthole. As the time passed and I continued my vigil, the temperature in the van climbed well past 100 degrees. I was now shirtless and soaked, wearing nothing but jeans and a shoulder holster that housed an unauthorized Beretta 9 mm pistol. Every ten minutes or so Joe would call me on the radio to check on my status. I casually mentioned to him that it was getting rather hot in the van, and he promised he would bring me something to drink. Another ten minutes passed, and the driver's door unlocked and Joe appeared with a paper bag containing what I assumed was water. As I thanked him, I looked into the bag to find not water but a six-pack of Heineken. I respectfully reminded Joe that we were on duty and that as good as the beer looked I probably should not have one. With one look and no words Joe reminded me that, in his culture, refusing such an offer was an insult. Realizing my error, I thanked Joe, opened a beer, and drank deeply from the green can, enjoying the best-tasting beer in my life.

After a few more hours, and having received the discontinue signal from the case agent, at Joe's insistence we departed the Bronx for his restaurant in Chinatown. Joe parked in the alley behind the restaurant and we entered through the back door, where Joe was greeted as royalty. He introduced me to his staff in Chinese and we were shown to the best table in the house. I was noticeably the only Caucasian in the place. Joe ordered for me, and it was the best-tasting food imaginable. I learned later that to be invited to Joe's restaurant as his guest was a great honor, afforded to few. That day will always stand out in memory as my best day in New York.

CAT SCHOOL AT LAST

Two years had passed since my arrival in New York in 1986. For that period of time I had been up to my knees in cockroaches, rats, and the general New York field office experience. I was growing weary of the inability of an indifferent management to offer an intelligent assessment of when I could expect to move on to a new assignment. In the old days of New York, meaning just a few years prior to my arrival, an out-of-district agent like myself had a twenty-four-month date of service. Being assigned to the New York office in the 1980s, however, was much like serving time in a foreign prison with an open-ended sentence; one never knew when the sentence would end, as there was no expiration of New York service date stamped on anyone's orders. Things were becoming more depressing by the day, not only for me but also for the many who wanted out. Then one day a miracle of sorts happened.

While sitting at my desk on a Thursday, going through my investigative notes from an uneventful interview of a potential suspect on Coney Island, the assistant to the special agent in charge (ATSAIC) called me into his office. He told me that the Counter Assault Team school that was to start on the following Monday at the Secret Service training center in Beltsville, Maryland, was one agent short. It seemed that at the last minute, a candidate had backed out, leaving an open slot. They needed to fill it now, and he asked me if I wanted to go. "Yes," I replied instantly, "I can go."

All of my future classmates had the advantage of having attended the preselection course a few weeks earlier and had been working out in preparation for the selection course. With no advance warning, I would be attending the most physically demanding school in the Secret Service. My boss was concerned that I might not be up to the challenge. Most marines, whether current or former, exist in a perpetual state of physical readiness. While I had not trained specifically for CAT school, I was certain that my normal physical fitness regimen would be more than sufficient.

I assured my boss that I would have no problem.

"Fine," he said, "go home and pack." By the way, he added; if you fail, don't come back. I had no intention of failing, because if I did, I knew I would be coming back, probably for many years.

On a Sunday, August 21, 1988, I checked into the Greenbelt Holiday Inn just outside of the James J. Rowley Training Center in Laurel, Maryland. Here my classmates and I would reside for the following three weeks unless we failed to make the cut. After everything I had endured to make it to this school, I was determined I would not be going home early. Short of a compound fracture or being killed, I would succeed.

Monday, August 22, 1988 found me and five other CAT hopefuls standing in the gym at the Secret Service training center in Beltsville preparing to take the CAT physical fitness test. Almost everyone who washed out of CAT training did so as the result of failing one event on this test, usually the pull-ups or the run. In order to pass the test, a student had to do ten dead-hang pull-ups, followed by forty perfect locked-out push-ups in one minute, followed by forty perfect-form sit-ups in one minute. Form was paramount in these events, and any repetition that did not meet the standards of the instructor's staff was not counted. These events were followed by the 1.5-mile run, which had to be completed in less than ten minutes and thirty seconds. At the conclusion of the run, the candidates returned to the gym, where all upper-body events were repeated, this time with the pull-ups done using the opposite hand position that had been used in the first set. For example, if the first set was done palms facing out, the next ten had to be done with palms facing in. All events were video-recorded for the record should a student fail and protest.

I had essentially been training for this test my entire adult life without knowing it. In the Marine Corps, pull-ups and running were the two main areas of fitness, and all marines feel as if they were born on a pull-up bar. While I had no pull-up bar to train on at home, I improvised by doing them on the open stairs at my apartment. If one stood underneath the stairwell and gripped the rear of a step underhanded, it made a pretty decent pull-up bar. Each day for the past two years I had trained under those stairs with the hope it would one day pay off. Now that time had come, and when my turn came to do pull-ups I was so jacked up with adrenaline and years of pent-up frustration over various delays in fulfilling my destiny, I practically vaulted myself through the ceiling on the first rep. In order to assure the required perfect form I did the ten pull-ups overhanded, practically in slow motion, coming to a complete dead hang for at least one second. The push-ups and sit-ups were easy, and when it came time for the run, I exploded off of the starting line like a Thoroughbred at the Kentucky Derby, almost expending all my energy by the halfway point in the run. While reaching the halfway point in near record time, I was so depleted that I almost failed the run, finishing at 10:20. Just ten seconds separated me from continuing in the program or going home. It was too damned close, and I vowed from that point on to pace myself a little better for the remainder of the school.

CAT school was three weeks long in those days, each week consisting of six training days, with each day running about twelve hours. The most difficult part of training was weapons qualification.

During this period, the standard Secret Service agent was required to qualify with a 210 out of a possible 300 points for each issued weapon. CAT agents, on the other hand, were required to score a minimum of 270 out of a possible 300, or 90 percent, with the M16 rifle, MP5 submachine gun, and the Sig Sauer pistol.

The CAT courses of fire for these weapons incorporated almost impossible time requirements along with multiple magazine changes that challenged anyone with less than near-perfect motor skills. Failure to meet qualifications with one weapons system constituted total failure. For CAT students, failure to qualify meant going home without a graduation certificate. For operational CAT agents, it meant leaving the program short of tour. In CAT, weapons proficiency was everything.

The M16 rifle and MP5 submachine gun courses of fire consisted of sixty rounds that began at the hundred-yard line. Within eighty seconds of facing a target, the CAT student was required to fire ten rounds from the standing position, execute a magazine change while transitioning to the kneeling position, where he fired ten more rounds, followed by an additional magazine change, with the final ten rounds fired from the prone position. The student then moved to the fifty-yard line, where he fired five rounds standing, then dropped to the kneeling position for five more rounds in a ten-second time period. The final phase of fire was at the five-yard line, where the student fired a magazine of ten rounds, two rounds at a time within three seconds each time he faced the automatic targets. This was followed by a magazine change, and then ten more rounds were fired on full automatic in bursts of two to three rounds. Failure to fire all rounds in the allotted time resulted in five points deducted for each saved round, and thirty points was the maximum that could be dropped.

The course of fire for the pistol was equally challenging, with the last six rounds being fired at fifty yards. Anyone who has fired a handgun can appreciate the difficulty of hitting a human torso–sized target from a distance equal to half a football field. Yet this is what every agent in CAT is capable of doing.

This was anything but target shooting at the neighborhood range where a person has unlimited time. The goal in CAT firearms training was to be surgically accurate while laying down a heavy volume of fire and demonstrating the motor skills necessary to conduct magazine changes in almost no time flat. Over time, with the firing of thousands of rounds of ammunition and hundreds of magazine changes, these skills become imbedded into the muscle memory so that in a crisis, when there is no time to think, training takes over.

Learning to quickly clear a malfunctioning weapon was also a critical part of the training, and we practiced clearing these stoppages until our hands literally bled. A CAT agent's primary weapon is the Colt M4 carbine, a variation of the M16 rifle. If one of these weapons malfunctions the team is now down one rifle, which can easily mean the difference is success or failure of mission as well as the life of the agent with the now useless piece. It is paramount to get the weapon up and running in short order.

The standard M4 malfunction drill taught by the Secret Service begins with the slapping of the magazine base with the heel of the shooting hand to ensure that the magazine is properly seated and that the top round on the magazine follower is in the proper position. M4 magazine bases tend to have sharp edges that can and did slice the palm of the hand. This drill was repeated sometimes up to fifty times consecutively or until the instructors felt the response was becoming automatic. After raw flesh was exposed on the hand from scores of magazine slaps, the student then looked forward to doing more push-ups that ground the bleeding hand into the pavement of the range. In the summer heat, with our hands constantly exposed to dirt, grease, and weapons solvent, everyone's shooting hand became infected and swollen. Gnats and all manner of insects loved our bleeding hands and elbows.

In addition to torn hands, another memento of CAT is something known as the CAT tattoo. This occurs when a hot expended cartridge casing ejects from a rifle and lands on the sweat-coated neck of the agent to the shooter's right. The hot piece of brass tends to stick to the skin. If it is not immediately removed, it can leave a second-degree burn—a permanent reminder of that day's training. Today, twenty-five years after our CAT class graduated, my friend and CAT classmate Scott Marble retains such a scar on the left side of his neck.

As time progressed, the instructors made the courses of fire more difficult by requiring us to sprint a hundred yards in full kit prior to firing in order to put us into oxygen deprivation simulating the physiological combat condition of hyperventilation. Some students when placed under this stress found the relatively simple act of conducting magazine changes in both shoulder weapon and pistol to be almost impossible as they fumbled to get their weapons on line. Wearing full kit and hyperventilating while the clock is running for qualification can make the hands feel clumsy, as if one were wearing gloves.

I was the first in my class to qualify with the M16 rifle, although I did not finish first for final qualification. That honor went to my good friend and Robert Redford lookalike Craig Carlson, who, twenty-five years later, is still movie-star handsome. Others had difficulty with the rifle, especially operating the weapon under stress, and it appeared that not all were going to make it to graduation. With the expert tutelage of the best firearms instructors in the world from the Uniformed Division, however, all pulled through.

We did most of our firearms training in the mornings, when we were at our most rested state. There comes a point of diminishing returns in tactical shooting that is directly proportional to fatigue. When the instructors observed everyone's scores in a steady decline, we stopped and cleaned weapons until they were factory-immaculate.

In the afternoons we conducted a never-ending series of immediate action drills simulating responding to an ambush both from vehicles and stationary positions.

A CAT team consisting of between five and six agents employs what is known in the military as fire team tactics. These tactics are based on the age-old but tried-and-true concepts of fire and movement and fire and maneuver. In each case, agents from the team attempt to envelope the enemy by moving out as a maneuver element while one or more agents provide cover fire for their movement. The iron rule: Never move out without cover fire. To do so is a sure way of getting killed.

We conducted this training in a crawl, walk, and run. In the crawl phase we studied diagrams of our tactics, then practiced and choreographed them in slow motion using unloaded weapons. In the walk phase we sped things up a bit by moving first at half speed and then at full speed employing both empty weapons and those loaded with blank ammunition. Here we also practiced exiting from a vehicle in response to an attack. The type of attack dictated what side of the Suburban you exited on as well as actions taken after deployment. This deployment from the vehicle by the team was triggered by the team leader's command describing the attack, which would be: "Left, right, front, or moving." After many, many repetitions over the first two weeks, by the third week we moved our training to Fort Meade, Maryland, where we would go to the run phase. In this, the most dangerous training in the Secret Service, we would use live ammunition.

Students under stress carrying live weapons jumped in and out of now moving vehicles—but also ran with those live weapons with a round in the chamber.

This was the phase of CAT school that has washed out more than a few. The work not only requires strength and stamina but is also a thinking man's game. No matter how well a student had performed up until now, if he did not display the proper situational awareness he would be sent back to his field office minus a diploma. Safe weapons handling had to be second nature, and certain violations were met with dismissal. Such infractions as sweeping, or pointing a live weapon at a fellow CAT student, or, worse, not keeping the finger off the trigger until ready to fire, would result in one warning. A second violation usually spelled the end for the student. One mistake in this type of training can be fatal, and through the years, there have been many close calls, prevented from becoming fatalities only by the focused attention of the superb CAT instructors.

In addition to live-fire exercises, where we fired live ammunition scant feet past one another, I was to discover that CAT was the only school in the Secret Service in which students experienced what it was like to be shot at. Part of our realistic training involved all CAT students standing about three hundred yards downrange with an instructor firing an M1 Garand rifle chambered in 30.06 at an impact zone within mere feet of where we stood. The purpose of this exercise was to familiarize the CAT student with the sound of a bullet as it traveled almost directly toward him.

The bullet from a high-powered rifle travels faster than the speed of sound. Therefore, when being shot at, the first thing a person hears is not the sound of the weapon being fired, but the "crack" of the bullet, which sounds like a bullwhip as it goes supersonic. So, the sounds of being shot at by a high-powered rifle are "crack," followed by "kaboom," not just kaboom, as most would imagine. The instructor firing the M1 was an expert rifleman, and we weren't concerned he would shoot us, although he always delighted in putting his rounds as close to us as possible without hitting someone. Close enough that we could feel the dirt from the impact of his rounds kicking up around us.

As August dragged on into September, the very long days wore on. Things became more difficult as knees continued to swell and elbows rubbed raw from firing on cement in the prone position became infected. Tempers and emotions were also being rubbed a bit raw at times, which is part of the training. CAT agents sometimes spend up to sixteen hours at a time together, confined in a Suburban, and weeks together on the road. Each student is constantly under observation from the staff, who look for breakdowns in emotional control. If a man is not a true team player and cannot get along with others under these conditions, he will not become a CAT agent. Some of us had to work on this as much as on tactics or shooting skills.

Other than one of my classmates who had survived Plebe Summer and Beast Barracks at West Point, none of my classmates were former military. CAT school was the most physically demanding thing some had yet to encounter, and few were accustomed to being verbally harassed. This was not a gentleman's school and was very paramilitary in nature. Although everyone in the class had been an agent for at least four years, we were treated by the staff as mere trainees and were constantly harassed, although nowhere near as badly as in Staff Sergeant McLean's program. For me it was like old times, although no one told me I was crazier than the enigmatic shit-house rat of Quantico lore. While some fretted and complained privately over the treatment, I took it all in stride with a smile and was just glad to be there.

After finally being deemed worthy as CAT material, graduation arrived. Much as my drill instructors in the marines had done, these Uniformed Division instructors transformed into human beings. The turnover rate in the CAT training department was almost zero, and these would be the same instructors who would continue to help train us for the next several years as we became operational CAT agents.

With a CAT graduation diploma in hand, I returned to New York to finish out what I hoped would be my last year there before transferring to Washington, DC, and CAT.

ESCAPE FROM NEW YORK

It was now spring of 1989, eight months after I'd graduated from CAT school. I was becoming more restless by the day, as I had received news from all my CAT classmates that each had reported to Washington for the beginning of his protection tour. Still, the light was most certainly at the end of the tunnel.

One day, with no warning, in late March 1989, my orders to CAT came through. I received an official T-number. I had survived the survivable accident that was the New York office, and it was time to pack up and head south to Washington. Not only was I getting out, but I was going to the assignment of my choice. Some who had transferred into New York at the same time as me had already gotten out, but to assignments they really did not want. They had essentially agreed to go almost anywhere just to escape from New York and then had buyer's remorse while others rode it out longer and did better with the next assignment.

As I began planning for a house-hunting trip to Washington, my supervisor approached me and asked if I had contacted the movers yet. I said I had not, and he told me to hold off. I told him what he already knew, which was that I had a T-number. My orders were official. He said that while headquarters had cut a set of orders with my name on them, the deputy special agent in charge (DSAIC) of New York had not approved the transfer, and for the moment, at least, I was not leaving.

My T-number was retracted as quickly as it had appeared. I was not going anywhere for the moment, and I was, understandably, disappointed. This was a power play by the DSAIC designed to prove a point. He was the number-two man in New York and could dictate when people would leave, and no one was going anywhere without his approval. With so many agents wanting out of New York, I suppose he felt the need to display this fact.

Later, the DSAIC who had rescinded my orders called me into his paneled inner sanctum, which overlooked the Hudson River. Not inviting me to sit, he demanded to know whom I knew in Washington at Protective Operations, the directorate in charge of all protective details. In light of my having received orders without his approval, he was led to believe I was somehow connected to someone in Washington. I told him I knew no one and that, if I did, I wouldn't still be sitting in New York.

I suggested that the answer to the mystery of my receiving orders without his being consulted by Washington was that I was a CAT school graduate, and CAT agents were needed to protect the president. After throwing an icy stare my way, the DSAIC dismissed me with the wave of a hand.

After I went home that day, my group leader, who was also somewhat exasperated with the situation, explained to the DSAIC that canceling my orders was damaging the morale of the entire office. Almost everyone wanted out, except perhaps the kids still living at home with their parents, and to see a man given orders only to have them practically torn up in front of him was causing trouble within the ranks. If a man could not escape from New York even with orders, what chance did anyone have of ever getting out? He apparently saw the logic in my group leader's presentation.

In August 1989, three years almost to the day that I had checked into the NYFO, I attended my going-away party. It was a fairly large turnout, and most of the people there were those I had, over the course of the past three years, drunk with, broken down doors with, suffered common hardships with, and risked all with. I would miss each of them. In spite of my southern heritage, which dated back to before the Civil War, there was no doubt that I had become part New Yorker and always would be.

After the party, I departed New York, watching the Holland Tunnel in my rearview mirror for what felt like the last time. I was finally on my way to Washington, DC, where I would protect the president of the United States as a member of one of the most elite counterterrorism units in the world: the United States Secret Service Counter Assault Team.

THE PROTECTION OF FORMER PRESIDENTS

As I headed to Washington, others, some by choice, others by force, were on their way to the protective details of former presidents Jimmy Carter, Gerald Ford, Ronald Reagan, and former First Lady Lady Bird Johnson. This courtesy offered to former presidents began with President Truman and continues today. I was extremely grateful to be headed for CAT.

I had nothing against any of these former leaders of our country or their agents; I simply had no interest in spending three years of my life and career providing quasi protection for private citizens who, in my view, should be paying for their own private security, an opinion I still hold today.

When a sitting president transitions into a former president, his Secret Service coverage takes on a completely different set of dynamics. Due to the conspicuous lack of threats against formers, his detail moves from a protective mission to more of a caretaker role. The offering of a full-blown 24/7 Secret Service detail to ex-presidents is a very expensive courtesy, not a necessity, as with a sitting president.

One of my instructors in agent school summed it up quite well by saying that, as long as an agent has to stand for hours in front of a door, wet, starving and freezing to death, the sitting president, not a former president, should be on the other side of that door. He also pointed out that, as a general rule, when an assassin awakens in the morning, he does not plan to kill a former president. He wants to kill the sitting president of the United States. Those words, spoken by a PPD veteran, confirmed what I already felt.

While law mandates that each former POTUS be offered protection until death, none is required to accept this service. Only the sitting president and vice president are required to have Secret Service protection, with Richard Nixon the only former president to have voluntarily given up his Secret Service detail in favor of private security paid for by him. Shortly after this historical event, the media asked former president Ford why he, too, did not give up his detail. He said that he had twice been the target of an assassination attempt. "Yes, sir, while president," said the reporter. When reminded of the fact, President Ford would move on to another topic. After leaving office in 1977, he suffered no more such attempts on his life and died of natural causes in 2006 at the age of ninety-three.

As of this writing, no former presidents in the history of the republic other than Teddy Roosevelt and George Herbert Walker Bush have had attempts made on their lives, and the one on Bush was weak at best. President Roosevelt had left office and was running again for the presidency, this time as a member of the Bull Moose Party. He was actually shot while preparing to give a speech on the back of a train. The round hit his speech, contained in a jacket pocket, before slightly entering his chest. With no Secret Service protection and after being shot, Teddy went on to give the speech.

As for the attempt on President Bush, it is a small footnote in history hardly worth mentioning. In 1993, after leaving office, George H. W. Bush was visiting Kuwait after Desert Storm when Saddam Hussein's forces made a very halfhearted attempt to blow him up by placing an explosive in the doors of a car he was to ride in. It was such a poor job they might as well have placed signs on the car that read, "Bomb in door." The usual suspects were rounded up and heads did roll in the literal sense. In keeping with the Kuwait government's interpretation of the speedy trial act, there were no appeals.

⋆ CHAPTER 8 ⋆

The Counter Assault Team

SOME BACKGROUND AND BRIEF HISTORY OF CAT

CAT, the Counter Assault Team, is the tactical unit of the Secret Service comprised of special agents whose stated mission is to neutralize organized attacks, multiple attackers, snipers from a known location, and rocket attacks against the president of the United States through the use of speed, surprise, and violence of action. The agents who comprise CAT are a unique group of individuals, arguably some of the best agents in the Secret Service. Each is physically hard and highly disciplined, and most delight (at times) in being politically incorrect when the opportunity presents itself. Some of the more genteel personnel in the Service feel that these are agents who should be locked away out of sight and released only in times of life-threatening crisis.

In addition to being Iron Man–fit, each CAT agent is an accomplished expert with all issued weapons, as well as small unit and individual tactics, and prepared to protect the office of the presidency by any means necessary. Each is a mission-oriented extremist. Upward mobility was not a concern for these men: When I joined the program, promotion was not possible within the unit. Of all the agents in the Secret Service, these men's motives for being there were perhaps the purist of all.

During my CAT tenure, while mutual respect between team members was always the norm, there was no political correctness in our small, highly selective group, and all had thick skins. Things were either good to go or not, with very little in between, and everyone was free to speak his mind to this end. If an agent was FUBAR (fucked-up beyond all recognition), he was made aware of this fact, usually in a very direct and insensitive manner. He could then unscrew himself or find another assignment.

Because of the physical prowess of these men, many people mistakenly underestimated their cerebral abilities. CAT agents are an eclectic lot in terms of background, education, and interests. Some speak a second language, and all hold degrees in a wide range of disciplines, including accounting, engineering, and law, with more possessing advanced degrees than not. Among their ranks are pilots, combat veterans, former teachers, military officers, and noncommissioned officers. One CAT agent and good friend actually built an airplane in the garage of his home and flew it for many years. This agent was of German heritage, and his airplane was adorned with correct German aircraft markings from World War I. On some days he could be seen flying low over the training center at Beltsville, waving from the cockpit, a white scarf streaming behind with the black cross of the German armed forces painted on the wings.

In contrast to their sometimes colorful demeanor, CAT agents also have impeccable party manners and look immaculate in a business suit, presenting an image all would expect Secret Service agents to portray.

With the constant threat of attack on America by radical Islam and other terrorist organizations, the United States Secret Service Counter Assault Team enjoys a reputation in the international law enforcement and counterterrorist communities as one of the most elite units of its kind in the world. In spite of this highly respected status, its beginnings were uncertain, and in the early 1980s many at the highest levels of the Secret Service lobbied for CAT's abolishment. Gaining acceptance in an organization such as the Secret Service, which had for years resisted the idea of an elite within an elite, was a long and painful process. The Secret Service is a very old and traditional organization, which for many years fought significant change of any sort, and for decades its mission remained essentially the same. It was a conservative, compact organization that had few missions, did them all exceptionally well, and considered protection strictly a gentleman's assignment rather than one for a paramilitary unit. Many did not feel the need for an expansion of mission by adding counterterrorism to the matrix.

As a result, some of the gentlemen of the Secret Service were not overly concerned with the threat of terrorism. Many had been on the job since Harry Truman or even Franklin D. Roosevelt, and there was not much progressive thinking going on during this time at the headquarters level. The feeling was that, during an attack on the president, the agents of the Presidential Protective Division could handle anything that came along.

Consequently, since assuming its mandate to protect the president with the assassination of President William McKinley in 1901, the Service had not changed a great deal in its methods. It used more agents, performed complex advances, and now had jets and armored limos to move POTUS about, but it primarily still only trained for the lone gunman scenario or perhaps a sniper. That was the way the Service elders saw the threat, and, just as the Service retained its use of revolvers until after almost every organization in law enforcement had transitioned to semiautomatic pistols, that was the way it would remain for a very long time.

While most at Secret Service headquarters saw no need for a centralized counterterrorist unit, in the late 1970s, it gave the authorization to large field offices, such as New York and Washington, to create their own versions of such a unit. These teams were field agents who worked their cases and performed normal investigative activities until a presidential visit or high-threat protectee came to their city. Then these agents would deploy in any vehicle that could hold five large agents and not embarrass the Service. This car would be positioned in the motorcade several vehicles behind the limo, and was used in the event of an organized attack. It was known as simply the "muscle car" and was the predecessor to modern-day CAT.

The initial CAT selection course conducted at the Secret Service training center in Maryland was primitive at best and only lasted one or two weeks. Some attack scenarios were conducted, but they consisted mostly of Uniformed Division firearms instructors firing blanks from the woods. CAT's early weapons were Smith & Wesson revolvers augmented by Uzi submachine guns, with one M16-wielding agent. That was the general composition, but there was no real standardization, from training to uniforms to weapons.

With no strong support from HQ for money and training, early CAT was a very haphazard affair. Training and focus of mission centered almost entirely on responding to an attack on a motorcade or airport tactics. There was little to no emphasis on urban deployment or countering an attack from inside a building. Retraining was left up to the agents, for the most part, back at their field offices, and was hit-or-miss. It was truly half-assed in every way, but it was a start and better than nothing.

The early teams that rode in the muscle cars did not really have to be tactical geniuses or even good at tactics. Their real mission was to deploy in case of an attack, to draw fire away from the protectees onto themselves, while the shift evacuated POTUS. Their true purpose was to be sacrificed, if necessary, in order to give POTUS time and the opportunity to escape from the kill zone. From the beginning of the program, the assignment attracted those with a sense of adventure and with a seemingly total disregard for danger, and there has never been a shortage of volunteers.

By the 1980s, terrorist attacks around the world were on the rise, and our brethren at the FBI saw the future far better than we. In 1982, the FBI established HRT, the Hostage Rescue Team. HRT was something of a SWAT team but with a much broader mission. In addition to the centralized HRT, based out of the FBI academy in Quantico, there were similar but less specialized teams in the major field offices. They had the budget, the personnel, and the all-important backing from FBI HQ. From the beginning, it was a first-rate operation.

The Secret Service was about one tenth the size of the FBI and seemingly always at odds with the Bureau over one thing or another, but there were those in the director's office who wanted to be seen as a smaller version of the FBI. While this vision was totally unrealistic, the Service had one thing the Bureau did not yet wanted desperately: presidential protection. And while its budget was comparatively small to that of the FBI, the Service always got the funds it needed by citing security concerns for POTUS. That was good, because it was going to need a lot of cash for a new program coming down the alley known as CAT.

Not wanting to be outdone by the FBI in this new field of counterterrorism, the Service responded by creating a new branch within the Special Services Division (SSD) called Special Programs Branch (SPB), also to be known as the Counter Assault Team (CAT). While SSD's main responsibility was taking care of the protective fleet of vehicles and had nothing to do with guns and killing terrorists, this newly created branch had to be put somewhere in the table of organization. CAT, an unconventional force, would answer to the SAIC of SSD, a completely conventional division that had no idea how to utilize its new, potentially highly lethal, group of men.

With the establishment of the Special Programs Branch, CAT had become a permanent protective assignment lasting two years, on average. The agents who comprised it would come from all over the country and would be based out of Washington, DC, with the muscle car concept now scrapped. After the two-year assignment, a CAT agent would usually move to the presidential or vice presidential detail, depending on the needs of the service. Later, CAT would attain divisional status, with its own SAIC, for a few years. Then it moved to PPD and, still later, back to its own division.

By the mid-1980s, training had improved immensely, as had the weapons carried. Now everyone in CAT would have an M16 assault rifle and the new Sig Sauer P226, a 9 mm pistol. Instead of six rounds (like the revolver), it held sixteen rounds. In an organization that still issued revolvers to its agents, carrying a Sig was a status symbol envied by all. Only CAT carried them, adding to the mystique of the program.

Although CAT now officially existed, the proper utilization of this new resource was an enigma to some supervisors. As a result, CAT in the early years was sometimes either improperly used or not used at all. For example, it did not accompany the president on all movements, and its presence was at the discretion of the presidential detail supervisor running the movement. It was not uncommon for PPD operations to call CAT notifying them of a POTUS movement but without requesting CAT assistance. CAT was being deliberately left out when its presence didn't suit the White House bosses or when its proper use was beyond the tactical knowledge of the conventional supervisor.

Especially frustrating was the fact that CAT was sometimes not used because of its threatening appearance. Some supervisors did not feel a Suburban full of muscular men armed with assault rifles was aesthetically pleasing and preferred CAT not be included in the motorcade. Since we normally operated with our windows down, upon arrival at a site, CAT agents usually had one arm hanging out the window. This sight so displeased some at high-level PPD management that we were ordered to procure lower short-sleeved shirts that would not accentuate the well-developed male bicep/deltoid musculature.

These exclusions and this attitude began to create friction between PPD and CAT. There were several additional causes for this friction. Much of it came down to the fact that many at PPD distrusted CAT, did not feel its massive firepower was needed, and were ignorant of its capabilities. Things had been fine for almost a century of protection without CAT, and many felt it was not needed now. Another reason PPD did not like CAT in the early days was the freedom we enjoyed. We were totally on our own, for the most part, and were having entirely too much fun for some on the detail.

We were an unconventional, independent lot, and almost everything we did spoke to that side of us. There was also some old-fashioned jealousy involved. On the road and away from Washington, CAT began to take over from PPD the reputation of being the Secret Service social elite.

MY CAT TOUR BEGINS

I checked into CAT from New York in August 1989 and officially began protecting the president of the United States, George Herbert Walker Bush.

On my first day, Randy Wood, the boss, called me into his office, where he welcomed me to CAT, congratulated me on my performance in CAT school, and then said essentially that I was a new guy and that he did not want to even hear my voice for one full year. I was just happy to finally be in CAT and had no problem playing a silent role.

Randy was a combat-decorated army officer and paratrooper who had served in Vietnam and had been an interrogator of Vietcong and North Vietnamese captures. He could be hard and demanding in many ways, but he also gave us a great deal of freedom to do the job as we saw fit. He loved his CAT boys and would go to the wall for us with upper management whenever any heat came our way, but he would chew us out if we were wrong about something. He was a firm believer in handling discipline internally, not putting our CAT business out for the world to see, and any of us would rather have taken a major beating than to draw his ire. He was a hard-to-know and complex man, but once he accepted you, he would never let you down. Above all, he was a great leader, and his men always came first, even at the expense of his own career, if necessary. During my Secret Service career he was the best leader and manager I knew.

I began my CAT career as all new arrivals do, spending the first year in the rear of the CAT truck watching the world while facing backward and learning how things worked in the program. My tactical duty was to provide a base of fire for the team in the event of an attack. My team leader was Phil Hyde, and unofficially my largest duty included always having Phil's personal bag available for him and stacking the gear bags of the remainder of the team in a neat and accessible manner. On days when I was not scheduled to work with my team, I was at our training facility at Beltsville, honing my weapons skills and working out to maintain CAT-level fitness.

By my second year in CAT, I had moved up to team driver and then was selected as assistant team leader. In 1992, Randy appointed me as the team leader in command of team one, the team I had started with as a new guy three years earlier. It now consisted of a new group of agents, the original agents having moved on to other assignments, either within CAT or elsewhere in the Secret Service.

Team leaders were usually chosen from the pool of assistant team leaders. I had been an assistant team leader for a year. There was no real leadership training per se. Teams went to guys who were considered technically and tactically proficient as well as those who had displayed some leadership. My philosophy of leadership was what I had learned as a marine officer and Randy had learned as an army officer: A leader is responsible for everything his people do or fail to do. When your men do well it is to their credit. When your men fail it is your failure. On more than one occasion I stood, not sat, in Randy's office, explaining failures of mine that would seem trivial to most. But to men such as Randy, no detail was considered too small.

Having been moved from Special Services Division to Special Programs Division, CAT was being assigned new leaders. Randy was now promoted to special agent in charge.

We had enjoyed our new designation as a division for about two years when rumors began to circulate that CAT was going to be placed under PPD. All in CAT had hoped it would not happen. We enjoyed our autonomy as a small elite unit and were not willing to give it up. Then, without warning, in the spring of 1992, the entire division was summoned to a large conference room in the New Executive Office Building, where the CAT office was located. The person ordering us to attend this meeting was the director of the United States Secret Service himself.

This individual, while highly respected, was the last of the authoritarian directors from the old school. He was not use to, and did not appreciate, being questioned by subordinates. He had vast government experience at the upper managerial level that included dealing with almost any situation a manager could encounter; all except situations concerning unconventional entities such as CAT.

All CAT agents appeared in the conference room of the New Executive Office Building, at Seventeenth and H streets, as ordered—dressed in suits and looking pretty. As we all sat awaiting our fate, the director entered, along with the deputy, and moved around the room, shaking hands with each CAT agent. We were respectful but resentful; we knew the purpose of the meeting: to abolish CAT as a division and place it under PPD.

The director began his remarks by stating, "CAT, as you all know it is over." He continued by stating that CAT was now a section of PPD. It had lost, its divisional status. The news was not well received. The director had assumed that most of us would approve of being placed under PPD, and he had never expected anyone to challenge him over the issue or voice any displeasure. He was somewhat agitated—I guess that would be the best way to describe it—when more than one agent spoke up. Each one made it clear that he did not want to go to PPD but would instead rather go to other assignments. The director forcefully responded that he could make that happen. Of that fact none had any doubt.

With our divisional status now gone, agent Alan Whicher was assigned as our new boss. After settling into his new role, he did a very good job leading the program. He had replaced a man who was loved by the troops and had been a near-impossible act to follow.

Alan was heavily praised for his good work at CAT and as a reward was given the ASAIC slot in Oklahoma City. He was doing his usual efficient job there when, on the morning of April 19, 1995, a disgruntled army veteran named Timothy McVeigh parked a truck filled with explosives in front of the federal building where the Secret Service office was located. When the truck detonated, Alan was killed, along with five other Secret Service employees.

KOREA

The Korean War began in June 1950, when forces from Communist North Korea invaded the south in an attempt to unify the Korean peninsula under the Communist regime, and it ended with a cease-fire, not an actual surrender or peace agreement, in June 1953. Technically, a state of war still exists to this day between North and South Korea. As anyone who watches the news knows, North Korea is extremely unpredictable and capable of both aggressive rhetoric and unprovoked deadly aggression. It is best not to unnecessarily provoke them.

President Bill Clinton visited South Korea in 1993, and in spite of this potential volatility, the president, or perhaps someone on his staff, decided that he should do a photo op on the Bridge of No Return.

This bridge runs perpendicularly through the 38th parallel of latitude separating the two countries of North and South Korea, and all American POWs that North Korea chose to release walked across the bridge to freedom in 1953. Since the cease-fire agreement in June 1953, the North Koreans have controlled the northern end of the bridge and the South Koreans the southern end. On the Communist northern side of the bridge, there is an observation post occupying high ground, which overlooks the south and provides a perfect view of any activities on the bridge. The area just south of the bridge is a UN observation post and was the site of past unprovoked violence by the always unpredictable forces of North Korea. This was the exact location where, one day in 1976, ax-wielding North Korean soldiers murdered two US Army officers, Captain

Art Bonifas and First Lieutenant Mark Barrett. This deliberate killing of two US Army officers by North Korea, while a blatant act of war that should have resulted in an immediate military response by the Ford administration, produced only the usual verbal outrage, with no action to follow. Seventeen years later, this area where the murders occurred would be the arrival point for President Clinton's motorcade.

As part of the cease-fire, no rifles were allowed in this area, and the closest significant American forces were one mile away. Even with this agreement, CAT was directed by PPD to go to the bridge and get into position. Armed with pistols, only we could monitor POTUS, the bridge, and the North Korean observation post. I took the word "monitor" and applied my own definition to it.

North Korea was briefed ahead of time that POTUS would be making the stop on the bridge. This was a diplomatic as well as an intelligent maneuver. The Communists would have gone ballistic over the sight of President Clinton and company on the bridge had they not known of it before the fact.

The night before the president's visit to the bridge, the commanding officer of Camp Bonifas (named for the deceased officer), a colonel, held a dinner for all Secret Service personnel on the trip. Over drinks in a secluded corner of the officers' club, the colonel, a veteran of both Vietnam and Desert Storm, described our situation in black-and-white terms, characteristic of military men. He stated to the team, "If attacked and you survive the assault, and chances are you will not, you will be acting as a speed bump for the North Korean regulars. We have a squad of shock troops waiting just outside the DMZ who will ride to battle, but they are ten minutes away. In any case, it will be the longest ten minutes of your life . . ." All on the team appreciated his honesty as we accepted this warrior's offer of another round of drinks and his toast to our success and to the survival of the team and the president.

The following day, my team—consisting of agents Mike Carbone, Charlie White, Lee Fields, and Jim Cobb—finished gearing up and mounted our Humvee for the move to the bridge. We had just rolled a few yards when the voice of command post agent and CAT school classmate Joe Clancy jolted me with its urgency. Joe's voice was usually calmer than calm, but on this occasion, the calm was accented with strain. I was aware from the tone in Joe's voice that something was wrong and already knew what it was before Joe announced it.

"Hawkeye from command post," Joe forcefully broadcasted over our encrypted frequency.

"Damn Joe," I said to myself while lowering the volume on my radio. "CP from Hawkeye, go ahead," I answered.

"Hawkeye from CP," Joe responded, "be advised that numerous North Korean soldiers have been observed moving into their sector of the bridge armed with AK-47 rifles."

As I turned and gave my team the "I told you so" look, I keyed my microphone and simply replied back to Joe, "CP from Hawkeye, roger that."

I had anticipated this entirely predictable event well in advance and had never had any intention of letting my team go to the bridge armed only with pistols. Before we left Camp Bonifas, I had given the order to carry our full complement of arms and ammunition—pistols, M16s, and a combined total of over a thousand rounds of ammunition—and I was prepared to assume full responsibility for that decision should the fact be discovered. In addition, I had given the order for each of my team members to carry their rifles with a round in the chamber, violating a major Secret Service regulation for long guns. Since we were not supposed to have our M16s to begin with, violating the round-in-the-chamber regulation was minor. Given how outnumbered we were, the extra second it would take to chamber a round under fire could mean the difference whether we or POTUS survived an ambush.

I felt the situation was serious—damned serious, in fact—and I was not risking my team or the life of the president based on a forty-year-old agreement I had correctly predicted would be broken by the Communists. Because North Korea had come to expect over the years that America is always naïve enough to play by the rules, the Communists likely expected us not to have rifles, and this incorrect assumption on their part tilted the odds in our favor a bit more.

Now knowing what we were up against, we moved out to the bridge, where we found the Communists in and around their observation post arrogantly brandishing their Kalashnikov AK-47 rifles, as reported by my good friend Joe Clancy. To our Secret Service way of thinking, the only reason they would commit such a violation of the no-rifle agreement was because shooting the president of the United States is much easier with rifles than with their Russian-provided Makarov pistols.

The terrain around the bridge, while somewhat improved since 1953, was probably much as it had been at that time. The area was a combination of dirt and asphalt road surrounded by fields and forests. The area was also mined, and it would only take driving off the beaten path a little bit to produce a big, flaming kaboom, so we moved carefully. After settling into the best position from which to deploy in case of attack, which in this case was not directly at the arrival point yet near enough to respond by fire and maneuver, we saw quite clearly the Koreans eyeing us with binoculars and trying to shake us up a bit by pointing rifle scopes in our direction. We counter-eyed them with our own binoculars, and although our M16s were scoped, we kept our rifles low and out of sight. Unlike our North Korean nemesis, we at least had concealed our rifles, giving no indication that we were possibly in violation of the meaningless clause in the 1953 cease-fire agreement.

The North Koreans we now traded game-face looks with were not members of just any foreign military. All were the sons or grandsons of the same men who had helped kill over fifty thousand Americans from 1950 until 1953. Each from birth was indoctrinated to hate America, its form of government, and its leaders, and had been taught that resuming the war with the United States was both inevitable and desirable. The shooting part of the Korean War had ended in 1953 with a truce, and we were technically still at war with

North Korea. If they wanted to resume the shooting war again, today would be the perfect day.

As irrational as the North Koreans could be, we hoped that they had manned the towers with officers under strict orders not to provoke a situation but rather to present a threatening appearance. We also knew that because North Korea was a fanatical Communist state, the possibility existed that one of these young officers might just decide that taking out an American president would be the thing to do. Even an accidental discharge could set off a gunfight, and those can happen at any time on either side. When dealing with North Korea, anything was possible.

By fate and necessity, our mission of fighting a delaying action while POTUS escaped was not much less than certain death should things break bad, and the colonel in charge of the area had as much as said so. None of us had any doubt that, in addition to the North Koreans in the observation post armed with AK-47s just yards from where the president of the United States would be standing, there were in all likelihood more soldiers in the tall grass on their side of the bridge.

This scenario was the quintessential example of why CAT existed and why we trained with such intensity. With a command from me that consisted of only one word, the team would be out of the vehicle and directing a heavy volume of pinpoint, accurate fire on the objective in less than four seconds. Regardless of our own fate in the seconds that would follow, the hope in such a situation was that we would accomplish our mission and that the president of the United States would live another day. Everyone on my team knew this. We accepted it as our job, and there were no complaints. We had no intentions of being mere sacrificial lambs or dying a glorious death, but we were confident that the five of us would produce many, many dead Communists if they decided to do something as ill-advised as killing an American president.

The mood in the CAT vehicle was serious, quiet, and confident as I announced our plan of action in the event of attack. The men indicated with grim smiles that they understood their assignments. I had total confidence that each would do his duty and respond per his training if called upon. We were brothers in arms who worked together, trained together, and traveled the world together. Now, if necessary, we would meet our fates together. We all shook hands and waited for the arrival of the president of the United States into what amounted to nothing less than a made-to-order kill zone. It was time to earn our pay.

As we waited for POTUS, we played eye screw with the Communists while scanning the area. Then, with no warning, everyone in the Humvee began to laugh hysterically, as if the funniest joke in the world had just been told. For one brief moment, we could have been anywhere other than where we were. All mirth died as quickly as it had begun as we saw the approach of the president's motorcade.

At the designated time, President Clinton and his shift arrived at the bridge. As POTUS emerged from the right rear seat, he was immediately surrounded by the shift. From our position, we could see a noticeable increase in activity and movement from the North Korean observation post. If a gunfight were going to happen, it was going to happen within the next few seconds.

The shift then began doing a constant series of radio checks with us. It was both ridiculous and irritating, but they wanted to be sure we had radio contact with them in the event an attack occurred. We didn't bother pointing out that, while there would be a lot of activity in such an event, no one would be talking on the radio. Any survivors from the shift would be covering POTUS and trying to evacuate him across the expanse of the bridge, while CAT did its best to turn the Communist observation post into a sieve by killing as many North Korean soldiers as possible.

I felt calm yet hyper-alert as the adrenaline took effect. I could feel my heart rate increase as my grip tightened on the hand guard of my rifle, concealed beneath the instrument panel of the Humvee. As we sat in our vehicle, we stared at the North Koreans and scanned the surrounding area while the Communists stared back. Meanwhile, President Clinton leisurely strolled along the bridge as if he were at

Camp David, with the satisfied, relaxed look of a man with no concerns.

After walking a little farther onto the bridge than he probably should have, practically into North Korea, President Clinton looked around the area for a few minutes and then returned to his vehicle, and we got the hell out of the zone.

TRAINING FOR THE WORST

In order to maintain our high level of readiness, we trained constantly. If we were not protecting POTUS, we were running immediate action drills, or working on the firing range or in the gym. As good at our work as we were, we were about to become much better: An agent newly placed in charge of CAT training was poised to take our training to new heights and set a new standard for CAT training that continues to this day.

Through this training program, our skills became as sharp as those of any police tactical unit in the world. There was, however, one problem with the training, and it was potentially lethal. CAT protected POTUS, as did the working shift, but at the time the two entities seldom, if ever, trained together.

In the event of an attack on POTUS, PPD shift agents had little idea what CAT was going to do or not do for them, and CAT really did not know what the shift was going to do, other than attempt to cover and evacuate POTUS, as was their job. In order to remedy this shortcoming, CAT and the PPD shift began training together regularly, and problems quickly surfaced that had to be corrected.

One of the first joint training exercises I participated in with CAT and the main presidential detail took place at Kennebunkport, Maine, at the Bush compound. President George H. W. Bush had agreed to allow the Secret Service full access to the compound for some realistic practice.

The first exercise required CAT to respond to the main house, kill the attackers, and consolidate its positions around the house. Within seconds of our securing the residence, a PPD agent ran around the corner of the house and promptly shot me with his training weapon, which fired blank ammunition. The bizarre thing was that this agent and I knew each other, and I had a label in large letters on my back: POLICE. In spite of this, he became so excited over the simulated attack, and so overcome with tunnel vision seeing a man in a black outfit, that he promptly blasted me with his Uzi.

The problem was not unique. Under stress, even in training, some people totally lose the ability to think clearly, and all situational awareness goes out the window. As a result, the confused person shoots someone known to him, because all he sees is a black uniform and a rifle. These exercises were invaluable in that they helped CAT and the shift become a harmonious unit. They also alerted us to the fact that certain agents had to be watched closely during time of stress.

CAT COLLATERAL DUTIES: PROTECTING THE VICE PRESIDENT

While protecting the president is CAT's main function, in some cases upon request CAT would accompany the vice president on high-risk trips, usually overseas. Many times these trips were as eventful as any with the president.

On a trip to the Far East in 1989 in support of Vice President Dan Quayle, my CAT team was in a motorcade en route to a planned stop, and I was working in the back of our Suburban providing rear security. I had just joined CAT about two weeks earlier, and this was my first foreign trip.

Although we had total intersection and route control, one of the many motorcycles that navigate the streets of the region had somehow gotten into the motorcade and was coming up fast behind us. The biker, who wore a backpack, was traveling parallel to the motorcade and accelerated as if he were coming up toward the CAT truck and limo, and then backed off and dropped back. It would not have been permissible to allow this interloper to pull past us and end up adjacent to the VP limo. Once there, the biker could damage the limo and perhaps the vice president in any number of ways.

At the approach of the motorcyclist, who this time looked as if he were going to try to move past us, Phil Hyde, my team leader, calmly turned to me and, with his Boston accent, said, "If he looks like he is going to go past us, take him out." As the biker began to move closer to the CAT truck, I aimed with my M16, placing the UltraDot sight on his chest with the barrel of my weapon clearly protruding from the rear of the vehicle. Upon seeing my rifle aimed directly at him, the biker abruptly decelerated and then moved back and out of our motorcade. Who he was or if he meant to harm the VP, we would never know. These types of incidents seemed to happen a lot in the Far East, mostly due to the maniacal manner of driving found there. In our work, however, we always had to assume the worst in such cases.

WITH THE VICE PRESIDENT IN HAITI

Some of the most dangerous moments in CAT occurred not on the mission itself but rather on the advance. In 1989, I was sent to Haiti to do a CAT advance for Vice President Quayle.

Haiti, adjacent to the Dominican Republic and south of Cuba, is the poorest country in the Western Hemisphere. There was a great deal of political unrest when Vice President Quayle visited, and things were tense from the moment of the advance team's arrival in the capital of Port-au-Prince. The airport was straight out of a bad movie, with one runway and the median strewn with the wreckage of several derelict DC-3s. The terminal building was a pockmarked reminder of other periods of unrest.

With the arrival of the advance team in an Air Force C-141, the Department of State regional security officer (RSO) briefed us. He said that over the past several days, more than one policeman had been captured and burned alive by the criminal element of the local population. Their method of execution was to corner the officer and, after he had expended all ammunition, place a tire over his head, pinning his arms to his side. They then filled the tire with gasoline and ignited it. I was armed with a Sig Sauer P226 9mm pistol, which by then was standard CAT issue, along with 5 magazines of 15 rounds each and an M16 rifle with 180 rounds of ammunition. After the briefing from the RSO, I carried them all.

In addition to relaying the information regarding the human torches, the RSO stated firmly that we should never under any circumstances step outside our vehicle in Port-au-Prince. In the event of a vehicle breakdown, we were to contact the embassy and request assistance. During this time, it was felt that any American caught on the streets could be treated to the same fate as some of the local police. I was determined not to be taken alive and, if cornered, would take as many attackers with me as possible before ending the episode on my own terms.

Each morning the advance team got into our armored Suburban at the El Rancho hotel and drove to the embassy. We had to drive straight through downtown Port-au-Prince. Locals surrounded our vehicle anytime we slowed down. The VP lead advance would drive, while I sat in the right front seat with my rifle, hoping the older, mechanically questionable Suburban would make it to the safety of the embassy yet again. Each morning we saw at least one dead body lying somewhere close to the embassy or floating in the ocean. Due to the heat, it did not take long for these unfortunate souls to notify us of their presence through the sense of smell before we could see them.

On this trip in 1989, there were other dangers in addition to the restless populace. One was the Anopheles mosquito. During this trip, we were warned about the malaria-carrying mosquitoes, which seemed to be everywhere and in great numbers. At night in my hotel room, which was nothing more than a small room with a cement floor, a bed, and a giant red bathtub, I slept very lightly, with a sheet wrapped up to my neck to deter the bugs, and my Sig pistol gripped in my right hand. Sleep did not come easily with the mosquitoes and the sound of gunfire, which could be heard all night, ranging in distance from very far to very close.

The most concerning part of the advance was a night move from the American embassy to the airport in order to meet the air force cargo plane that was bringing the vice president's armored cars, as well as additional agents and my CAT team. For the moment this was, for all intents and purposes, a land without law, and CAT was the only protection that could be counted on if we were ambushed.

We arrived at the airport without incident at about 2:00 a.m., when most everyone in the area was sleeping. This was done by design in order to avoid a broad-daylight spectacle of the VP's limo and follow-up being driven from the airport to the embassy. The cars were to be garaged until his arrival two days hence.

My team came off the plane with their rifles, and we formed a CAT team in my vehicle to protect the motorcade on the way back to the embassy and then proceeded to the hotel, where all six of us were treated like royalty by other agents sent to assist in the visit. No one was shy about voicing their gratitude for our presence, and that night our bar tab was taken care of by others.

On game day, as we awaited the vice president at the airport, we were pretty apprehensive. Since our arrival the week before, we had seen virtually no police or anyone from the military. Today, however, there were large numbers of Haitian militia armed with M1 Garand rifles surrounding the airport and pacing the tarmac.

The M1 had been the main battle rifle of the US military from 1942 until around 1962, when it was replaced with the M14. Close to six million M1 rifles were produced, and although the weapon only fired eight rounds of 30.06 ammunition before having to be reloaded, many nations around the world, including Haiti, were happy to receive it as a gift from America. While these rifles were old and beat, they were lethal.

As I wandered over for a look at the soldiers and their weapons, I noticed that some of the ammunition clipped to their rifle slings was black-tipped, indicating armor-piercing ability. This was a major concern to a Secret Service agent for obvious reasons. In civilized countries that were longtime allies, such as Great Britain, this would have presented no issues for us. Haiti did not fall into this category, however, and seeing so many Haitians armed with rifles with an effective range of well over five hundred yards and ammunition that could punch through armor was of concern.

History had taught us that there was always cause to view armed foreign military at political events with suspicion. Egypt's President Anwar Sadat was assassinated by his own military in 1981 during an outdoor political event. America had never lost a vice president to assassination, and I was determined that today would be no different. We were taking no chances.

When confronted with questions regarding the addition of the armed Haitians, the Haitian government counterpart explained to the airport site agent that these last-minute troops were a "reaction force" should the airport or the motorcade be attacked. This move was not a part of the agreement with the Haitian government but typical of how the Service sometimes finds itself manipulated in third-world countries like Haiti.

After all plans are agreed upon between the Secret Service advance agent and the local government, on the day of the visit they are usually not worth the paper they are written on. I always wondered if this was indifference or ill intent: a desire to abuse the most powerful country in the world simply because it was possible to do so. There was little one could do when the protectee was on final approach and the formerly friendly, "no problem" counterpart all at once became an arrogant, dictatorial monster.

Days prior to a visit by POTUS or VPOTUS (the vice president of the United States), if things became too heated between the host government and the Secret Service, the nuclear option was to simply tell the host government that the president or vice president would cancel the visit due to security concerns. To avoid the embarrassment of such a cancellation, the host would usually concede—until the day of the visit, when it was too late for the protectee to back out, like now.

As Air Force Two finally arrived and parked with all eyes on it, the CAT Suburban slowly and with little notice moved into a position where the so-called reaction force of the Haitians present could be observed and, if necessary, neutralized.

Sometimes a decent show of force is as good as the use of force itself, and the unwanted militia behaved themselves in a quiet, docile manner, seemingly afraid to handle their rifles or even look at us.

As the motorcade began to move, CAT abruptly repositioned and waited until the second truck full of Haitians drove past. We then cut in front of the second vehicle behind them, placing us in a perfect position to respond to any unforeseen event. Although we were severely outnumbered, six highly trained CAT agents with M16s each holding thirty rounds, with an additional thirty-round magazine clipped alongside and access to hundreds more, were certainly a match against these poorly disciplined and undoubtedly ill-trained militiamen. Also, even if the militia meant no ill will, in the event of an attack on the motorcade we did not want them to try to help. Having them deploy and open fire probably in all directions would have been as dangerous as an actual ambush.

We maintained this position in the motorcade for the remainder of all movements. Although the Haitians had reveled in the power of pulling a fast one at the last moment by placing these two trucks in our motorcade, giving the Secret Service no choice in the matter, we simply countered this potentially dangerous move with a move of our own, which left the Haitians no choice but to play our game. There was a saying in the Secret Service that you either played ball with the Secret Service or the Secret Service would ram the bat up your ass, and this was certainly our game.

A Department of State official informed me later that the Haitians were not happy about our posturing. I advised the diplomat that we were not posturing but rather placing ourselves in the best position to take out the Haitians, if necessary, and that we couldn't have cared less about their feelings. Our job was to ensure that the vice president left Haiti alive, not to make friends. The diplomats could work out the hurt feelings later at the next embassy party over martinis and hugs.

With the visit concluded and the VP now safely airborne en route back to Washington, DC, the advance team formed up at the airport to await our transportation back to civilization, an old, noisy C-141 like the one we had flown in on. We sat on the tarmac under the broiling, merciless sun, leaning against our gear bags until we heard the unmistakable whine of the four big jet engines that would take us out of this hellhole and back to America.

After landing, the pilot, an older major wearing the star and wreath on his wings signifying that he was a command pilot, voiced some concern about the current airworthiness of his plane but said that there were no backups available. After some consultation with his copilot and flight engineer, he decided to give it a go if we were willing. We were all were willing to take a chance on this plane and crew rather than be left in Haiti for another night.

We boarded the plane, which had been sitting in the sun for more than an hour by then, and the interior was well over 110 degrees. We took our seats in the stifling heat, and the major came back to our area and announced that there was no water on board and asked if we would be willing to share whatever we had by pouring it into the cooler at the front of the passenger compartment. Not enough water in this heat was serious, and several agents were already showing signs of becoming heat casualties. No one hesitated, and a line formed so that agents could pour whatever water remained into the communal supply. As a result of sharing, there was enough water for all on the trip back to DC. That was one of the things about Secret Service agents. An agent might try to steal your date, but he would give you his last dollar, last beer, or the last of his water merely for the asking.

After stepping off the world's slowest jet and seeing home again, I was, as always, thankful to God for allowing me to have been born in the United States rather than in a country like the one we had just left behind. That feeling of gratitude always surfaced after I returned from countries such as Haiti. Years later I would have the same feeling after returning from a place even worse than Haiti—Afghanistan.

WITH THE VICE PRESIDENT IN THE PHILIPPINES AND KOREA: NECKTIES AND CARPET-TACK BOMBS

Agents in general, and especially CAT people, had a pretty gregarious sense of humor, almost to the man. The CAT sense of humor was designed to keep the teams loose and could surface at any moment.

Just prior to a 1989 CAT trip to the Philippines, there had been a lot of unrest among the people, and the local police had used tear gas to quell the violence. More trouble was expected. On this trip, we were supporting the VP. Dan Quayle was due to arrive at the airport in the late evening. That night, as we stood around the CAT truck waiting for Air Force Two, a rotund, rosy-cheeked, little vice presidential staffer bashfully wandered over to our truck. He was more than a little concerned about breathing tear gas should the police throw any. It seems he had asthma.

All CAT agents had been gassed more than once, either in CAT school or in the military. It was unpleasant but no big deal, but of course, we had gas masks and staff did not. I tried to explain to the staff person that in an open area or in a motorcade, he would not even notice the gas should it be deployed. He was not satisfied. I patiently explained that the wind dissipates the gas very quickly. Worst case, if he did get a whiff, it would be gone and over before he knew it. He was still not satisfied. I was trying to assuage this man's fears as best I could, but he would not believe me. Exasperated, I finally said, "If they throw gas, urinate on your tie and wrap it around your face; that will protect you better than anything else." He was now satisfied.

While this method of gas protection was utilized in World War I, I was puzzled as I watched the young man wander over to the jungle tree line, where he removed his tie and began relieving himself on it. I was astounded that he would actually do it, but, after all, he had asthma. He was quite thorough in his mission and must have had to go for quite some time. He then walked past the CAT truck with a new swagger in his step, born of the confidence of the field-expedient gas mask around his neck like a bandanna. He thanked me for my help and rejoined his group, where we saw them discussing something obviously of great importance.

In a few minutes, the same jungle area was lined with male staffers relieving themselves on their ties. Each then filed past the CAT team sporting their modified neckwear. The VP landed and boarded the motorcade, and we proceeded to his next stop with no tear gas being thrown. If there had been gas, however, the vice president's staff was prepared.

Even serious incidents could produce humor. On a VP trip to Korea around the time of the Philippines trip, the locals had been throwing carpet-tack bombs at police, and some injuries had occurred. Essentially these were not much more than big cherry bombs wrapped in tape and carpet tacks. We had been warned about them and had been told that, on the trip up to Camp Bonifas with the motorcade, where we would meet up the next day with the VP, who was arriving by helo, we should keep the windows rolled up.

It was late at night, and we were sitting in our truck in the motorcade waiting to move north to Bonifas. The weather was warm and humid, so our driver had his window down for the time being to allow some air in. The cars started to move, and our driver pressed on the accelerator, at which time he started screaming, "God damn, God damn!" Phil Hyde, our team leader, turned to him and said, "Calm down," and then asked what the problem was. It seems that our driver's sunglasses had fallen from behind the sun visor into his lap. In the dark, he thought it was a carpet-tack bomb. When he and all of us realized what it really was, we laughed until we could not breathe. "Damn, man," he said, "I thought I was about to get my balls blown off."

We made it up to Camp Bonifas, and, other than a few male staffers relieving themselves on their ties and our driver relieved that he had not lost his manhood from a dreaded carpet-tack bomb, the entire VP trip to Korea went without incident.

After the VP departed for Washington, DC, the rest of the team moved from the DMZ back to Seoul in the CAT truck. Phil Hyde and I were going to move back down to Seoul via an army UH-1 helicopter, or Huey. He and I had been sitting in the Camp Bonifas officers' club trading stories with some outstanding Airborne Ranger army officers when our Huey flight crew arrived.

Our crew of pilot, co-pilot, and crew chief entered the bar, and introductions were made. Our pilot was one of the few, or perhaps the only, Warrant Officer 5 (WO5) in the US Army. He was the most senior aviator in all of the army, with over thirty years of flying experience.

After some small talk with the crew, the WO5 headed for the door, and my team leader and I got up to move to the Huey, leaving our beers on the bar. The grand old man of army aviation shook his head and, smiling with his pale blue eyes, crinkled around the edges from thousands of hours of flying into the direct rays of the sun, told us to bring our beers with us. We had to comply because, after all, he was the aircraft commander.

It was a clear, warm afternoon, perfect for flying. The doors to the Huey were open, with the calming wap-wap noise of the rotors echoing through the helicopter and the wind swirling through the crew compartment. I sat directly behind the old Warrant Officer, whose neck looked like leather that had been left in the sun for about five years and was splattered with scars from wounds received more than twenty years earlier. He had probably dodged and caught as much lead in Vietnam as any man alive. I had asked him back at the club how many times he had been shot down. He smiled and said, "Too many to even count." The old WO5 was a true American hero and a damned nice fellow, too.

CAT FLOURISHES

Time moved on, and so did the never-ending flow of CAT agents to the presidential working shift, as more and more of the older agents moved out of the White House and on to other assignments. It was becoming common for almost entire shifts surrounding the president to be made up of former CAT agents, and they were all excellent. CAT agents began to run PPD. Three of the most recent SAICs were former CAT agents.

When I returned to PPD/CAT in 2003 to become the ATSAIC, I scarcely recognized the operation. There were now twice as many teams as had been there when I left in 1993, and the caliber of the agents was beyond outstanding. These agents were bigger, smarter, and far better equipped than those in the CAT I had been a part of in the late 1980s and early 1990s. CAT had come light-years since its initial inception and had become one of the most highly respected branches of the Secret Service. The truly extraordinary agents who make up CAT are a force to be reckoned with and a source of pride for all Americans. When the day comes for CAT to deploy in a live-fire situation to save the life of the president—and that day will come—I have complete faith that they will succeed.

CHAPTER 9

The Agent Who Loved Me . . . Eventually

During my four years assigned to the CAT team, I experienced many exciting and interesting episodes that would provide memories for a lifetime. The most important, however, was not any adventure involving the protection of the president. It was my marriage to another agent, which occurred in November 1990.

My decision to get married came as a shock to many, as I was a thirty-five-year-old confirmed bachelor, or so everyone—and I—believed. With my busy career and a great social life, characteristic of a single Secret Service agent, marriage did not seem to be in the cards. I had totally dismissed the thought.

Over the years I had sat in vehicles, command posts, and squad rooms listening for hours to the complaints of married agents about their wives' reckless spending, jealousies, and petty complaints, as well as the challenges of trying to be a father while being away from home a great deal of the time. It seemed that many Secret Service wives did not understand or were unwilling to accept the fact that the mission came first and family came second. Nor did they seem to understand that, when a man had been working out of state or country for twenty-one continuous days or longer, upon arriving back home he did not want to hear the complaints of the standard suburban housewife. Before being tasked with yard work and going to the PTA meeting, he merely wanted, in varying order, conjugal relief, a good meal, a cold beer, and some sleep.

Most of my fellow agents had married prior to joining the Secret Service, and their wives had no idea what was coming in the way of demands of the profession—separations, long hours at work, and so on. Husbands were torn between the mission and maintaining domestic tranquillity. To be a married Secret Service agent seemed like a tremendous amount of work and trouble. The job made being a good father and husband seemingly impossible. In each case where a decision had to be made regarding career or family, either the family or the Service got the short end. I knew I loved the Secret Service but merely enjoyed the company of attractive women. I was a confirmed bachelor, and nothing could possibly change that. I was, however, about to come face to face with the reality of "never say never."

On a cold Sunday evening in November 1988 I had just returned to my apartment in New Jersey after spending Thanksgiving leave at my parents' home in Georgia. As I walked in, dead tired from the fourteen-hour drive, I opened a beer and noticed the blinking light on my answering machine. It was a message from a senior agent in the New York field office, who stated that on the following day I was to begin motorcade advance preparations for the visit of Mikhail Gorbachev, general secretary of the Communist Party of the Soviet Union, and his wife, Raisa, who were visiting New York. The message also instructed me to meet and bring to the office a female Secret Service agent sent from the San Francisco office to assist in interpreting Russian for the advance team. My instructions further stated that she would be standing in front of the Vista Hotel adjacent to the World Trade Center at 8:30 the following morning.

Monday morning came, and after willing myself out of bed and surviving the ninety-minute gauntlet of death from New Jersey to Manhattan, I pulled up in front of the Vista Hotel, where I parked the Secret Service 1981 Pontiac LeMans and waited. I soon found myself looking at one of the most attractive women I had ever seen. She was standing on the steps of the hotel and appeared to be waiting for someone. I dismissed the thought that she could be my contact. While admiring her and listening to *Imus in the Morning* on the radio, I continued to wait for my assignment to show up.

The object of my attention was tall and statuesque, over five feet ten inches, with jet-black hair, high cheekbones, and dark Italian eyes, combined with a posture, figure, and demeanor that unmistakably said she was a woman of refinement. Probably European, I thought to myself, perhaps in New York on a modeling assignment. I sat in my car staring at her—leering, in fact—but realizing that whoever this lovely creature was, she was totally out of my league and could only be admired from a distance, as one would admire a beautiful painting or a statue.

As I continued to stare, she stared back. "Busted," I thought. She then began moving down the steps of the Vista toward my car and me. Apprehension turned to near panic as she opened the door to the car, got in, and said, "Hi, my name is Donnelle" while flashing a perfect, blinding smile and offering me a feminine yet athletic hand to shake. With some difficulty I stammered out my own name.

Up close, she was even more beautiful. Over the next several days, her beauty, along with the scent of her perfume, drove me nearly to distraction from the business at hand of moving Russians safely around New York. I could see that this assignment was going to take all of the professional discipline I possessed.

As luck would have it, she was assigned to me as my interpreter for the duration of the visit, which lasted several days. Her Russian language skills were very good, and the beauty of the Russian language as spoken by her was almost at times too much for me to endure. It was obvious that my KGB counterparts were equally impressed.

During those few short days she and I worked closely together, and while I tried hard to impress her with whatever charm I could muster, she seemed totally immune and uninterested. Even so, we became friends, and when it came time for her to return to San Francisco, I sadly thought I had probably seen the last of her.

Over the course of the next year, Donnelle and I stayed in touch by telephone but never saw one another. The turning point in our relationship occurred when I was transferred from New York to Washington, DC, and the Counter Assault Team.

My first several CAT trips were to the San Francisco area, where she was still assigned. It seemed that everywhere I turned she was there, and in spite of our conflicting assignments we managed to see one another occasionally. Each time I saw her I felt more and more that this was someone I wanted to have a relationship with, although I fought the emotion, as the entire situation seemed too improbable to seriously pursue—impossible, in fact.

With each encounter, however, my affection for her began to grow, but if she shared that affection, it was not noticeable. Due to circumstances, timing, geography, and her seemingly built-in emotional deflector shields, we seemed to be on a path of friendship only. I had noticed one thing for certain, however: This woman had the kindest eyes I had ever seen, and my determination to resist pursuing a serious relationship with her was diminishing each time I looked into them.

During the late spring of 1990, Donnelle was sent from San Francisco to Washington for the purpose once again of using her Russian language skills during a visit from Mikhail Gorbachev, by then president of the Soviet Union. As usual, I took up as much of her time after-hours as possible.

One of the benefits of socializing with other agents is that we all have the same security clearances and can talk shop. The inability to discuss certain things with non-agents ends many relationships before they begin. Donnelle and I talked for hours on end, never seeming to run out of things to say.

After arriving one evening at our usual meeting place, the Old Ebbitt Grill just down the street from the White House, I asked how her day interpreting for the Russians had gone. She said that the Russians had been, as always, entertaining to work with, and she related an incident that had happened that day.

She had been interpreting when she was approached on the south grounds of the White House by the five-man Russian equivalent of a Secret Service Counter Assault Team. Although Donnelle spoke very good Russian, the team leader said, in heavily accented English: "All day we have been called CAT. We do not know why we are called CAT. Can you please tell us why we are called CAT? Is this bad?" After writing on a piece of paper in Russian an explanation that CAT was an American acronym for Counter Assault Team, the Russian seemed pleased and said, "Thank you, we now know why we are called CAT." As he showed the piece of paper to his team, chests began to expand as each Russian CAT member smiled and nodded, obviously proud of the new designation.

As she told this amusing story, the thought went through my head that one of the most important things in a relationship, and one that had always been missing, to any large extent, in my previous relationships, was having things in common with the other person. We had much in common and each could talk openly about the job. If only she were not assigned three thousand miles away.

One evening after dinner at the Old Ebbitt Grill, lubricated with twelve-year-old Scotch and inspired by several minutes of staring into those eyes, I unexpectedly blurted out, almost to my own horror, "Hypothetically, if I were to ask you to marry me, what would you say?"

"Hypothetically, perhaps," she said. She then volunteered that she would be in Dallas the following month assigned to protect George W. Bush, son of President George H. W. Bush.

"I didn't know we were protecting him," I said. "Doesn't he own the Texas Rangers baseball team?"

"Right," she offered, "and stop changing the subject." She continued that if I were serious, nonhypothetically, I could come to Dallas and ask her to marry me in June. Always one to think things through, she obviously wanted me to do the same.

In the sober light of day, I discovered that I apparently was serious and that my feelings had not changed. On a hot June evening in 1990, I found myself in Dallas, Texas, holding an engagement ring while asking this Italian American beauty if she would indeed marry me. To my astonishment, she accepted. To my further astonishment, I was now engaged to be married, and very happy about the entire situation.

Two Secret Service agents marrying one another is not as easy a proposition as it sounds. She was stationed on the West Coast and I in Washington, DC. Donnelle accepting my proposal was only half the battle. In order for this to work, the Secret Service was going to have to cooperate.

At the time, there were relatively few couples employed by the Service. There was in those days a Service policy that tandems could not serve in the same office or division, which made marriage between agents difficult. Most of these tandems were located in large cities, where one partner worked in the main field office and the other in a smaller resident office. An example would be the Los Angeles field office and the Riverside resident office. Another option that others in our position had elected but which was unacceptable to us was for one spouse to resign. Donnelle and I were both career agents, so we would have to find another way. Administratively Donnelle was assigned to a field office that fell under the Office of Investigations, and I was assigned to CAT, which fell under Protective Operations. It was, in a sense, like working for two separate agencies.

One afternoon I sat in my boss's office at CAT and tried to explain the situation to him. He scratched his head, asked if I was insane, and then sent me to see the assistant director of Protective Operations, who, after patiently listening to my plight, agreed to ask the assistant director of Investigations to arrange for Donnelle to be transferred from San Francisco to the Washington field office, where she would conduct criminal investigations and do temporary protective assignments. There was one catch. We had to be married, not merely engaged, before he arranged for this transfer. It seems that in the past an agent had used the marriage card in order to be transferred to his girlfriend's city of residence and then never married her. This amounted to a very expensive waste of a transfer, so the Service wanted to see a marriage license before spending a hundred thousand dollars on Donnelle's move.

As our wedding date neared, it appeared as if one or both of us might not make it to the ceremony for any number of reasons. Three days before we were to be married Donnelle was in Colombia and I was in Haiti.

It all somehow came together, although I have no idea how. On November 10, 1990, we were married in Gainesville, Georgia, with both a Catholic priest and a Baptist minister in attendance. November 10 is the Marine Corps birthday. Being married on that particular day ensured that I would never forget my anniversary. Semper Fi.

After our honeymoon to Hilton Head, South Carolina, we moved into my small condominium in Gaithersburg, Maryland. Because one of us was usually gone most of the time, our marriage seemed like a never-ending honeymoon or the greatest date in the world. It is a date that has lasted for over two decades and produced the finest son anyone could wish for.

★ CHAPTER 10 ★

Human Shields and Operant Conditioning

One of the questions people ask most frequently of Secret Service agents is whether they are actually willing to take a bullet for the president. Most agents will simply change the subject or deflect the question with humor. For the record, the answer is yes, but few agents will publicly admit it, and none enjoys discussing it. In my own case, as an agent applicant I was made aware very early in the selection process that this possibility existed and that if I was not willing to lay down my life for the president I should apply for a job elsewhere. The subject never came up again in twenty-one years of service. It was simply understood.

Although it has the potential to become so, being a Secret Service agent on PPD is not a suicide mission and no agent is expected to unnecessarily give up his or her life for the president. One of the most popular myths about Secret Service agents is that they swear an oath to die for the president. A complete urban legend as no such oath exists, this is exactly what all commit to the moment they become a Secret Service agent.

For me personally, no one ever elected to the office of the presidency was worth dying for, yet the office of the presidency was. Presidents are only people who live and breathe like anyone else, but the office of the presidency must be protected at all costs. Consequently, the person occupying that office by default becomes worth dying for regardless of party affiliation or the personal feelings an agent may have. For anyone considering the Secret Service as a career, this must be part of his or her belief set. If it is not, the Secret Service is not the career he or she should pursue.

Psychologists will affirm that it takes a special type of person to willingly sacrifice his life for that of a president—or anyone else, for that matter. To this end, the Secret Service tirelessly seeks highly dedicated, motivated, intelligent, and patriotic young people, then trains them until certain responses become automatic, removing thought, heroics, or cowardice from the equation. While interviewees may be adamant and swear that they would die for the president if necessary, there is no way to prove the claim. But the training that is received by all agents assures it.

Secret Service agents are trained to cover and evacuate a protectee during an attack, not necessarily to dive in front of a bullet like Clint Eastwood's character in the movie *In the Line of Fire*. In an attack on POTUS the idea is to get him out of the kill zone and for everyone to survive if at all possible. If even one agent is taken out of action during an attempt on the president's life, the odds of POTUS surviving decrease exponentially. It is therefore more beneficial to POTUS for as many of his agents to survive as possible.

In order to ensure that its agents will respond correctly in situations that are life-threatening to the president, the Secret Service subjects its agents to repetitious training until certain responses become automatic.

Assassinations and attempted assassinations are usually over in less than three or four seconds. In such events, no one has time to think about what to do. Rather, one reacts according to training. The training that all agents initially receive and then continue to receive throughout their careers is a form of operant conditioning, whereby a person reacts automatically based on exposure to certain stimuli and events.

Agents, for example, are trained in how to disarm assailants who are armed with knives and handguns. The exercise is done so many times in training that if an agent faces a real gun or knife, he or she should automatically attempt to disarm the person without thinking. This super-repetitive training removes any thought process associated with the reaction, and responses become totally automatic, whether the situation is real or training. This response must be instantaneous if such situations are to end successfully.

While it takes years of training to produce such flawless response, Secret Service agents are anything but Pavlov's dogs responding to a bell. And, contrary to assertions by some very shallow, uninformed people, Secret Service agents are not brainwashed. Agents receive the best executive protective training in the world, and the success of this training has been proven on many occasions.

It was this training that saved the life of Ronald Reagan on March 30, 1981. On that day, John Hinckley, who had embedded himself inside the press pen with the media outside the Washington Hilton, fired six rounds from a .22-caliber revolver at President Reagan. Of the six shots fired, four found a human target.

One slug hit Washington, DC, policeman Thomas Delahanty, one hit the presidential press secretary, James Brady, and one hit the president after ricocheting off the limo. The other struck Secret Service agent Tim McCarthy. Of the four persons shot during this attack, it was McCarthy who was hit because he responded in a controlled fashion, while others were largely accidental victims, in the wrong place at the wrong time, as it were. McCarthy, who was standing in his assigned position next to the limo door, moved at the sound of the first round into a cover position blocking POTUS from the attack and, due to his training, became a 200-pound human bullet trap.

The entire episode was over in less than three seconds. Even so, the sound of the sixth and last round had not finished echoing off the buildings surrounding the Washington Hilton when SAIC Jerry Parr had pushed President Reagan into the backseat of the limo. These responses were the quintessential examples of operant conditioning produced by years of training, and while Pavlov's dogs might have been interested in the tires of the limo, they would have had trouble opening and closing the doors.

Another example of the effectiveness of Secret Service training occurred on September 4, 1975, when agent Larry Buendorf, while assigned to PPD, disarmed Lynette "Squeaky" Fromme as she pointed a loaded Colt .45 semiautomatic pistol at President Gerald Ford in Sacramento, California.

While escorting President Ford on a walk to the capital, Buendorf saw a hand come up holding a gun. Per training, he sounded off, "Gun!" Ripping the loaded Colt out of Fromme's hand in the prescribed manner, he pulled it to his chest while the remainder of the detail evacuated President Ford to a safe location. He had practiced this hundreds of times with a dummy weapon held by an instructor. This time it was a live weapon in the hand of a person intent on killing the president. Mr. Buendorf's response to the potentially lethal situation was perfect.

Presidents are, of course, not the only persons protected by the Secret Service. As we have seen, beginning in 1968, after the assassination of Robert Kennedy, the Secret Service began protecting major presidential candidates. Protecting a presidential candidate can be more dangerous than protecting the president, as the Secret Service discovered on May 15, 1972. At a shopping center in Laurel, Maryland, a man named Arthur Bremer shot presidential candidate and former Alabama governor George Wallace five times. Also wounded in the attempted assassination of Wallace was Secret Service agent Nick Zarvos, who was hit in the throat by a .38 Special bullet.

Due to the continuous training received throughout their careers, agents do not differentiate during an attack between the president and anyone of lesser office. The process is designed to work regardless of who the protectee is.

Agent Clint Hill shielding President and Mrs. Kennedy seconds after the assassination. (*Public domain*)

Running is a big part of agent training. Here I am with a class running the perimeter of the training academy. (*Personal collection of Dan Emmett*)

Pugil stick training to simulate bayonet fighting. (*Photo by Corporal Jess Levens, USMC*)

Climbing rope with a class on the obstacle course. (*Personal collection of Dan Emmett*)

As a first lieutenant home on leave, December 1979. (*Personal collection of Dan Emmett*)

With Senator Kennedy at Hyannis Port, Massachusetts, on Election Day, 1984. (*Personal collection of Dan Emmett*)

The Bridge of No Return, looking into North Korea. The Communist observation post is visible in the upper left-hand corner of the bridge. (*Personal collection of Dan Emmett*)

My CAT team in Korea preparing to move to the Bridge of No Return. (Left to right: Agents Charlie White, Jim Cobb, Mike Carbone, the author, and agent Lee Fields.) That is North Korea behind the yellow line. (*Personal collection of Dan Emmett*)

Donnelle and I with President and Mrs. Bush at the White House Christmas party 1992. (*Photo courtesy of The White House*)

With President Bill Clinton in Georgetown, 1993. President Clinton loved large crowds; the larger the better. That is me on the far right wearing the game face. We had just emerged from the Sequoia restaurant in Georgetown on a Sunday morning into a large crowd and had been in one place far too long. (*Photo courtesy of The White House*)

Keeping an eye on things with President Clinton in the pressroom at the White House. (*Photo courtesy of The White House*)

Donnelle and I with President Clinton at the White House Christmas party, 1994. (*Photo courtesy of The White House*)

All presidents I protected were always cordial to their agents and families. Here, my son and I say hello to President Clinton in the Oval Office. (*Photo courtesy of The White House*)

From inside a CAT truck following Air Force One, tail number 27000, with President George Herbert Walker Bush inside. Note the crack in the windshield from a previous encounter with this jet. Although the engine thrust was less with this airplane than the larger 747, it was still formidable. Damaged windshields were not uncommon from following too closely. (*Personal collection of Dan Emmett*)

Marine One departs the White House. (*Photo courtesy of The White House*)

President Clinton and I leaving the White House for a run through downtown Washington, DC, where anyone could be waiting with a gun. (*Photo courtesy of The White House*)

A 1993 Cadillac armored limousine first used by President Clinton. This vehicle sported a 450-cubic-inch engine. Although long retired from service, the actual weight remains classified. (*Photo courtesy of The White House*)

SATC 138 at Fort Meade obstacle course, 1995. I am at the far left. John Mrha is at the far right. (*Personal collection of Dan Emmett*)

With President Bush in the Oval Office. (*Photo courtesy of The White House*)

Leaving the White House as an agent for the last time. (*Personal collection of Dan Emmett*)

☆ CHAPTER 11 ☆

The Boldness of the Presidency

A SECRET SERVICE CHALLENGE

At times both sitting and former presidents voluntarily engage in optional activities that could result in death or serious injury. Frequently, the Secret Service watches these exhibitions knowing full well it has no control over the outcome. Since it is the mission of the Secret Service to protect these men from all harm, certain activities can be of grave concern to the Service. The Secret Service will usually voice quiet concern over such activities, yet in most cases the will of the president overcomes that of the Secret Service.

In these delicate situations, the Secret Service does its best to protect a man who does not always wish to be protected. There are times when presidents are very happy to have the Secret Service by their side. At other times, the president pushes back and strives for a small degree of independence from the necessary yet burdensome presence of his full-time protectors.

Many of our presidents, including John F. Kennedy and George H. W. Bush, have documented histories of physical courage exhibited during military service. It is unfortunate that such men's deeds of heroism seem to have a finite shelf life with voters. As such, a president and his advisors many times will take risks to remind voters that the man they have elected or who wishes to be elected by them is strong and brave enough to hold the office he holds or seeks.

Not to be left out, former presidents who were forced to control their impulse for adventure while in office often present great security challenges by engaging in acts they could have never gotten away with while in office.

Politics aside, there are other reasons these men engage in sometimes unnecessarily dangerous behavior. Eight of the last ten presidents were military officers. Five served in combat. As commander in chief of the armed forces, the president of the United States presides over the boldest group of men and women in the world, our men and women in uniform. Because they are constantly around such high-speed individuals, some presidents occasionally seem to feel a need to be seen, in the eyes of these warriors, as "real men"—not just politicians in Brooks Brothers suits wearing expensive watches but rather equals in nerve and boldness.

And, part of this behavior is simply in a president's DNA. Men who become president of the United States tend to be super-competitive risk takers. While this trait of personality may mellow with the years, it seldom goes dormant and is never extinguished.

Neither Democrats nor Republicans seemed immune. This is true of those who possess a history of tangible physical courage, such as Presidents George H. W. Bush and John F. Kennedy, and of those with a background strictly in academia and politics.

PRESIDENT JOHN F. KENNEDY

One example of the type of man who becomes president is John F. Kennedy, who, as a naval officer during World War II, commanded a PT boat. A mere eighty feet in length, these boats built for speed and maneuverability were constructed primarily of wood. Propelled by two enormous General Motors engines that dined on highly flammable 100 octane aviation fuel, they made a huge explosion when hit by enemy gunners from the Japanese destroyers they were sent up against.

After losing his first boat, PT-109, and recovering from the experience, he rejected going home to Hyannis Port to the safety and celebrity of a returning war hero on survivor's leave. Instead, he requested and was granted command of another PT boat and continued to do battle with Japanese forces.

JFK's exploits were driven by his desire to serve America and by his love of adventure. Prior to the war, Kennedy had no political aspirations. His political career was formulated and moved into action by his father, Joseph Kennedy Sr., who was grooming JFK's older brother, Joe Jr., for politics. When Joe was killed as a naval aviator, JFK moved up to take his place in the future Kennedy political machine. After becoming president, JFK was known to take inordinate risks from time to time, most notably immersing himself in large crowds of people where anyone could have killed him.

Some believed JFK had a death wish or that he could see his future. Part of this belief is based upon President Kennedy's favorite poem, "I Have a Rendezvous with Death," by Alan Seeger.

I HAVE A RENDEZVOUS WITH DEATH

I have a rendezvous with Death
At some disputed barricade,
When Spring comes back with rustling shade
And apple-blossoms fill the air—
I have a rendezvous with Death
When Spring brings back blue days and fair.

It may be he shall take my hand
And lead me into his dark land,
And close my eyes and quench my breath—
It may be I shall pass him still.
I have a rendezvous with Death
On some scarred slope of battered hill,
When Spring comes round again this year
And the first meadow-flowers appear.

God knows 'twere better to be deep
Pillowed in silk and scented down,
Where Love throbs out in blissful sleep,
Pulse nigh to pulse, and breath to breath,
Where hushed awakenings are dear . . .

But I've a rendezvous with Death
At midnight in some flaming town,
When Spring trips north again this year,
And I to my pledged word am true,
I shall not fail that rendezvous.

Perhaps President Kennedy also felt because of his World War II adventures at the age of twenty-six commanding a PT boat, combined with being the youngest president in America's history, he was invincible. He was not.

True to the words of Seeger, he did not fail that rendezvous.

PRESIDENT GEORGE H. W. BUSH

Another president who was no stranger to risk taking was President George H. W. Bush.

A naval aviator during the same war JFK served in, he flew low-level bombing missions against the Japanese in his Grumman Avenger from the deck of a small carrier. Awarded the Distinguished Flying Cross for his skill and courage under fire, he parachuted into the Pacific Ocean after his torpedo bomber was fatally struck by ground fire. The life raft in which he floated while awaiting a rescue that might never come drifted very close to the Japanese-occupied island of Chichi-jima, which he had just bombed. Japanese officers who were known to cut out and eat the livers from their still living captives inhabited this island. Fortunately, the American submarine *Finback* plucked the future forty-first president of the United States from the ocean, saving him from such a cruel fate. Lieutenant Bush then became an accidental submariner until the *Finback* could deliver him back to his ship.

President Bush never quite got over his love of physical danger, as demonstrated by his numerous parachute jumps since leaving office. Even though he is a former president, he is still a protectee of the Secret Service. During these jumps the Secret Service could do little more than wait on the ground hoping the parachute of their charge would not fail.

WHO IS RESPONSIBLE, POTUS OR THE SECRET SERVICE?

If things should go wrong during these elective adventures, the president or former president would in all likelihood accept responsibility should he live. Officially, however, the Secret Service will take full responsibility, not POTUS. In other words, if a president should be killed or seriously injured in an incident of his own making, the first question asked would be: Why did the Secret Service allow this to happen? The director of the Secret Service would in all liklihood go to Congress and accept full responsibility for the accident. Careers would suffer accordingly.

I am frequently asked the question, Who has the final say regarding the president's activities, the president or the Secret Service? The answer is both, with the president by far having the most control.

For example, the Secret Service may discourage but will not openly defy the president or former president if he wishes to engage in a dangerous act such as shaking hands with a group of people who have not been screened for weapons, or landing on an aircraft carrier in a jet. The Service should, however, remove—by force, if necessary—a president who wishes to shake hands with a group of people known to harbor a hostile gunman. In other words, barring specific knowledge of tangible, imminent danger, the president usually does what he wishes to do while the Secret Service does its best to protect him.

The bottom line is that many who have occupied the Oval Office are bold, aggressive men who, at a young age, tasted danger and liked it a great deal. Once the opiate of danger has been ingested, it can become as addictive as any drug, no matter how well-educated, old, or intelligent the user may be. There is no cure for this addiction but only temporary fixes.

★ CHAPTER 12 ★

Presidential Protective Division

The Presidential Protective Division is the most important and prestigious division in the Secret Service. When an American president is assassinated, it is a catastrophic event not only for the United States but the entire world. An attack on the president of the United States is an attack on the United States itself. Consequently, PPD is a place where failure can never be an option and little short of perfection is tolerated. The PPD agent standing next to the president is the last line of defense against anyone or anything that might attempt to harm the chief executive.

When I was selected to become a part of PPD, the fact was not lost on me that I had just become a member of one of the most elite groups of men and women in the world belonging to the most highly regarded protection organization in the world. And, while some were selected based upon politics, most of us were there because we were very good at our profession and had distinguished ourselves over several years of service performing well at everything asked of us.

For me, being selected as a member of the PPD working shift in 1993 was as euphoric an experience as was my initial selection as an agent ten years earlier. Just as there is a long selection process to become an agent, so too there is one to become an agent on PPD. For me, the process lasted ten years.

After the initial buzz wears off from having made the first team, a feeling of overwhelming responsibility takes over. The realization that the life of the president of the United States will rest in your hands for the next several years is indeed awesome and invites reflection. The next reality that sets in is the harsh nature of the assignment, known only to those who have been members of this select club.

While a member of PPD, an agent's life completely ceases to be his or her own and becomes sole property of the Secret Service and the office of the presidency. The term "family-friendly," which has become so popular in today's more warm and fuzzy federal government, will never apply to those entrusted with the life of the president. Single agents fare much better in this assignment than those with spouses. While an agent may be married with children, for the duration of an assignment to PPD there really is no family outside the Secret Service family. An agent may have a house in which his spouse and children live, but his true home is the White House.

The PPD agent is free to plan all of the family outings, vacations, dinners he wishes but should never be disappointed or surprised when such plans have to be canceled, sometimes at the last possible moment. In some cases, such plans have been scrapped as an agent and family were heading for the airport to enjoy a long-overdue vacation together. For the agent it is all a part of the job; for the spouses and children of these agents these occurrences are all but impossible to understand. There is a question that married PPD agents hear at home more than any other: "Why can't they find someone else?" This is usually accompanied by the sounds of crying children who cannot fathom why their trip to the beach or ballgame is not going to happen.

On one occasion, my CAT team was flying to an assignment out of the Baltimore/Washington International Airport. As the team gathered in front of the terminal, one of my agents pulled up curbside along with his wife and infant son. As the CAT agent got out of the car and kissed his wife good-bye, his son promptly threw up on the wife and began crying. The little guy had been running a fever all morning and was now pretty ill, as was his wife. "Sorry, honey, gotta go," he said, and disappeared into the terminal, leaving behind a sick wife and child.

In December 1992, President George H. W. Bush, who had just lost the general election to Bill Clinton, was scheduled to travel to Russia and France on January 2 and 3, 1993. This trip had been planned for quite some time. The advance teams had already deployed, and those not involved were looking forward to at least one or two days with their families for Christmas. At the last possible moment, President Bush unexpectedly made the decision to begin his trip with stops in Saudi Arabia and Somalia on December 31.

In order to cover advances for these new stops and to man the required CAT teams and working shifts, scores of PPD agents with approved leave for Christmas were about to get a hard shot of PPD reality. This trip was going to require all agents on the detail. Many agents who had already arrived at their holiday destinations were called and told to pack for a foreign trip.

As the CAT operations agent during this period, it was my responsibility, after shredding a work schedule for thirty-six agents I had spent five days writing, to write a new one in a matter of hours. To make the schedule a reality involved calling several agents back to Washington from their holidays. This was one of the most difficult assignments I was ever given. All agents whose Christmas leave was canceled were of course frustrated with the last-minute change, and in each case I patiently listened to those frustrations for a minute or so before having to terminate the agent's sentiments in order to provide him with his travel itinerary. The deafening echoes of exploding spouses, emotionally crushed grandparents, and upset children could be heard all the way back to the White House.

Prior to volunteering for PPD, all agents understand that such things as the December debacle will occur. Yet when the reality of it all sets in, some change their minds and ask for transfer. In most cases these early transfers are requested in order to save marriages, because while the agent may be all in the game, his or her spouse may not be. Generally these transfers are granted not because the Secret Service is concerned about preserving marriages but rather because the safety of the president of the United States cannot be entrusted on a daily basis to anyone who is not 100 percent committed to the mission.

What makes these types of events endurable is the fact that everyone on PPD is making the same sacrifices. Because of common hardships, unbreakable bonds form between these remarkable people that will last a lifetime and in many cases longer than the marriages of some agents.

To the casual observer, seeing the president accompanied primarily by muscular, menacing-looking men and athletic, serious-looking women makes the job of the PPD agent appear glamorous and exciting. Thoughts of James Bond, martial arts experts, license to kill, fast cars, and martinis come to the minds of many. This image is an illusion, however, as I believe anyone reading this will have realized. The reality is quite different.

Legions of people have asked me throughout the years to describe exactly what it is like to be one of the Secret Service elite who protected three presidents. In terms of the actual physical experience, I explain that if one were to forgo sleep for twenty-four hours, skip lunch and dinner, stand outside of one's house in the rain at 3:00 a.m. for several hours, cab to the airport, and board a plane to a large city for a four-hour flight, then repeat this regimen for several days in a row, one would begin to simulate the experience. To make the simulation complete, fail to attend a child's birthday or graduation, and miss the holidays or your wedding anniversary.

Of course, there is a great deal more to being on PPD, but uncertainty and extreme fatigue are constant companions of the PPD agent. This is why the job is for the young and why burnout usually occurs at the four- or five-year mark of constant presidential protection.

While the public sees agents with the president during public functions, seldom seen by anyone outside the detail are the agents working the midnight shift who after getting off at 8:00 a.m., have to double back for the afternoon shift beginning at 4:00 p.m. I recall arriving at Andrews Air Force Base from Russia in the late afternoon already dead tired from the trip and jet lag, then going home to quickly shower and dress for the midnight shift back at the White House. The following morning, after going home and sleeping for a few hours, I was back at the White House for the evening shift. In that instance I worked three days with roughly four hours of rest. This was not an uncommon occurrence, and all agents, not just on PPD but also on all Secret Service details have experienced this unavoidable abuse on more than one occasion.

A PPD agent's life revolves around an eight-week schedule. Like that of a factory worker, the routine is essentially shift work. Each agent assigned to the president works for a two-week period on day shift, followed by two weeks on midnight shift, and two weeks on the evening shift. At the end of this six-week cycle the agent goes into a two-week training phase, after which the cycle begins again. The changing of shifts every two weeks, combined with constant travel to different time zones, is, as one would expect, very hard on the body.

In addition to the agents who are directly assigned to the president, there are various sections within PPD, not all of which can be discussed here. These sections primarily include the First Lady's detail and transportation.

After an agent has been on the working shift with the president for a period of time, he will then be moved to a section for approximately one year, then moved back to the working shift. This at least gives the agent a break in routine and allows for a more normal existence. Still, there are the trips to every corner of the world, announced and unannounced, which never end. It is all part of protecting the president of the United States, and those of us who have survived the experience will all say it was worth it. I have never heard former PPD agents say they wished they had done any protection assignment other than PPD.

FROM CAT TO THE SHIFT

When PPD absorbed CAT in 1992, everyone on CAT became members of PPD. While few of us wanted to be adopted by the detail and lose our divisional status, the change removed a lot of the guesswork. If a man wanted to move over to the working shift after his time in CAT was up, he was free to do so as long as he was deemed competent. Most of us went to the shift when our time came to leave CAT, while some moved to other places. I had loved my assignment in CAT. It was the best four years of my career, but four years was a long time and I was ready to move on.

One day while in the CAT office, I was called to the offices of PPD in the Old Executive Office Building. There I met with an assistant special agent in charge to discuss my future. "Dan, your time is up in CAT. Where do you want to go next?" the ASAIC said to me. "You can have almost any assignment you want in the Secret Service."

I replied, "I want to stay on PPD and become a member of the working shift."

He smiled and said okay and told me to report the following Monday.

With CAT behind me and my new assignment as a shift agent on PPD a given, I had in ten years as an agent attained all of the major career goals I had set. No matter what the future might hold, through planning, tenacity, and luck I had managed to land the prime assignments sought after by most young agents but realized only by a few. I would now join the ranks of such notable agents as Clint Hill, Jerry Parr, Tim McCarthy, and Larry Buendorf, as well as the thousands of anonymous agents who had since 1901 directly protected the president of the United States. After paying my dues and learning the basics of my profession for a decade, it was now my turn to help safeguard the leader of the free world up close. No more cockroaches or muddy dogs. I was going to the White House.

THE NEW GUY, AGAIN

In June 1993, on my first day as a PPD shift agent, I reported to W-16, the Secret Service command post in the West Wing. Briefing for the shift was at 6:00 a.m., but I was always at least five minutes early. I found out that morning that everyone else was ten minutes early. I met my shift mates, and although I knew each of these agents, my shift leader introduced me and then we briefed for the day. I was happy with the lot I had drawn. These were good men, two of them former CAT agents.

After the briefing, we moved from our command post in the West Wing to the main mansion, where I had worked so many CAT midnight shifts over the past four years. We relieved the previous midnight shift, which was very glad to see us, and moved to our posts.

The senior agent on the shift, whose position was officially known as the shift "whip," walked me around to each post, explaining the responsibilities. Although I had worked in the White House for four years as a CAT agent and had filled in from time to time as a shift agent, I did not know what the permanent shift responsibilities were or the general shift routine. While an ace in CAT, I was essentially a shift "new guy" that happened to know how to move around the White House without getting lost, at least most of the time.

For a new agent on PPD, there were always tough moments in learning the routine. Each day there seemed to be a never-ending list of new things to be learned, some of which were written and others not. Most information that did exist in writing was provided on small flash cards reminding the agent of what his actions should be at each post. Also issued was a series of flash cards depicting the various formations used in walking with the president.

I had been on the shift about two weeks and was learning just enough about my duties to be a menace. One morning I was posted on the ground floor of the White House when the elevator light came on indicating that "Eagle," the call sign for President Clinton, was on the way down in the elevator. The door to the elevator opened, and out came the president in a suit dressed for work. I quietly announced over my sleeve microphone, as was standard operating procedure, "Eagle moving to the Oval." Off we went, with me leading the POTUS to his office for another day of whatever presidents do. He did not need to be led, of course, but there always had to be an agent close by.

All was routine, and as we reached the Oval Office, I opened the colonnade door leading inside the oval office, with Eagle close behind. As we entered, I did a quick look-see to make sure all was in order and then exited through what I thought was the door leading to the hallway between the Oval and the Roosevelt room. It was not. I instead exited through the door leading into the private dining room of the Oval Office, which was located next to the door I was supposed to use.

There was no one in the small dining room other than me standing there trying to decide what to do next. I should have taken another second or two to decide, because I made the wrong decision. I turned and reentered the Oval Office to find a surprised and somewhat annoyed-looking President Clinton. I tried to look as though this were all somehow planned, as I said, "Good morning, sir, all clear," and then exited through the correct door, leaving behind a puzzled POTUS.

No one knew about this minor but embarrassing incident, and, being new, I was certainly not going to inform on myself. Phil Hyde, my old team leader in CAT, was a big proponent of the old question: "If a tree falls in the forest and no one hears it, does it make a noise?" My going through the wrong door was a tree that had made no noise, and I was going to leave it that way.

ADVANCES AND STAFF COUNTERPARTS

Before the president leaves the White House for any reason, a security site advance is performed by the Secret Service at the location to be visited. It can be as simple as merely finding an arrival point for the motorcade, a bathroom, and the route to be walked, or it can be complex, like a two-week advance in a foreign country with multiple venues.

On each site advance, an agent is assigned a counterpart from the staff of the protectee to work with. This staff person is responsible for creating the protectee's itinerary—activities on site, sequence of events, who the greeters will be. The agent is then responsible for preparing a security plan around the itinerary.

After receiving the itinerary from the staff advance counterpart, the site agent designates an arrival and departure point for the motorcade, and a location for the emergency motorcade. He designates several different rooms to be used by the protectee, route of travel for the protectee and an emergency egress route, posting of agents, police, and other security assets. He coordinates with explosive ordnance disposal teams and local fire department and does many other things that cannot be listed here. In short, it is an enormous responsibility, and one must be able to keep several things in the air at once in order to be a successful site agent. For a trip to be a success for both agent and staff, it is essential that the two work together in harmony, not in opposition.

A few months after joining my shift, I was assigned to do my first out-of-town advance for President Clinton. The stop was a library in Sewickley, Pennsylvania, and it was fairly simple as far as presidential advances go. By this point in my career I felt experienced and confident enough to handle such a venue but getting to this level of experience had taken time, with some hard learning experiences along the way.

As I sat in National Airport reading the latest edition of the

Washington Times and waiting to depart for my first PPD advance as a member of the working shift, I remembered my first experience as a site advance agent, during the 1984 campaign. It was a near disaster but a great learning experience and my first encounter with a less than straightforward volunteer staff counterpart.

Before Sarah Palin there was Geraldine Ferraro, the first woman to be nominated by her party for the office of the vice presidency of the United States. She ran with Walter Mondale on the 1984 Democratic ticket against Ronald Reagan. Just out of agent school, I was assigned to proceed to Raleigh, North Carolina, to conduct a site advance for Ferraro. The site was considered major and would have been a challenge for an experienced agent. This was during the middle of a presidential campaign, and there were no experienced agents to be found.

When my supervisor gave me the assignment, I told him that I was happy to have it but wondered why I had been chosen. With no hesitation, he replied, "Because you are the only agent available."

"You mean one of the few available," I replied.

He looked up and said, "No, the only agent available in the entire state of North Carolina."

The site was a large outdoor courtyard shopping mall, with stores on the left and right and streets running along the northern and southern boundaries. Ferraro would be speaking at an outdoor rally at one end of the courtyard. Not only was I in over my head, but my staff counterpart was on his own agenda.

He was in his late fifties and dressed as one would expect an older liberal intellectual to dress: baggy pants, rumpled tweed sport coat, wrinkled button-down shirt, shoes that had not seen polish since JFK. He had long, gray thinning hair and a reddish complexion, and he wore round wire-frame glasses. He looked as if he just stepped out of a Berkeley political science classroom where he had been teaching that socialism was superior to capitalism. I am certain that he immediately sensed my inexperience, and I could also see that he was going to try to take advantage of that inexperience. In the business, this is called "getting rolled."

For about the first two days of the advance, my Timothy Leary clone pushed for things that probably should not have been done, but I was as green as an agent could be. Although I was relatively certain he was taking advantage of me, I could not put my finger exactly on any one thing that would point to that. Not long out of agent school, and with no real experience or a senior agent to mentor my advance, I was winging it pretty hard.

On the third day of the advance and the day before the visit, I thought that we had pretty much nailed everything down. As we stood looking at the site, my elder counterpart volunteered that he was going to place a gigantic banner behind the podium welcoming Ferraro to Raleigh. He said that he had already ordered it and that it should arrive at any time.

While I was inexperienced, I knew that he should have run this by me beforehand. My counterpart from the Raleigh Police Department was also standing there and firmly offered that such banners violated city ordinance and were therefore not permitted. As far as I was concerned, that settled the issue. Not for the professor, however. Realizing that he was losing this engagement, he elected to try a flanking maneuver. He offered that the banner would serve as an excellent barrier to block any sniper's view from behind Ferraro. Snipers? Where was this coming from, and what the hell did this man know about snipers? A little too smugly for my taste, he volunteered that he had vast experience in such matters and that he had done site advances for JFK and RFK. I suppose this comment was designed to impress and intimidate the police officer and me, but it failed to do so. I was at the end of my endurance with this pompous ass. He had opened the door, and I couldn't resist. I then observed that both men he had just boasted about doing sites for were dead, killed by assassins. The police advance officer burst into laughter and the bohemian pseudo-intellectual turned red and stormed away. The banner never happened.

That same year I was tasked with conducting a fairly simple advance for Lady Bird Johnson at an elementary school in Texas. Part of this advance, as with any other, was to obtain a holding room. Here protectees can review their notes before proceeding with their schedule or just collect themselves for a few minutes. This is Secret Service protocol doctrine.

I was working with a very young volunteer staff counterpart, who advised me that Mrs. Johnson would not need a holding room, as she intended to move directly from the cars to the event. I nodded but obtained the holding room nonetheless. The Secret Service, not staff, dictates such things, and it was a good thing I made the decision I did. Upon the arrival of Mrs. Johnson, the panicked young staffer practically screamed that we needed a holding room—that Mrs. Johnson did not want to immediately move to the event. I just smiled, letting the staffer believe that we had no holding room, per her unheeded, meaningless orders, and then led Mrs. Johnson to her holding area. My instincts were correct on this day, and I had learned an unbreakable rule of advance work that would serve me well in the years to come: Always carefully consider any direction or advice offered by a protectee's volunteer staff, and always stick to Secret Service procedure.

Experience is the best teacher, and I was getting a lot of it that would serve me well throughout my career when the protectee was the sitting president of the United States, not a candidate or former First Lady. I was learning that advances were the most difficult part of protection and that the hardest part of the advance was dealing with staff. Every advance was different, and there always seemed to be a new staffer who did not understand his role. It was like going on a never-ending series of blind dates: You never knew what you were going to get, but you knew it was usually going to be unpleasant. I learned that in many cases staff was as ignorant of what their job was as I had been in Raleigh, and that they needed to be dealt with firmly and professionally right off the bat. For a young agent to become too friendly with some of them was immediately perceived as weakness, which they would exploit. In time I learned to strike the right balance of firmness and friendliness, but one always had to be on guard.

A NEW ADMINISTRATION

On January 20, 1993, William Jefferson Clinton moved into the White House, and along with him came a staff so different from that of George Herbert Walker Bush's that they could have been from another planet. This was my first experience with a Democratic presidential staff. Starched white shirts, conservative hairstyles, and blue suits had given way to denim, long hair, and Dockers.

In direct contrast to the departing Republicans, most of whom were at least forty years of age, President Clinton's staff had a mere handful of experienced, mature professionals. The remainder were young people possessing no significant work experience. Some were younger than us by a decade or more, and many were initially disrespectful of the Secret Service. Much of this attitude had to do with their youth and immaturity. Unlike their outgoing Republican counterparts, none seemed to own a watch.

To many of these young people, who were now in charge of planning POTUS's schedule and who played a large part in the day-to-day running of the White House, this seemed to be nothing more than a grand adventure not to be taken too seriously.

On top of their seemingly youthful arrogance, the junior staff could also be dangerous in an adolescent sort of way. President Clinton was visiting Russia in December 1993, and I was along for the trip as a member of my shift. I had been preposted at an event. A young staffer walked by and into the secure area about to be occupied by POTUS. This was not a concern, as I knew the staffer, who was wearing the proper lapel pin identification that allowed total access to the area. The rub was that the Russian KGB agents assisting us did not understand our identification system and had no idea who this young man was.

As the staffer was walking by, a KGB officer named Yuri grabbed him by the arm to stop him. The staffer jerked away from Yuri and continued on his way, as if he were dealing with a Wackenhut security officer in Toledo. As Yuri was about to do his worst, I put my hand on his shoulder (gently) and explained to him (he spoke English, as most do) that the young man was one of the president's staff and that he had access to the area. I also asked that he not officially detain or confront the young man. Out of professional courtesy he reluctantly agreed, but first he said, in a heavy Russian accent, "Dan, he is big asshole." I had to laugh, and while I certainly agreed with Yuri's assessment of the young staffer, I withheld comment. This request on my part to leave the neophyte unmolested by the KGB would cost me several rounds of vodka later when I was off duty with my Russian friend. I always appreciated the directness of the Russians.

I later confronted the young staffer and in a tactful manner told him he had come very close to being taken into custody by the KGB for his immature, unprofessional behavior. He glared at me and replied that they couldn't do that to him because of his position on the presidential staff. I informed him that he was in Russia, not America, and that they could most certainly detain him if they wished. He stared at me for a moment and then rolled his eyes and walked away. Resisting the impulse to grab him by the collar and shake him around a bit, I maintained my professional decorum. I then thought of Yuri's comment regarding the young man and smiled.

While the young staffer offered no gratitude for my having plucked him from certain embarrassment and physical discomfort, I did not intervene in the situation for his sake. In fact, it would have been entertaining to watch the KGB agent teach the young man a lesson in humility. While it is every agent's job to protect the president from physical harm, it is also every agent's unofficial duty to protect the president from potential embarrassment when possible. For one of the president's staffers to be hauled away by the Russian authorities would have created embarrassment for President Clinton and would have required Department of State intervention as well as resulting in a media event. Even so, from that point on, I decided to never again intercede in any matter on behalf of this boy trying so desperately yet unsuccessfully to be accepted as a man in a world of which he had no understanding.

Another example of the maturity issues the Secret Service encountered with junior staff occurred in 1993, when I was sent to conduct an advance for POTUS to Hilton Head, South Carolina. The site was a hotel ballroom where President Clinton would address a group of supporters from a stage. Secret Service doctrine is, and probably has been since the days of Teddy Roosevelt, that there will always be a means of evacuating POTUS from the rear of any stage he occupies. This is not negotiable in any way, and staff is well aware of the doctrine.

I was working well with a young female staff counterpart, and all was going according to plan until I left her unattended for a few minutes. When I returned, I found that she had blocked the rear of the stage, our avenue of escape, with a movie-like set made of plywood. I had just explained to her not one hour earlier that we needed a clear exit to the rear of the stage, and she had agreed. Perhaps she had not understood. This is when I came to realize that young volunteer staffers were not unlike first graders: You should not turn your back on them for more than a few seconds.

I patiently explained that the set had to be moved and why. She crossed her arms and proceeded to raise her voice and tell me that the set was going to remain where it was and she was not going to move it. This was probably some sort of verbal judo nonsense learned in a classroom, but she was about to learn that much of life is learned outside academia and that there was no school solution for what was coming her way.

I once again tried to explain why the set had to go, or at least be modified to give us a way out using the rear of the stage. I used the word *modified,* hinting that we could compromise but that we needed our way out. Once again, my patient attempts to reason with her were met with childlike emotion born of a past where no one in authority (probably beginning with her parents) had ever said no to her about anything. I was now dealing with a spoiled child rather than a presidential staff person, and I was very quickly losing what patience I had remaining. Finally I said, "Okay, I am going to go call the lead staff advance." This was her boss. One could assume that the lead staff advance would be a little older than the site counterparts. I would turn the matter over to the two of them. They could battle it out.

As I walked away to make the call, I heard the sound of running footsteps behind me. I turned to see my assertive counterpart in tears, begging me not to call her boss. This young woman had tried to intimidate and bully a security professional with her drama-queen performance to get what she wanted. She had been testing me. It had probably worked most of her life with college professors, boys, and her parents. It did not work against the Secret Service, and I was unmoved by her tears. While I had first agreed to compromise, I was no longer in the mood and directed her, in a voice that could be heard for some distance, to get rid of the entire god-damned set—all of it, and right now! She did, and from that point on, we had no more issues.

She began to really work for me, doing whatever I directed, as I was no longer asking or suggesting but telling. I was also teaching her, and without realizing it, she was learning. I suspected she was probably a nice person, but like most of the staff was young and immature and just needed some discipline, someone to say no occasionally. In this case, the task fell to me.

The visit went well, and when POTUS departed, the lead staffer congratulated her. The young woman hugged me and thanked me for all my help—and then asked if we could get together later on. I declined.

As fate would have it, I worked with this same woman again a few months later at a major site much more complicated than the one in Hilton Head. She was a totally different person—much more mature, confident, and emotionally stable. This time we worked together instead of me directing her or her trying to roll me. There were no problems during the advance or at the site. This staffer had begun to grow up and would be an asset to the president and the Service, but there were still too few like her.

The young staff's worst quality by far was total disorganization, which for the Secret Service was a major issue. They seldom had even a basic idea of POTUS's itinerary or sequence of events on the first several days of any advance. As a result of the staff's total inefficiency, we had a lot of time to roam around for the first few days of the advance. You always paid at the other end, however. About two days before POTUS's arrival, staff would come up with at least a half-assed itinerary, at which time we would put it all together. The result was that, although we had been in place for days, we now had only about forty-eight hours to do our advance.

Before agents could do a motorcade advance, for example, they had to run the routes to be used on game day, which required having to have a point of origin and a destination. To do a site advance you had to have a site. We usually had neither for the first several days of the advance. Other than the date and place of Air Force One's arrival, we had no idea where the president was going to go, what he was going to do, or whom he was going to meet with. The only person, then, who could really even begin his advance was the agent responsible for the airport arrival.

My most memorable journey plagued by disorganization was a trip to England for the fiftieth anniversary of D-Day, June 6, 1994. President Clinton was going to do a swing through Europe, a trip that included visiting the Normandy beaches where so many Americans had died in the effort to save the world from Adolf Hitler. My job was to do the motorcade advance for President Clinton's trip to Cambridge, England. Eventually he would visit the American cemetery there, where there were several thousand empty graves of American airmen lost over Europe. They had taken off from English airfields. One of the most noteworthy names on the wall was that of Joseph P. Kennedy Jr. Joe had been killed on a mission to take out German submarine pens in France. His name was on the wall because there had been no body to bury. He had been blown to pieces along with his Martin PB4Y, the navy version of the B-24 Liberator. Cambridge cemetery was primarily for aircrews, and most of the graves held nothing.

The advance team arrived in the beautiful town of Cambridge in the middle of the afternoon two weeks prior to the visit. We had the usual meeting with staff and received the usual announcement that there was no itinerary as yet. We took the news as we always did, then moved across the street from the hotel to a pub where we decompressed from the flight over. After a couple of drinks I traded the bartender a Secret Service baseball cap for a porcelain water pitcher bearing the logo of Famous Grouse Scotch. The trip slogan became a line from a W. E. B. Griffin novel: "If you are going to drink you have to get on the bird," meaning the Famous Grouse.

With not much to do until staff pulled an itinerary out of the air, I decided to call my wife and invite her to come over and visit. Another agent invited his wife, and we all had a great time touring the English countryside. Our driver was from Cambridge and one evening he invited us for dinner at his home, where we enjoyed his wife's cooking and his daughter played the clarinet. These were intelligent, well-educated people who lived a happy, simple life with few amenities. I envied them.

Finally the staff came up with a schedule, enough at least for us to go to work. My wife and the other agent's wife spent the days visiting Buckingham Palace and other sites while the advance team tried our best to put together a security plan in a very short amount of time.

This lack of purpose and organization by staff never seemed to change, although the Service and the staff eventually grew used to each other and the relationships began to improve. There were fewer and fewer instances like the one in Hilton Head as the staff matured somewhat, thanks in no small part to being around adult professionals in the Secret Service. They began to understand the reasons for the things we did, and some even began to develop a basic respect of authority. They realized that we were anything but the hired help, and that a smart staffer would befriend an agent as much as possible, whenever possible. They were learning that with power comes responsibility. This change also occurred because the POTUS chief of staff worked well with the SAIC of PPD, laying down the law among the junior staff to stop being adolescent pains in the collective ass of the Service and start playing ball. If anything, junior staff was an intelligent lot. In the end, albeit somewhat reluctantly, most got on board the team bus.

FOREIGN COUNTERPARTS

Advance counterparts on foreign trips could be anyone, including hastily vetted foreign nationals, but the advance was still coordinated by the presidential staff. One such trip was to Aqaba, Jordan, where I coordinated motorcades for President Clinton's visit to the region.

The C-141 flight with the president's cars and some advance agents to Jordan was the roughest of my career. Prior to leaving Andrews Air Force Base, I had lunch with agent Charlie White, who had been on the Korean DMZ adventure, at a dive in Washington named Stoney's. Stoney's was demolished not long after, probably due to substandard sanitary conditions. I picked up a bug there that rendered me practically useless for the next forty-eight hours. I spent the entire flight from Andrews to Spain moving between my less than comfortable seat and what passed as a lavatory on the C-141. By the time we landed in Spain I was so dehydrated and weak from expending all bodily fluids from every orifice that walking was a chore. The flight from Spain to Aqaba was hardly better.

Our hotel in Aqaba overlooked the Dead Sea and looked like something out of a 1939 Humphrey Bogart movie. Upon arrival we had a quick meeting with all the advance personnel and presidential staff to try to get an idea what President Clinton's itinerary would be. As usual, the staff did not know, and their ineptness in this case worked to my benefit, as I slept a full twenty-four hours trying to recover from my visit to Stoney's. Had we been back in the United States, I would probably have been hospitalized, but this was PPD and the show had to go on.

Being the motorcade advance on this trip, a large part of my job was the planning and running of routes that the POTUS motorcade would be using. I was issued a Jordanian counterpart who had been vetted by the American embassy and bore an amazing resemblance to Sirhan Sirhan, the man who had killed Bobby Kennedy.

In the States, you usually did your advance with a local cop who knew every street and every possible way to move from point A to point B. In this case, I had the young Jordanian, who always needed a shave and wore the same dirty T-shirt and jeans each day. He had dark, piercing eyes and a two-inch scar running down his right cheek. His demeanor suggested he was capable of cutting a man's throat and leaving him for the vultures should it become necessary. As with any foreign counterpart, the Secret Service had to assume that people such as this were part of the host country's intelligence service or, worst-case, a terrorist organization. I never trusted him entirely and was never comfortable with the amount of sensitive information he was acquiring.

After two full days with my Jordanian counterpart running all of the routes the president of the United States would actually be traveling the day of the visit, including routes to the hospital, police stations, and possible safe houses, my assistant disappeared and was replaced with a Jordanian policeman. I asked our main Jordanian counterpart from the US embassy what had happened to my guy. I reminded him that this young man knew every inch of the POTUS motorcade routes, that it was too late to change them, and that it was perhaps not a good idea for him to be at large.

The Jordanian diplomat, smoking a cigarette that would make a

Lucky Strike seem tame, informed me that his government had acquired some information that had caused them to be concerned about my counterpart's allegiances. "But not to worry," he said, "he has been taken care of."

I was never sure what that meant exactly but had a good idea what it might mean in that part of the world. I guess my counterpart had not been vetted well enough.

On the day of the visit, as the presidential motorcade navigated its way through the narrow ancient streets of Aqaba, I could not help but scan the open windows of the stucco homes. I half expected to see one of my former counterpart's clones lean out of a window with a rocket-propelled grenade launcher and put a rocket into the limo. I never saw him again, however, and maybe no one else ever did either.

VELVET COVERED STEEL

When POTUS's visit to Jordan ended, our advance team was put on a bus at the Jordanian-Israeli border and driven all night to Jerusalem, where we would assist with a second visit. The good shepherd provided to watch over us by the Israeli government was a female Shin Bet or perhaps Mossad agent. She gave her name as Rachel.

Rachel was quite different from most women I had ever met in the security field. She had wild, wavy brown hair and a dark tan from the Israeli sun. She also had the most unusual scar running down her perfectly sculpted right bicep. It was jagged and uneven—not a surgical scar but one caused by something from her unknown past. Although we were all armed, she was our protector as we rode in our bus on a brilliantly moonlit night through the Israeli desert.

Growing up in a country that had fought for its survival on more than one occasion and was surrounded by countries that wished their homeland exterminated, Israeli women were raised somewhat differently from American women—or women from almost anywhere.

A certain number of Israeli girls grew up learning how to use weapons, load ammunition magazines, and kill their country's enemies, while many American girls grew up playing with dolls. Biologically, Israeli women and those from other countries were the same, but that is where the similarities ended.

At some point, we stopped at a small country store in the middle of nowhere. Rachel told us to get whatever we wanted, including beer. Back on the bus, almost everyone had a couple of beers. We had just completed one of the most stressful and dangerous advances of our careers, and we needed to relax a little. I had finally gotten rid of my bacterial friend from Stoney's, and the cold beer went down very well. The bus was not large, but there were only ten or so of us, so we each had our own row. It was a great time to reflect on the last mission and just enjoy traveling through the land where Jesus once walked.

We were fatigued, but our minds were still wound up from the last assignment and would not allow us to rest. No one talked and no one slept, but each merely sat alone with his or her own thoughts. The moonlight illuminating the ancient desolation was almost as bright as noon and was too beautiful to miss.

After several hours of driving and with the sun rising, we arrived at our hotel in Jerusalem. As we got off the bus and said good-bye to our lovely and most certainly lethal guide, Rachel shook hands with each of us with a soft but firm grip and then disappeared back to her life of serving Israel.

THE MEDIA

The First Amendment to the Constitution of the United States guarantees freedom of the press. The founding fathers deemed this right to be so sacred they put it at the top of the Bill of Rights. The media are an inseparable component of the White House's daily operation, present both there and anywhere the president travels. The media have a difficult job, as does the Secret Service, and while both entities must coexist, it is the Secret Service that sets the boundaries the press must operate under when at the White House or in proximity to the president.

There are three types of media that cover the president's activities, and each presents its own set of challenges for the Secret Service. The press pool is the smallest group of media that covers the president and is comprised of journalists almost everyone is familiar with by sight. These are senior members of their networks who ask the president questions in the White House during presidential press conferences. They include CNN's Jake Tapper and until recently, Helen Thomas, of UPI, who covered every president from Eisenhower to Obama. This group travels in the presidential motorcades as well as on Air Force One and is by far the easiest group to work with due to their seniority and familiarity with Secret Service procedures and requirements. Each is issued a White House pass that enables him or her to enter the pressroom of the White House 24/7. They all have designated work areas in the West Wing.

The next group of media that covers the president is larger and is made up of primarily Washington, DC–based reporters on the White House beat. They can also travel in presidential motorcades, but, unlike the press pool, which travels in small vans, this group usually travels in a large bus and is accompanied by cameramen and sound operators. This group flies ahead of Air Force One in a chartered commercial-sized aircraft and lands ahead of the president. They then move to their respective sites. This group can be more challenging for the Secret Service to oversee than the press pool due to their large numbers and the amount of bulky equipment they travel with.

The third and by far the most problematic group is the local media. These reporters and technicians work in local TV and radio stations, and many are young and inexperienced. This is the largest group, and they are usually placed on a flatbed trailer at outdoor events and in the very rear of indoor events. Unlike the pool and traveling press who understand the rules set forth by the Secret Service for media conduct, the locals are not used to working with the Secret Service and are issued temporary press passes that are only good for the event they are covering. They are unaccustomed to being directed by men in suits with wires in their ears, and maintaining group integrity with these individuals is like herding cats, a near impossibility.

I personally liked and had great respect for many members of the media. Most were highly professional and thoughtful. On one trip to Russia, President Clinton was scheduled to visit a forest where Joseph Stalin's troops had murdered and buried thousands of people. It had been raining a great deal in the region, and my wingtips were not exactly the best choice for slogging through a marshy killing field. On Air Force One prior to landing and boarding the motorcade to the forest, a senior ABC reporter looked at my shoes and said, "Dan, those shoes you're wearing will never do. Here, take mine." He was wearing waterproof duck boots that fit me perfectly. Here was a senior ABC reporter wearing jeans and black wingtips, while I was dressed in a navy blue suit and wore brown duck boots. The Secret Service could also return the favors at times.

One morning while in Switzerland a young reporter was suffering from a case of self-inflicted dehydration due to the previous evening's activities. On the press bus he asked, practically pleading, if anyone had extra water and would be willing to share. While none of his colleagues seemed to have any water to spare, an agent gave the young man his reserve bottle to get him through. Since agents are accustomed to working in a state of dehydration and malnourishment, it was not a problem for him.

While the vast majority of the White House media respected the rules set forth by the Secret Service and understood their purpose, others could occasionally be a challenge to work with. There was at times a tense relationship between the media and the Secret Service that could ignite with little warning. This state of affairs arose due to polarization of purpose. While it is the job of the media to cover every public move POTUS makes, one job of the Secret Service is to keep the area in which POTUS operates as "clean" as possible, meaning clear of unnecessary bodies and paraphernalia. Here lies the primary conflict between the media and the Secret Service: The media always seems to be in the way, there are too many of them, and they are a constant distraction to security.

Each time an assassination attempt is made against the president, successful or unsuccessful, the Secret Service reevaluates its procedures. A new procedure was created after John Hinckley shot President Reagan. It was the creation of a position known as the press agent.

The main purpose of this assignment is to see to it that no assassin embeds himself in the press area, as John Hinckley did when he shot President Reagan. As President Reagan exited the Washington Hilton Hotel, Hinckley casually joined the White House press corps and, standing squarely in their midst unnoticed, shot the president. The more practical everyday purpose of the press agent is to ensure that the press hurries along and does not delay the motorcade's timely departure.

Some in the media played a game, pushing the envelope as far as they could in order to get their story or photo. Generally, the worst-case scenario for breaking the rules would be receiving a verbal admonishment from the press agent. This meant really nothing to the offending reporter or photographer as long as he or she got the shot or the story. Too many such admonishments could result in a complaint being filed by the Secret Service with the reporter's network, but this was a very uncommon occurrence. The bottom line for the media was to get the story or the shot that could win a Pulitzer. Most journalists are as mission-oriented to their calling as agents are to theirs, and they are willing to go to jail if necessary to get their stories. Receiving a colorful reprimand from an agent was a small price to pay.

In most cases during a motorcade departure, everyone, including the president, is in his or her vehicle ready to move out, while the hapless members of the media struggle to get into their vans with cameras, microphone booms, and all other manner of equipment. Many tend to move without much purpose, and, absent the constant prodding from an agent, they would take close to forever getting into their vans. Each agent on the working shift takes turns with this assignment. I never enjoyed it. My job as I saw it was to protect the president, not herd the media, making sure they did not get into mischief.

THE WHITE HOUSE PRESS PASS

While few members of the media appreciated being told where they could and could not go, they knew it was a part of the game they had to play in order to keep their White House press credentials. This Holy Grail of press passes was issued by the Secret Service and was the hammer held by the Service over the media. It could be used against out-of-control behavior, and the hammer did fall on occasion.

One day I witnessed an agent literally rip a press pass from the neck of a photographer who had pushed things too far on too many occasions. With the loss of the coveted pass, the photographer was now no different from the general public and was escorted from the area. Rather than ride in the press van, he was forced to take a series of taxicab rides from site to site, where he could observe only from the general public area.

Although such encounters perpetuated the sometimes adversarial relationship between agent and journalist, it was in most cases not personal: An agent could be chewing out a journalist one minute and sharing a joke with him five minutes later. It was all a part of the game, not unlike the game between defense attorneys and the prosecution, who might battle it out in a courtroom and share drinks that evening.

The end of my official association with the press occurred as the result of a physical confrontation I had with a print reporter while working a rope line with President Clinton. President Clinton was on a trip that had a lot of stops. We had been on the road for several days, everyone was tired, and as usual practically all of the staff was testing everyone's patience with their "golly gee whiz" approach to things. As POTUS moved down this particular rope line, the limo paralleled along behind him in the event we had to move him quickly out of the area. My job was to walk alongside the limo manning the left rear door, which was cracked open and ready for use if necessary.

All in the media are well aware that no one is to get between POTUS and the door of the limo. On this day, however, a very large print reporter continued to do so. It was a problem because if Rich, the detail leader, had to grab POTUS, turn him, and push him inside the limo, the reporter would be in the way. Twice I put my hand on this man's shoulder and firmly but politely asked him to move away from the door of the limo. Twice he ignored me. The third time I did not ask. I turned him around and, with all my strength and weight—I weighed about ninety pounds less than he did—shoved him out of the way. He went spinning toward the crowd. While the reporter knew and understood that he had pushed the boundaries too far and that the consequences he faced were simply the cost of doing business, some did not take it as well.

This rope line was so chaotic and was moving so fast that no one seemed to notice the interaction—no one except one of President Clinton's senior staff. I say *senior* in the sense that she was fairly high up the staff chain of command, although she was only in her thirties. She also did her share of getting in our way a great deal of the time, moving in our formations with a sense of irritating entitlement and no purpose.

After President Clinton had finished working the rope line, everyone boarded Air Force One for the trip to our next stop. We had been airborne for about an hour when my shift leader informed me that the senior staffer had complained to the special agent in charge of PPD about my tossing the reporter and wanted me removed from

PPD. The boss reportedly calmed the staffer like a father would calm down a hormonally driven teenager, and the incident died. The word from him to me through my shift leader was, however, to stop grabbing reporters. I never "grabbed" another reporter because I was never again assigned the job of press agent.

THE DEATH WATCH
Camera 1

On November 22, 1963, President John F. Kennedy was gunned down in a motorcade while riding through Dallas, Texas. While many onlookers snapped photos or rolled motion picture cameras, only one actually captured the headshot that killed President Kennedy. Even this footage was incomplete—it missed the first round that passed through the president's back and exited the throat. No meaningful media footage exists of the actual assassination.

Since that day a specially designated vehicle has been in every major presidential motorcade to ensure no such opportunity is missed again. The vehicle is known as Camera 1, or "the death watch." Riding on the tailgate of Camera 1, or with his or her head protruding from an open hatch, a camera operator films nothing other than the presidential limousine during all movements. The sole purpose is to ensure that a future attack on the presidential limousine is filmed in high definition.

THE CAMEL'S NOSE IN THE TENT
The Journalistic Media

One cold night, as an Arab sat in his tent, a camel gently thrust his nose under the flap and looked in. "Master," he said, "let me put my nose in your tent. It's cold and stormy out here."

"By all means," said the Arab, "and welcome." He turned over and went to sleep.

A little later the Arab awoke to find that the camel had not only put his nose in the tent but his head and neck also. The camel, who had been turning his head from side to side, said, "I will take but little more room if I place my forelegs within the tent. It is difficult standing out here."

"Yes, you may put your forelegs within," said the Arab, moving a little to make room, for the tent was small.

Finally, the camel said, "May I not stand wholly inside? I keep the tent open by standing as I do."

"Yes, yes," said the Arab. "Come wholly inside. Perhaps it will be better for both of us." So the camel crowded in. With difficulty in the crowded quarters, the Arab again went to sleep. When he woke up the next time, he was outside in the cold and the camel had the tent to himself.

This old Arab fable is in my view a very accurate metaphor for how, beginning in the mid-1990s, the media began to move into the once enigmatic and clandestine world of the United States Secret Service.

When I became an agent in 1983, the Service was a total mystery to most, and virtually no substantial amount of information about it existed outside the organization. The culture of the Secret Service during that era dictated that agents never publicly discuss weapons, numbers of agents, training, and tactics—and never under any circumstance did we publicly discuss out-of-school incidents regarding the people we protected. To do so was to violate an unwritten code of silence observed by all agents and to risk being terminated. This old school mentality has been rendered largely obsolete due to the number of TV specials that have been produced over the past several years about the Secret Service.

In those days, there was no contact between the Secret Service and the media unless it was completely necessary. There seemed to be just enough contact to perpetuate one of the most powerful weapons in the Secret Service inventory: mystique. That is why most of the Service was stunned when our training facility at the James J. Rowley Training Center in Beltsville was opened to Joan

Lunden in the late 1990s for her *Behind Closed Doors* special. Enter the camel.

Prior to the airing of this TV special, agents would have been expected to hold out under torture to protect the information that was freely offered up to Lunden. Authorized at the highest levels of the organization, the show became the camel's nose under the tent flap in terms of allowing the media into every space occupied by the Service. Now the entire camel roams almost at will.

When Lunden rode the camel into the Secret Service tent, her mission was to obtain as much information and gain as much access to the inner workings of the Secret Service as possible. She succeeded beyond her producer's wildest dreams, using all of her people skills to get that information. For those of us trained since being sworn in as agents to reveal almost nothing about our work, we could scarcely believe what we were witnessing.

The Joan Lunden special was filmed during my tour as an instructor at the James J. Rowley Training Center. Subsequent to this filming, it became the norm for journalists from various magazines, film production companies, authors, and almost anyone who wanted to film a TV special about the Secret Service to regularly be on campus.

There were times when so many of these visitors were on site that regular training had to be canceled and special agent class members used as extras in the productions. It was not unusual on some days to be standing for an hour or more at the obstacle course with an agent class waiting for the signal to begin the course while some cameraman filmed away. Even more irritating to me as an instructor was being forced to give up certain students for on-camera interviews, which caused them to miss class and require makeup instruction.

While the office of public affairs turned down the vast majority of such requests, it granted just enough to interfere—significantly, at times—with our normal training schedule. In order to better facilitate these productions, a member of the training staff was given the collateral duty of coordinating these media events.

During this time many agents began to feel that the Service had lost touch with its mission by allowing this type of unnecessary exposure. Many, thought that this "glad to see you, come on in" attitude toward the media was unwise. In the "new" Secret Service, headquarters was attempting to present a picture of agents as approachable and friendly rather than mysterious and menacing. With these productions, the Secret Service had moved from the shadows into the bright light of day while the camel cozied up inside the tent.

Lunden's production became one of the first of what many of us deemed potentially harmful video presentations about the Secret Service. We believed that their existence was a danger to both agents and protectees alike. All terrorist attacks and assassinations begin with intelligence gathering, and there is no better source for information about the Secret Service and how it protects the president and others than these irresponsibly detailed documentaries, available to anyone with a personal computer.

The CIA refers to this type of gleaning of Intelligence available to anyone "open source." For potential enemies, it means poring over any type of information available to the public, such as newspapers, magazines, the Internet, and, yes, the Joan Lunden special, to learn as much as possible about the Secret Service.

THE WHITE HOUSE CHRISTMAS PARTY

Perhaps the one night of the year PPD agents and PPD spouses or significant others look forward to most is the annual White House Christmas party. For an agent, being a POTUS party guest is a perk of being a member of PPD. For one night of the year, an agent is treated as a presidential guest rather than as a presidential protector. Other than high rollers from headquarters, the only Secret Service agents invited to these galas are PPD agents. Including PPD at these gatherings is the president's way of saying thank you to the men and women who would sacrifice anything necessary to protect him and his family from harm. These parties were great for agent morale and almost made up for all the bad coffee consumed while trying to stay awake during the previous year's midnight shifts.

Each invited agent is allowed to bring one guest to the party. Few date invitations can equal being invited to accompany a Secret Service agent to the White House for cocktails, dancing, and a photo op with the president and First Lady. Bringing a parent to this special event will usually even the ledger for any misdeeds of youth not yet forgiven. In my own case, the complete absolution of youthful transgressions came when I arranged a meeting between my parents and President George Herbert Walker Bush in 1992 as he passed through my hometown of Gainesville, Georgia. While the White House photographer's equipment malfunctioned and no record exists of the meeting, it was a moment my parents cherished for the rest of their lives.

In order to accommodate as many of the presidents' best friends as possible, there is not one White House Christmas party but several—in fact two almost every night during December, leading up to Christmas. In all, there are approximately fifty parties.

The evening begins with entry into the White House via the East entrance, where all guests must show invitations to a representative of the social secretary's office and pass through security screening prior to being admitted into the mansion. Secret Service agents are of course exempted from this screening because as agents we were all armed to begin with and were expected to have our weapons.

The guests then move through the East Wing of the White House until entering the lower level of the main mansion, where they are met by an impeccably dressed, physically fit commissioned officer of one of the armed forces. The officer directs the guests up a well-worn set of marble stairs that has been trod upon by millions since it was installed in 1953. Guests proceed to the state floor of the mansion, where the festivities take place. I recall at one party that this post was manned by a Navy SEAL lieutenant who was preparing to leave the navy due to numerous disabilities. At the age of twenty-six he had sustained so many broken bones and torn ligaments as a SEAL that he was no longer medically qualified to perform his occupational specialty. Being around such men has always humbled me, and I felt he should have been the president's guest instead of me.

On the state floor, everyone is treated to the sight of magnificent Christmas decorations and several live Christmas trees towering twelve feet or more. Each tree is heavy with ornaments and bursting with the aroma of fresh pine. Prior to moving about at will on the state floor of the White House—including the East Room, Red Room, Green Room, Blue Room, and the State Dining Room—guests are invited to indulge in the open bar, manned by a white-jacketed bartender. In the State Dining Room, guests will find an enormous table that runs almost the length of the room adorned with a white linen cloth that supports what is without doubt the mother of all hors d'oeuvres settings. The main attraction at this stop is the shrimp, practically the size of small lobsters, resting in silver bowls of ice.

A variety of music is provided in the East Room by a military orchestra made up of musicians whose talents rival that of any orchestra in the world. Here couples may elect to just enjoy the music, or if so trained may waltz, tango, foxtrot, or just sway to and fro. This is where mine and Donnelle's Arthur Murray training always paid off.

It is generally around this time that the president and First Lady descend the main stairs leading from the second-floor residence to the state floor, where they mingle with their guests. There is never any doubt as to when this occurs, as almost everyone, except the agents, begin to move in that direction at once, hoping to have a few seconds of private time with POTUS. From there POTUS and

FLOTUS move to the photo op area, where they graciously stand for an hour or more as each guest is announced by a permanent member of the White House staff prior to having their photo taken with the president and First Lady.

The photo op is generally the grand finale of the event and after the last guest has posed, things start to thin out as the Uniformed Division begins herding people out of the building through the North doors and the portico of the White House. Being lucky enough to attend even one of these events provides a very special lifetime memory, and Donnelle and I were privileged to have attended six such evenings during our careers.

PRESIDENTS AND THEIR SECRET SERVICE AGENTS: A UNIQUE RELATIONSHIP

I have been asked so frequently about the relationship between president and agents that I felt the need to include some information about this topic, as the answer is both multifaceted and, at times, complicated.

Presidents exist in a world in which many of the people who surround them are there strictly for personal gain, and loyalties can be bought with promises of power. Given their constant association with these kinds of individuals, I believe presidents find it refreshing when they realize that their agents have a pure commitment and dedication to something greater than themselves. Perhaps another thing that some presidents have realized and admire about their agents is that, although they themselves may be president, more than a few could not have met the qualifications to become a Secret Service agent.

One of the most misunderstood relationships in the world is that of an American president and the Secret Service agents who surround him. In spite of the mutual respect between agents and a president, the relationship is not one of friendship and can be misinterpreted at times by all but the most professional of agents.

This is a relationship so complex at times that it is a bit enigmatic even to agents who, over the years, have seen more than one president come and go. More than complex, it can also be extremely awkward for both new president and new PPD agent alike. Rookie PPD agents, when spoken to by POTUS for the first time, can be a bit starstruck and tend to talk a bit too much. This trait needs to be recognized by the new agent and avoided. In no case does POTUS's reaching out to speak to an agent constitute a wish to be friends with that agent. Any agent who mistakenly believes that such a gesture is one of friendship will not last long on the detail.

This unique relationship of protector and protected is based on the premise that the president goes about his business of being president and the Secret Service goes about its business of doing all within its power to keep him from harm while he performs his duties both official and unofficial. This simplistic explanation, however, is just that, and the reality is a great deal more complex.

Secret Service agents occupy a unique position in the dynamics of a presidential administration. Agents are so physically close to the president on a daily basis that they hear and see almost everything the president sees and hears. Yet, unlike the presidential staff that interacts with POTUS and monitors his activities, Secret Service agents stand silently and seldom offer input into situations other than those that are security-related. If asked by POTUS about a situation, especially political, the agent should be brief and friendly yet noncommittal.

Secret Service agents do not initiate conversation with a president other than to perhaps offer an initial greeting, and then only when the situation merits. Should the president wish to engage the agent in conversation, the agent is certainly obligated to respond out of respect for the office of the presidency. The agent must not become too chatty. In many cases, POTUS is merely being cordial and does not wish to engage in long conversations. In order for the agent to appear engaged and approachable, he must exercise care. In most cases any conversation between POTUS and agent should be over within seconds after its beginning. Over time, every agent should get the feel of when to speak and when to remain silent. This is a very delicate balance, and mastering it can be critical to career survival.

On one occasion, a First Lady asked an agent a superfluous question as she escorted a group of women through the rose garden. The agent went well beyond the required response to the point of practically becoming part of the tour group. One week later the agent was promptly reassigned to a post other than PPD. The best policy for a rank-and-file agent on PPD, especially a new one, is to speak as little as possible to POTUS or FLOTUS while appearing approachable.

The relationship between a PPD supervisor and POTUS is entirely different from that of the worker agent. The agent who rides in the right front seat of the limousine occupies a completely unique place in the universe than that of his subordinates. The PPD supervisor is a senior agent who, in addition to being in charge of the detail, is the main contact between POTUS and the Secret Service. Cordial conversations between this agent and POTUS frequently occur, usually in the limo, although I have seen this relationship stretched on occasion. Just as the shift agent must know his place in the hierarchy of things at the White House, so must the senior supervisory agent in charge know his place. This relationship by its very nature draws POTUS and his senior agents closer than that of the working shift, but it still should not be misconstrued as friendship.

Familiarity between POTUS and FLOTUS and their agents can become a detriment to security and should be avoided. While presidents and First Ladies are well aware of what their agents' jobs are in terms of security, and each has paid staff that attends to their personal needs, agents can sometimes be placed in difficult positions requiring tact and diplomacy. For example, I am aware of a situation in which a First Lady asked her agent in charge to have an agent retrieve her makeup bag from the limousine. This, of course, is a staff function, but for whatever reason, the staffer was not as close at hand as the agent. Rather than the agent saying, "Sorry, that is not a Secret Service function," which would undoubtedly have caused unnecessary friction, he nodded, then sent out a radio call to his detail to locate the First Lady's staffer and pass along the request.

Contrary to popular belief, the Secret Service does not work for the president and is, at least in theory, the most apolitical of all government agencies. This detachment serves a purpose. If an agent becomes too close to a president, closeness may cloud the professional judgment of the agent during crisis. Also, as law enforcement officers, it should not appear as if the Secret Service is the president's personal police force. Unlike staff who do work for POTUS, although paid with taxpayer dollars, Secret Service agents work for the director of the Secret Service and the secretary of the Department of Homeland Security. While a POTUS staff member's job is tied directly to POTUS, an agent's career will eventually move from PPD to other parts of the Secret Service.

An agent is assigned to PPD, not to the man who is president. When a president leaves office, the agents who have protected him do not then move on to his former presidential detail but rather remain on PPD, where they protect the new president. I saw this firsthand in 1992 as a PPD agent in the George H. W. Bush administration. When President Bush lost the general election to President Clinton, he picked up an entirely new group of agents, while his old protectors, including me, watched over President Clinton.

Some agents on PPD protect people other than the president. In spite of these smaller details within the main presidential detail, all have one thing in common: Each protectee has a direct line to the president, and some are not hesitant to use it.

In this regard, agents who watch over the president and First Lady's children have a particularly difficult task at times. Historically, children of POTUS have represented a wide range of ages and temperaments, from the very young, such as Caroline Kennedy, John Kennedy Jr., and Amy Carter, to adults, such as the Reagan, Ford, Johnson, Nixon, and Bush children. In between are teenage and college-age children such as Jenna and Barbara Bush and Natasha and Malia Obama. Each one of these famous children of presidents has his or her own distinct personality. They may not wish to be controlled by the Secret Service in any manner. While POTUS may not always enjoy the restrictions placed upon his activities by the Secret Service, he understands the necessity for it. Children of POTUS sometimes do not.

Most of these individuals have Secret Service protection not through their own wishes but rather because their father, the president of the United States, has directed it. As such, some are resentful of the sometimes imposing always felt presence of the Secret Service in their lives, a presence that makes a normal existence all but impossible. The threat against these children of POTUS is not so much assassination as kidnapping. One can imagine the impossible situation a POTUS would be placed in should his child be abducted and held in return for demands that could never be met. In this sense agents assigned to the seemingly more benign children's details must be as vigilant as those assigned to POTUS. It can be difficult when a child calls his or her father—the president—to complain that the Secret Service is ruining his personal life, and the president, in turn, asks the Secret Service to give his child more space. Too much space can be the same as no protection at all, and the agents will bear the responsibility should something happen to his charge.

A PPD agent must be a hybrid of bodyguard and diplomat and must be prepared to handle any crisis that might arise, be it a gunshot or a complaining adolescent.

AROUND THE WORLD WITH POTUS

Most think of traveling to locations such as Europe with the president while staying in the finest hotels as being glamorous and exciting. If you are an agent on PPD, however, traveling to exotic, faraway places means working long hours while experiencing jet lag and sleep deprivation and trying to keep your nutrition level to a point where you can function. Biorhythms get totally out of phase, and regularity habits kick in at the worst possible times.

On one such trip to Europe, I had been preposted by my shift leader in a large ballroom of a hotel where POTUS was to have a private, off-the-record meeting, meaning no press. It was a grand room and hotel, very old and ornate, with enormously high ceilings and priceless artwork—all very European.

As I waited in the empty room for POTUS, my internal mechanisms began to rumble. This was trouble on a large scale. I knew I had to find a men's room, or even a ladies' room. For the first and only time in my Secret Service career, I abandoned my post and fled to the men's room across the hall from the room POTUS was due to arrive at any minute. The odds that an assassin would appear in the next two minutes were probably zero, while the certainty that I had to find a men's room during that time was 100 percent.

I rushed into the ornate men's room and found a beautiful stall. Two minutes later, back in phase, I quickly reassembled equipment and myself and then ran to the door of the men's room to return to my post. I flung open the door and literally ran into the president of the United States, William Jefferson Clinton, almost knocking him down. It seems his internal clock was still on Washington time, the same as mine. As I moved aside to allow him into the men's room, I quickly thought of a cover for action and blurted out in my most professional voice, "All clear, sir." He said, "Thanks, Dan," and entered to tend to his presidential business. My shift leader nodded to me, and we left the leader of the free world alone in his now-private bathroom.

As I moved back to my post across the hall, it occurred to me that my shift leader thought I was checking out the men's room for POTUS. It was too perfect, and I let him continue to think that forever.

I quickly learned that foreign trips on PPD were seldom exotic or exciting. On some trips, we could be in one of the most beautiful cities in the world and never really see the place, depending on what shift we were working. On one such trip to Budapest, I was working the shift from 4:00 p.m. to midnight. It was already dark when we arrived, and we never left the hotel during my shift. We could just as easily have been in Cleveland and not known the difference.

After the anticipation of looking forward to a foreign trip to a nice part of the world, I frequently found that, after the flight and working twelve or more hours, in some cases all I wanted to do was sleep in the too-small beds in the too-small European hotel rooms. Once I had to store my bags in the hallway of the hotel, as there was not enough space in the Barbie doll–sized room.

The saying in the Service was that no matter where you go, once you arrive, there you are. Generally speaking, that summed it up for me as far as foreign travel went.

SKORPIONS AND SYRIANS

All Secret Service agents constantly live with the reality that their lives are expendable and can be exchanged at any time for that of the president. That reality permanently resides in the back of an agent's mind, where it is not dwelled upon yet is always there.

In every Secret Service agent's career, however, there are incidents that bring this reality home. One such incident occurred on a trip to Switzerland in 1993. President Clinton was meeting with various heads of state, including the Syrian president and dictator Hafez al-Assad.

While the president of the United States traveled with just the number of agents needed to efficiently protect him, Assad, it seemed, traveled with every armed agent in Syria, most of whom were probably related to him.

Dictators such as Assad also traveled overseas with almost all of their military leaders. These men dressed in uniforms resembling something out of a cartoon, with more medals and awards than

Audie Murphy, although not as well deserved. The idea was that if all his military leaders were with him, there would be no one to overthrow the government in his absence, although I saw this happen once while protecting the president of Sudan in 1983.

With regard to the meeting between President Clinton and Assad, the Secret Service was concerned about having so many armed Syrians in a relatively small room just feet from POTUS. Because of this concern, an agreement had been reached with the head of Syrian security that Assad's detail would not be armed during the meeting. The thought behind this request was twofold. One, we did not trust the Syrians in general. Two, in any situation where gunfire might erupt, Syrian protocol was to empty magazines indiscriminately in all directions. With the Syrians unarmed, neither of these things would be an issue.

The problem was that the Syrians, would as almost all people from the region, outwardly agree to almost anything and say, "No problem, no problem," when in fact they had no intention of following through with whatever it was they had no problem with. In most cases, they were not even listening to what was being proposed.

As a result of this known trait in their culture, my shift leader ordered me to prepost in the room with President Clinton and Assad, for the express purpose of neutralizing any threat to POTUS regardless of who posed it. Translated, that meant kill the Syrians if necessary. When I asked for clarification of his instructions, he merely nodded. I suppose I should have been flattered to be chosen for such an assignment, but I realized that if I did have to shoot the Syrians, like them, I would be experiencing the last day of my life.

As directed, I preposted in the conference room, and as Assad entered, so did his security detail. As expected, they were not unarmed. Nor were they even trying to conceal the fact. It was as I slowly moved behind them into the best possible firing position that I noticed their Skorpion machine pistols.

The Skorpion was a .32-caliber weapon with a ten- or twenty-round curved magazine that fired fully automatically, giving it little accuracy in any situation, especially in a packed room. It had a small folding stock that, when extended, came down over the forearm for added stability. The weapon itself was prone to malfunctioning and was really a piece of junk, but in such a venue, it would be deadly, and many individuals would be shot, including, perhaps, the president of the United States.

As President Clinton and Assad sat at the front of the room side by side and I stood behind the Syrian security agents, all of my senses were on full alert, peaking and then receding with every movement of my potential targets. If I had to respond to the Syrians, it would be the quintessential example of surgical shooting, taking out specific targets one by one in a room packed with innocents as well as the leader of the free world. In CAT, I had practiced this type of scenario many times and had fired thousands of rounds of ammunition preparing for such a challenge.

I repositioned a bit in order to ensure that POTUS and Assad would not be in my line of fire in the event I was forced to shoot and actually missed. As bad as a shootout in this small room would be, it would, of course, be catastrophic beyond imagination if a Secret Service bullet from my pistol struck either POTUS or Assad.

Due to the exceptional training received through the years from both the Marine Corps and the Secret Service, I felt confident. As in similar situations I had encountered, I knew I had done all I could do to prepare for whatever might now occur. A calm came over me as I stood ready to do what was necessary to protect the life of the president of the United States.

After what seemed like an eternity, the meeting finally ended uneventfully. I held my position until each of the Syrian security agents had exited the room and then returned to our command post, where I sat in the first chair I saw. This incident left me knowing two things for certain: The Syrians were not to be trusted, and, had they drawn their Skorpions, it would have been quite a mess.

AIR FORCE ONE

When it was time for PPD to travel, we traveled in a style that even the wealthiest could not buy a ticket for. We traveled on Air Force One, operated by the US Air Force Special Air Mission (SAM) squadron.

The call sign "Air Force One" for presidential aircraft was first used by the Eisenhower administration in 1953 after an incident in which a commercial aircraft operating in the same airspace as Ike's had the same call sign. Since that time, the call sign Air Force One has applied to any air force aircraft carrying POTUS. It makes no difference if the plane is one of the Boeing 747s built specifically for POTUS or a smaller Grumman Gulfstream business-type jet sometimes used by POTUS for short hops, when using a full-size 747 is not practical. Technically the call sign could apply to a Cessna Bird Dog two-seat single-engine aircraft if POTUS were aboard. If it is an air force plane and POTUS is aboard, it is Air Force One. If POTUS is not aboard, the airplane will have a normal air force call sign.

Presidents using airplanes for official travel is a relatively new phenomenon, with FDR being the first president to fly while in office. He had no designated airplane in the beginning and flew a commercial Pan Am Clipper on one overseas flight. Two US Army Air Corps aircraft later were designated for him, but the Secret Service deemed one not usable due to its safety record and the other was used only on one occasion. President Truman had two different aircraft assigned to him during his presidency but did not use them a great deal. Most notably, it was aboard one of these aircraft that he signed the bill that created the US Air Force as a separate branch of the military in 1947.

While Eisenhower had flown on one or two occasions in jets as POTUS, JFK was the first president to actually use a jet for travel on a regular basis. It was symbolic, in a sense. Presidents like FDR, Truman, and Ike were old and slow men who traveled on slow propeller-driven aircraft. JFK was more like the Boeing 707. Both airplane and president were young, good-looking, and in a hurry to get places.

The first jet aircraft that would become the standard Air Force One (AF-1) was a Boeing 707, tail number 26000. In the beginning, this jet did not have the familiar blue, white, and gold paint scheme now identified with AF-1, nor did it have the large emblem of the president of the United States on the forward part of the fuselage. It was painted orange and white, with the letters identifying it as belonging to the US Air Force. Not long after JFK entered office in 1961, tail number 26000 was given its new colors, which remain today the standard paint scheme for presidential aircraft.

The plane that took Kennedy on his most famous trips—including Berlin, where he made the "I am a Berliner" speech—was the 26000. It would also take him home for the last time on November 22, 1963, this time in the aft end of the plane, in his coffin with Jackie sitting by his side.

In 1972, Richard Nixon took delivery of a new AF-1, another Boeing 707, with the tail number 27000. It then became the primary AF-1, and 26000 remained as the backup, but as operationally capable as 27000. Both of these aircraft would be used interchangeably as AF-1 until President George Herbert Walker Bush took delivery in 1990 of two new Boeing 747s, tail numbers 28000 and 29000. They are identical, and both are still in service today.

After the new 747s arrived, Boeing 707, tail numbers 26000 and 27000, were relegated to backup duty. They were not retired completely from service until the mid-1990s. Both of these aircraft now reside in museums, with 26000 having served seven presidents and 27000 five.

A NEW AIR FORCE ONE AND THE DISAPPEARING WINDSHIELD

There was a world of difference between the older 707s and the new, much larger 747s. In addition to being significantly larger and more comfortable, the 747 engines had a great deal more thrust than those on 707. This initially caused some problems for CAT, dramatically brought to light quite unexpectedly one day.

One of CAT's main duties is protecting AF-1 on arrivals and departures. When the big jet is taxiing for takeoff and sitting at the end of a runway, or when it comes to a complete halt on landing rollout and is no longer able to immediately lift back into the air, it becomes a gigantic fuel-bloated target of opportunity. It is the mission of CAT to defend AF-1 during these times of total vulnerability against attacks of all types, from an organized act of aggression involving multiple attackers to someone running out of the woods to plant a charge on the landing gear. In order to provide this protection, the CAT truck must drive very close to AF-1 as it moves about on the ground, and must be able to give chase down the runway during takeoff and landing. The noise in the CAT truck and buffeting from the engines' thrust are tremendous, as CAT drives just yards behind the airplane. It was discovered quite by accident that this procedure had to be modified with the arrival of the larger 747s.

One of the first departures of 28000, one of the new 747s, occurred in 1990. The plane took off from Andrews Air Force Base and from the CAT truck, the new airplane seemed twice as large as the old AF-1. As AF-1 taxied, an uneasy feeling began to spread through the vehicle when it was noted that the buffeting of the CAT truck from merely following the airplane during its taxi to the runway seemed as intense as the buffeting from the old Air Force One at full power.

On this departure of 28000, with George Herbert Walker Bush on board, the CAT Suburban as usual upon takeoff fell in to provide coverage behind AF-1—and it fell into a hurricane force of jet blast. The tremendous power from the four massive turbo fan engines, each providing 43,500 pounds of thrust, proceeded to blow the front windshield of the CAT truck into the laps of the driver and team leader.

Most sane, rational people, including Secret Service agents, would have called off the mission at that point, but CAT does not fall under this category. In best CAT tradition, which always includes finishing its mission, the truck continued to trail AF-1 down the runway, with the hot jet blast and dirt and debris ripping through the truck like a windstorm and the smell of burning jet fuel permeating every nostril in the vehicle. Due to the deafening roar of the engines, the sound of five CAT agents screaming and laughing in unison could not be heard, even by each other.

As the jet lifted off, the CAT truck turned off the runway onto the taxiway for its trip back to the ramp with no front windshield. A debriefing was later held, at which time it was decided that CAT airport tactics were to be modified. CAT would continue to provide chase for AF-1 but from a greater distance.

MARINE ONE

As with Air Force One, the president must be on board a marine helicopter in order for the call sign to be Marine One. Otherwise, the helicopter retains a standard Marine Corps identification. The army and Marine Corps once shared the duties of flying the presidential helicopter, but in 1976, the marines took over exclusively in this area. Much old footage exists of Ike and JFK flying in Sikorsky H-34 helicopters with "ARMY" on the fuselage. In such instances, the call sign of the helicopter would have been Army One.

The Marine Corps squadron tasked with the honor of flying the president is HMX-1, based out of Marine Corps Air Station Quantico. "H" stands for helicopter, "M" for marine, and "X" for experimental, denoting the squadron's original mission of testing new, experimental helicopters. While the squadron flies many different types of helicopters, it transports POTUS primarily in Sikorsky VH-3 Sea Kings.

MY FIRST FLIGHT ABOARD AIR FORCE ONE

In an agent's career, there are certain things that will always stand out and be remembered forever. One of the most memorable events in my career was the privilege of flying on Air Force One, especially for the first time.

Flying on AF-1 was always special, and for many reasons. Nothing symbolizes the power and prestige of the presidency and the United States more than this magnificent aircraft. It is also special because only a very small percentage of Secret Service agents ever fly on AF-1. For a Secret Service agent to fly in this airplane, he had to be assigned to PPD, and our numbers were relatively few compared to the total number of agents in the Secret Service.

My first flight on AF-1 occurred in the summer of 1993 at night. My shift and I began this adventure by driving from the White House to an off-site landing zone, where we boarded our own HMX-1 helicopter for the trip to Andrews. There we would board AF-1.

We arrived at the landing zone and proceeded into the HMX-1 complex through a gate manned by a heavily armed marine. After checking our credentials, the marine waved us through the gate; we found a parking slot and got out and entered the ops building. Our helicopter arrived shortly thereafter and settled into its landing zone, whereupon the pilot disengaged the rotors and let them come to a stop, but with the engine still running at idle, which created a low whining noise. Cleared by the marine in HMX-1 operations, we proceeded out of the building to board the green Sikorsky VH-3 with the white top and "United States of America" painted on the aft end of the fuselage.

As I approached the waiting helicopter with my shift, I was immediately impressed by the beauty and sound of this unique flying machine. I remember the wonderful smell of burning jet fuel, the noise of the engine, and the perfect marine sergeant at the bottom of the aircraft's steps. On the carpeted steps were the words "Welcome Aboard Marine One" on removable Plexiglas placards in large letters as bold as the marines who flew these machines.

As we boarded the helicopter, the marine sergeant in full dress blues who stood by the forward steps saluted. The salute was a standard courtesy rendered by the marine aircrew for anyone who boarded their helicopter. As a former marine officer, I instinctively returned the squared-away sergeant's salute, although it was not part of protocol. Protocol or not, as a former marine officer, it was a habit I would never break.

No sooner were we in our seats than the recruiting poster–perfect sergeant climbed in and pulled the entry hatch shut, fastening the latch behind him. He then leaned into the cockpit, where he talked briefly with the pilots before strapping into his seat. The pilots engaged the rotors and began to increase power until the rotors were spinning above us with a comforting but muffled sound and the bird began to vibrate from the torque of the turning rotor shaft. The crew quickly completed their pre-takeoff checklist, and very suddenly the helicopter began to rise as the pilot applied power and pulled up on the collective stick.

Up we went into the purple night sky and began to circle slowly over Washington. We flew in a type of holding pattern as we waited for Marine One bearing POTUS to lift off from the White House, at which time we would fly together in formation to Andrews.

The sun had just set on this clear night, and Washington was brilliantly illuminated, with the monuments standing out like giant white carvings placed on a toy landscape. The noise of the VH-3's engine was muffled by the sound insulation, and thus it was amazingly quiet—so quiet, in fact, that you could actually carry on a conversation with the person next to you without yelling. I had last flown in a marine helicopter in 1981. It was another product of Sikorsky, a CH-53 Sea Stallion that was so loud one could not talk over the noise. It also had a noticeable puddle of some type of fluid on the floorboard. The 53 was designed to carry marines and their equipment into battle or anywhere else they needed to go. It did not need to be clean, quiet, and pretty. The presidential VH-3s, however, were designed to carry POTUS and his entourage in total comfort and style.

After circling for about twenty minutes and watching the same sights pass underneath several times, I could feel we were changing heading. As I looked out my window, I could see the red and green lights of Marine One rising up to meet us from the direction of the White House. As it neared, I could clearly see the shape and outline of the president's helicopter as it took the lead; we flew along in a trail position. Along the way, we changed the lead position more than once for security purposes.

As we began our approach into the Andrews Air Force Base area, I could feel changes in the pitch of the rotors as well as in the power setting. We came in from the west and descended lower and lower until we were in hover just feet above the concrete, and then the marine aviator flying our helicopter touched down with scarcely any notice. We taxied to our position, where the pilot parked the aircraft and shut down the engines. The recruiting-poster sergeant unlatched the door and lowered it. He then turned and nodded to us, indicating that we were free to leave the helicopter and go to where we would begin the next part of our adventure. We quickly disembarked the Sikorsky, and as we left, the pilots, still seated, turned to their left and right to wave good-bye to us.

In about five minutes, Marine One was hovering over the tarmac and landed just as gently as had our helicopter. The pilot disengaged the rotors and shut down the engines. The front door opened and dropped into position, at which time another perfect marine sergeant, in the same perfect dress blues, walked down the steps and to the rear of Marine One. There he unfastened and lowered an identical set of stairs for the passengers in the rear of the helicopter to descend.

Down the rear stairs descended the Secret Service detail leader and another agent, who picked up their designated places on the tarmac. Next came President Clinton, who walked down the front steps, where a marine saluted him. He began the short walk from Marine One to the front stairs of Air Force One. Ascending the front stairs and pausing at the top, he waved and disappeared inside.

At this point, we were free to board Air Force One, but not immediately. The agents always board the rear steps of the aircraft. At the bottom of the stairs standing on the tarmac is an air force sergeant with a list of all who are supposed to be flying on AF-1 that day. After you provide your name to the air force sergeant, he checks you off the list, and then you run up the stairs and onto the plane as it is only moments from moving out.

I stepped up to the sergeant, gave him my name, which he checked off, and up the stairs I went to the Secret Service compartment of the airplane, located toward the rear of the plane. This was just in front of the compartment used by the White House traveling press corps. I then prepared for my first flight aboard Air Force One.

I took my coat off and hung it in a closet next to our own lavatory, while keeping my gun and radio on. Even though we were on AF-1, we were still working and expected to respond to any crisis if needed. POTUS was up front in his area, watched over by the detail leader, where two seats are designated for the Secret Service.

I sat down in an oversize first class type of seat, which was standard throughout the plane. My shift mates sat down as well. The next thing I noticed was our shift leader closing the door that separated our compartment from that of the media. Our compartment had its own movie screen, and we began looking at the movie choices for the flight. All we had to do was select the one we wanted and push the button that corresponded to that movie, and it would run automatically.

As I settled in, an air force enlisted person came by and cheerfully offered sodas, coffee, and snacks. This, I happily realized, was par for the course on AF-1. If it were mealtime, they would bring sandwiches that always tasted better than anything from the best restaurants. This great service provided by the air force was especially welcome after a long day out with POTUS in large crowds, some of whom had not been through metal detectors. We would frequently arrive back at the plane exhausted and a bit stressed from a long day spent keeping the leader of the free world alive. No sooner would we take off our coats than the air force steward would be there with drinks, snacks, lunch, or dinner.

As I sat watching the movie selected by our shift leader and drinking a Coke, the engines of the airplane began to spool up, and we began to move. AF-1 taxied for what seemed a long time as it moved down the taxiway toward the end of the runway. I looked out my window and saw CAT move back and into its trail position to protect us from unwanted attention while on the ground; I hoped they would stay back far enough not to lose another windshield.

We moved directly onto the runway after being cleared for immediate takeoff by the tower and began the takeoff roll. The engines came up to full power, and their combined thrust pushed us back in our seats as we continued to accelerate down the runway. We were picking up speed very quickly but still lumbering down the runway as only this gigantic plane could lumber. Upon reaching the required speed, the pilot rotated the nose, and up we went into the night sky. Sitting toward the rear of the plane, it seemed as if we were going straight up as we heard the motors that powered the flaps and landing gear push them into the up position and then heard the solid "bump" of the landing gear doors closing. We were in the air, and I was now flying for the first time on Air Force One.

As comfortable as it was to fly on Air Force One, an agent was still technically working and was expected to be able to respond to an emergency if necessary. Also, Service protocol dictated that an agent should remain as alert and professional on Air Force One as in the White House. Consequently, one could never really relax during these flights. On this flight, as would be the case on many others, as we watched our movie, I looked and saw President Clinton standing in our section preparing to move into the next compartment in order to conduct an impromptu media session. Our shift leader opened the door separating us from the media, and the president went in, with the shift leader trailing. After the president answered a few questions from the White House traveling press, he moved back through our compartment, where he stopped briefly to offer some friendly words to our shift before returning to his compartment.

In a while, the sound of the engines lessened, and the plane's nose began to drop. This was the obvious sign that we had begun our descent, and it was our signal to start getting ready. For security reasons, such as avoiding shoulder-fired heat-seeking missiles, AF-1 always came in at a fairly steep rate of descent, and the pilot got the plane on the ground as soon as possible. On this, my first flight in AF-1, I was still putting on my jacket when the main landing gear hit the runway. It was dark and I was a bit startled when we landed, not realizing how close we were to the ground.

The entire shift was up and walking around while the pilot braked and went to reverse thrusters. We were bouncing and staggering around as if we were riding a rough section of train track. The plane had no sooner braked to a halt than our rear door was opened by a crew member and we ran down the stairs and out into the waiting night to protect the president of the United States. I had completed my first ride on an HMX-1 helicopter and Air Force One as a full-fledged member of the Presidential Protective Division.

REVERENT RUSSIANS AND FLYING IN THE BACKUP

As I noted earlier, there are two identical VX-25s, or 747s, outfitted for POTUS travel. Within the United States we usually only took one. On overseas flights we always took both of them, with one designated as the primary and the other as the backup. We took two because we needed the room to transport extra staff. And, in the highly unlikely event that the primary had mechanical difficulties, POTUS could easily switch to the backup.

On the same trip to Russia in 1993 on which I saved the staffer from Yuri, my shift had completed its assignment, and, rather than fly home commercial, we were lucky enough to be manifested on the backup plane. We were all dead tired after a week of protecting President Clinton in the streets of Moscow, Kiev, and other cities around the old Soviet Union, where he would frequently stop the motorcade, get out, and move among the Russians. The people were dumbfounded that an American president would be so open to them, as were we agents. We did, however, have the distinct advantage of being in a country not long out of the grip of Communism. In those days, people still automatically and without question moved when a security official said to move.

We were driving through the streets of Moscow on the way to the airport. Our shift was due to relinquish its responsibilities to another shift, and they would fly home on AF-1 with POTUS. We were feeling pretty good, although tired, heading for the homestretch on this marathon trip. Suddenly President Clinton ordered the driver of his limo to stop. I was in the follow-up vehicle with the rest of my shift when we saw the limo's brake lights illuminate and the giant car begin to slow. We then heard the voice of the detail leader call out, "Halfback from Stagecoach, Eagle wants to work the crowd"—Eagle being President Clinton.

As the cars halted, the detail leader emerged from the right front seat of the limo as we on the shift moved quickly to our positions. The detail leader opened the right rear door, from which President Clinton emerged into the freezing Moscow air. We went to our designated formation, working the president very tightly.

As we moved toward the large crowd now surrounding the motorcade in the street, we expected to be mobbed. Rather than swarming us, however, everyone who had been moving on the busy streets of Moscow began to quietly move to the sidewalks and stand motionless and mute. What the hell?

The hell was that as soon as we had stopped, a large, fierce group of men, many of whom looked like Dolph Lundgren from *Rocky IV,* materialized. Almost stereotypically Russian, they wore greatcoats, traditional big furry hats, and large boots. They were also armed with SKS carbines and AK-47 rifles. These men looked like pure evil, with cadaver-pale skin and blank, expressionless faces. They scarcely had to speak in order to control the crowd. Perfect crowd control—no muss, no fuss. Many of these people remembered the bad old days when to disobey a policeman, or even to move too slowly when given a command, could result in a beating, imprisonment in the famous Lubyanka prison, run by the KGB, or worse.

President Clinton shook hands with the people who stood reverently on the sidewalk. We knew, however, that the only thing standing between a mob scene and us were these Russian policemen, whom the masses were obviously terrified of.

President Clinton finally seemed to grow tired of shaking hands with the Russian citizenry—or perhaps he realized Russians couldn't vote in American presidential elections—and he returned to his limo. As we began moving back to the follow-up vehicle, I walked past one of our evil protectors. This one had the face not of Dolph Lundgren but of Lurch from *The Addams Family.* He extended his large gloved hand halfway to shake mine, and I returned the gesture without hesitation.

We arrived back at the airport and pulled up next to Air Force One, where our relief shift met us and immediately took over. We gratefully acknowledged the passing of the human baton known as POTUS and started heading over to the backup plane parked about fifty yards in front of us. On the way, I spotted a familiar figure adorned in boots and a full-length greatcoat: It was my wife, who was on the trip as an interpreter. Prior to boarding the plane, I was able to say a few brief words to her. I think I asked her if she had remembered to unplug the iron in the laundry room at home before she left for Russia. Then a quick kiss good-bye and back to work. She would be returning to the United States via commercial aircraft, and I would see her again in a day or two. Being married to another Secret Service agent was never dull.

After giving our names to the air force sergeant at the bottom of the stairs, we staggered on board, numb from the cold and bone tired. Upon collapsing in our seats, we were greeted by the always cheerful air force steward, who offered the usual Cokes as well as beer. Since we were now off shift and POTUS was not onboard, we were free to relax as if we were flying first class on British Airways. For any taxpayer who might wonder, we paid for all meals and drinks ourselves.

FLYING THE PRESIDENT'S CARS

When POTUS travels out of Washington aboard Air Force One, his limousines travel via air force transport. Although both aircraft are operated by the US Air Force, there is a world of difference in the ride.

During the 1980s and 1990s, Lockheed C-5 Galaxies and C-141 Starlifters were used to fly the presidential cars. Both of these giants were designed to move entire military units and all of their equipment anywhere in the world quickly. They were also perfect for moving presidential limos and support vehicles, along with legions of personnel, anywhere in the world. The 141s carried the basic package of spare limo, limo, and follow-up. The C-5s carried six to eight vehicles and were used more on overseas flights.

The C-5, in addition to carrying major cargo, can also carry passengers, with an upstairs deck containing ninety-plus airline-type seats. In addition to delivering the POTUS vehicles to where they needed to go, it was also the most economical way to transport the many agents needed to stand post on the middle perimeter of a POTUS event. For the cars, it was a great way to go; for an agent flying the C-5 or C-141, it was always misery, which one learned through experience how to adapt to.

Old and worn-out, first by constant use in the Vietnam War, then by constant use in Desert Storm, the 141s should have been retired to the desert storage area in Arizona years before, but the

C-17, which was to replace the C-141, had yet to go operational in sufficient numbers to help our mission. As a result, the tired C-141 by necessity flew onward in support of the president.

The 141s were noisy and slow, and the temperature inside was impossible to control. From your feet to your knees, you were numb with cold. From your knees on up, you were burning alive. Earplugs were necessary to avoid permanent hearing loss, although I did not escape that damage due to these and other loud noises, much to the annoyance of my wife, who has to yell at me in a noisy setting to be understood.

Another downside to the 141s was that they always broke, thankfully never in the air, but usually when you really needed to go somewhere in a hurry. It was more common than not for a replacement bird to be flown in from the closest base and the cars and people moved from the broken-down plane to the one that could still fly.

On one memorable landing, we hit the runway hard—very hard. The three armored vehicles were straining at their chains, and everyone was thinking about what would happen if one broke loose. Even though we had no window to look out of, it was obvious that we were going faster than the normal landing speed. The brakes were squealing, and we could smell them burning. Thankfully, we finally came to a stop, and the pilot turned off the runway onto the taxiway.

I spoke to the aircraft commander after we shut down, as the rear end of the plane was opened to disgorge the cars. He was happy to talk about what had happened, because he was obviously proud of having kept us from crashing. It seems we almost ran off the end of a runway while landing because the power bus that operated the flaps failed. With no flaps to help slow our airspeed during final approach, we landed at too high a speed. The talented young captain managed to get the mammoth airplane stopped just before going into the weeds.

There were other close calls as well, but no actual crashes of the 141 with Secret Service personnel or cars onboard. In spite of its mechanical glitches due to old age, only 22 of 285 were lost due to accidents during its entire service life, an incredible safety record for hours flown.

The routine to get the cars on the planes and into the air was standard. The day of the lift, several Secret Service personnel from PPD transportation section would meet at the main Secret Service vehicle garage, where all protection vehicles are stored and maintained. In the 1990s the facility was located at the Washington Navy Yard. The current state-of-the art facility is at a classified location, although Joan Lunden and her camel have been there.

All three vehicles—limousine, spare limousine, and follow-up—would depart the garage together en route to Andrews Air Force Base. Before leaving the garage, the checklist of items to be carried in each vehicle was verified, such as the proper number of Heckler & Koch MP5 submachine guns, radios, first aid kits, and so forth. After confirming that all equipment was in the vehicles, the package departed the garage and made its way to Andrews, where the cars were driven onto the plane.

The air force load master of the crew always did a perfect job of chaining the cars down securely, but it was the responsibility of the designated agent to drive the limo to ensure it was done correctly. It always was, and the checking of tie-downs by the agent was always a mere formality. The proper securing of the cars was absolutely critical. Should one come loose at anytime in the flight, especially during takeoff or landing, the monsters would crush people and cause damage, possibly causing the loss of the aircraft.

Fuel could not exceed one-half tank in the cars to be flown because of the sloshing about of the fuel during times of turbulence and the expansion of air inside the fuel tanks at altitude would cause spillage. Occasionally the level of fuel was incorrect, and those sitting too near would suffer nausea from the smell of gasoline fumes.

When the Secret Service was aboard their airplanes, the air force always went the extra mile to be as accommodating as possible.

To ride in a C-141 Starlifter or even the newer C-5 Galaxy was uncomfortable at best for overseas flights lasting ten or more hours, and we always appreciated the courtesy and professionalism of the Military Airlift Command.

After takeoff, we would walk around the airplane and visit with each other, while those who discreetly brought their own beverages onboard would indulge in quiet moderation to help the sleep process. After tiring of yelling over the noise of the engines, we would return to our seats, which were either standard airline seating that could be put in or taken out on pallets depending on the mission or—God forbid—the dreaded nylon web sling seats that folded down from the longitudinal axis of the airplane. Eventually everyone would try to sleep for a while until arriving at the next location.

Sleep did not come easily going to our destinations but coming back to the United States, everyone always went out immediately. Going back to my marine days, I could always sleep anywhere, either sitting up or lying down. One did not lie down to sleep on the floor of a car plane, however—it could be fatal.

These airplanes were very cold close to the floor. There was virtually no insulation between the thin skin of the airplane and the subzero outside air temperature. Returning from one overseas trip, an agent lay down in the aisle to get some sleep. He did sleep, almost forever. While sleeping on the freezer-temperature floor, his body lost a great deal of heat, and he suffered hypothermia. He was discovered shivering uncontrollably, and the airplane had to land as soon as possible in order to get him to a hospital. Had the air force not done such a great job of getting the plane to an alternate landing field where the agent could receive immediate attention, he would not have survived.

A FLYING TREASURE SHIP

There were two major advantages to flying the car plane on overseas trips. One was that you did not have to bother with the annoying process of clearing foreign customs and immigration, as the American Embassy handled that formality. The other was that it provided the perfect means of getting all of your shopping items, no matter how bulky, back to the United States. Once you got your purchases back to the plane, the air force would load them all for you as long as nothing was alive, illegal, or potentially harmful to the plane, crew, and passengers.

Many places we visited around the world offered excellent shopping at great prices. In places such as Korea, the Philippines, and Europe, there were great deals on almost any item you could think of. In some countries, you could buy anything from machine guns to people. Of course, we stuck to things that would be legal to have in the United States. We were, after all, federal law enforcement officers who valued our great jobs. No one was going to risk losing that job trying to smuggle contraband back home.

On one trip, an agent brought home an entire brass bed. Another lugged home enough wine to keep him from going to the package store for quite some time. Most of us settled for smaller things we could carry on the plane or store in one of the cars transported on the plane. In CAT, we usually took our own Suburban on overseas trips. The vehicle would be loaded up with all types of great merchandise acquired while on the trip.

CAT always became instantly popular on such trips, as everyone wanted to use our truck to store their purchases. We were all in this together, so we usually allowed other agents the use of the truck, unless by team vote it was decided that for any number of reasons the person making the request should not be allowed to use it. The criteria included, first and foremost, whether the person was a CAT hater or CAT supporter. In a case where the supplicant was voted to be a CAT hater, he would be told that there was no room for his purchases. Once such a decision had been made, there was no possibility of reversing it other than by unanimous team vote.

On one such occasion after we rendered our opinion, a rebuffed agent became indignant, claiming that the truck did not belong to us but to the government, and that he could store his things in it if he wanted. We, in turn, reminded this young GS-7, who still had wet ink on his graduation diploma from agent school, that while the truck technically belonged to the government, it was assigned to CAT. He stormed away, mumbling something about CAT guys, and found storage for his items elsewhere.

Upon our return to Andrews Air Force Base we would clear customs with our purchases just like other international travelers, then head to our homes, where we would present our latest acquisitions to our significant others. The responses to some of these purchases did not always go as expected.

GAUDY TREASURES

Almost every agent who has ever been on a foreign trip has in his or her home some hideous item purchased overseas and brought home on the car plane. A lot of these items looked great and had terrific novelty at the time of purchase. Upon getting them out of the country from which they were purchased and back home, many such items lost their shine almost immediately.

Once, in Turkey, I bought what I thought was a great-looking brass vase I thought my wife would love. After getting it home, I proudly presented it to her as a sign that although I had been halfway around the world, I was thinking of her. She took one look at the thing, and it was immediately relegated to the garage until picked up by Goodwill.

On the same trip, I purchased a giant water pipe. The enormous thing sat on the floor in our downstairs television room for about one day. In very short order, it joined the brass vase in the garage, along with an assortment of other tacky items, such as swords from Saudi Arabia recently rediscovered in our last move. Two men who did some work on our home are now the proud owners of these implements of destruction. The lethal-looking items may now adorn their respective residences, or lie under their beds to be used in the event of a home invasion. (Perfect, if a roving band of killer nomads break down the door demanding your women.) They could also quite possibly be in a garage awaiting the Goodwill truck.

GIFTS FROM CHINA

Not all souvenirs traveled via car plane. In 1998 my wife returned home from a three-week assignment to the People's Republic of China (PRC) with an unusual surprise. After Donnelle arrived home from her marathon flight, I asked what she had brought me from the land of Godless Communism. She said that the trip had been a busy one and that there had not been much shopping. She then produced several red metal butane lighters with Mao Zedong's image emblazoned on the side. When opened, the lighters played the anthem of the PRC. She then produced a Chairman Mao cap complete with a red star on the front. Nice, but not memorable.

A week or so later the phone rang. It was a shipping company from Baltimore, calling to let us know that our item from China had arrived at the Port of Baltimore and was being trucked to our house. Item from China? I pressed my wife for information, but she was not talking.

About two hours later a moving truck arrived in front of our home. The rear door opened and the two-man crew struggled to unload a rather large and heavy crate. As they pulled free the packing nails and began to remove what appeared to be at least fifty pounds of foam and bubble wrap, a brown, earthenlike thing began to emerge. When the last of the packing was removed, I saw a . . . terra-cotta warrior. The thing was easily six feet tall and weighed several hundred pounds.

The site that Donnelle had advanced for President Clinton was the location where the terra-cotta statues had been discovered, and the area had been turned into a museum of sorts. The warrior that arrived at our home was a full-sized reproduction, and the Chinese were selling these things to anyone who had the cash.

For some reason that remains unknown even today, we named our warrior Frank. He was a bit hard to get used to. Walking through the house in the dark, I would sometimes forget he was there and nearly go into cardiac arrest as I bumped into him.

Frank protected three of our homes over the next several years. Unfortunately, due to being moved so many times, including his trek from China, his base had cracked. It was only a matter of time before he toppled over, crushing anyone who might be near. Our son was five at the time, and we feared that Frank might one day accidentally kill him. So we made the painful but sound decision to dismiss Frank from service and find him a new home.

Once the decision had been made to dismiss Frank, the big dilemma became what to do with him. We wanted him to go to a good home, one in which he would be appreciated, as he had been while in our charge.

Our next-door neighbors were lovely people from South America who had always loved Frank. Each time they came over, they remarked how great Frank was and how they wished they had their own terra-cotta warrior. When we offered up Frank to them, they were speechless. They insisted on buying Frank, but to sell him seemed immoral. We explained that we would not feel comfortable accepting money. Finally, they accepted him gratis. That was in the fall of 2003.

In 2008 my wife was in the area of our old home and, to her delight, there was Frank still standing tall in the open foyer of our former neighbors' home. A smaller version of Frank that came with the full-sized statue still stands in front of our fireplace, a reminder of the most unusual overseas purchase in our combined forty-two years of service.

RUNNING WITH THE PRESIDENT

In addition to its normal protective duties, from 1992 until 1997 the Secret Service was dealt the challenge of keeping presidential candidate and later president of the United States Bill Clinton alive as he regularly pursued fitness on the open, unsecured streets of Washington, DC, and the world. Agents who ran with President Clinton were participating in what was potentially the most dangerous assignment they would perform while in the Secret Service. In this case the question would be: Would you take a bullet as well as a speeding car or a city bus for the president?

Bill Clinton became a candidate for president of the United States in 1992 and had not spent a great deal of his life in pursuit of fitness. During the 1992 campaign, he began to run as a form of exercise and a way to meet voters. One way to do this as a candidate was to run in public places, where the people were. His habit of running presented, over time, a large and unusual security challenge to the Secret Service.

In order to properly protect candidate Clinton during these public runs, at least one or two agents had to run alongside him, close enough to deal with any threat that might present itself. And they had to run with a pistol as well as a radio. In the beginning, this was not too difficult a challenge. Clinton was still a candidate, and only a couple of agents were needed, as his detail was much smaller than that of a sitting president. These two agents did not need to be especially fit, because Mr. Clinton did not run very far or fast.

The whole running thing with Clinton was as much about media coverage as it was about fitness. The important thing was for then Governor Clinton to get out and be seen, to appear fit, healthy, and energetic, all desirable traits in a president. As time progressed, he lost weight and actually began to get into a rudimentary level of fitness. He also began running farther and faster, and the Service was becoming concerned. Pretty soon the Service would need to find agents who were actually in good physical condition to run with him.

On January 20, 1993, William Jefferson Clinton, former governor of Arkansas and now a regular jogger, was sworn in as the forty-second president of the United States, and it appeared that he had no intention of stopping his runs. Prior to Bill Clinton's presidency, no president in the history of the United States had engaged in any serious physical fitness activities. Their Secret Service agents did not need to be aerobically fit, they merely had to be in good health.

Most pre-Clinton PPD agents were generally healthy, with their weight in proportion to their height, but many did not work out to any great extent. Up until the Clinton years and the relatively new threat of terrorist attacks, PPD had been largely a gentleman's assignment, where looking the part combined with good instincts and reactions was almost all that was needed. The mere practice of being perfectly groomed on PPD with a great-looking collar and tie knot was about to change, and the responsibilities of the PPD agent were about to expand to also include being physically fit. Agents would now be required to run as far as three to four miles with the president, bearing the extra weight of a gun and a radio.

Secret Service management had hoped that after inauguration, President Clinton would stop running, at least in public. To the contrary, however, and much to the concern of those responsible for his direct safety, not only did Clinton not stop running, he ran more. To double the horror, he insisted on conducting his runs not within the safe confines of the White House grounds Harry Truman described once as "a prison" but in broad daylight on the streets of Washington, DC. The issue had now become deadly serious. The president was regularly running the mean and always potentially dangerous streets of Washington during morning rush hour. Anyone who wished could stand within a few feet of the president as he ran by.

There is always a degree of risk in trips, even when the president is leaving the White House encased in an armored vehicle. Taking the president running down Pennsylvania Avenue at peak rush hour, around the reflecting pool at the Lincoln Memorial, or through Rock Creek Park, where anyone could be lying in ambush, was beyond dangerous; from a security standpoint it bordered on insanity.

The most concerning part of this morning ritual was that President Clinton was running regularly enough so that his routine was entirely predictable to all who cared to observe. Each year the Secret Service spent millions of dollars protecting the president utilizing metal detectors, K9 explosives-detecting dogs, counter assault teams, counter snipers, ballistic shields, armored vehicles, and by carefully screening guests. Yet anyone who wanted to harm the president did not need to defeat these complicated measures. They could simply sit on a bench having coffee and wait until the president ran by, at which time he would be completely vulnerable to attack. The odds were that eventually someone would be waiting.

Having fully digested the grim reality that the president had no intent of modifying his morning fitness regimen, the Secret Service set out to formulate a security plan that would give President Clinton some degree of protection as he ran among pedestrians and traffic with dangerous regularity. Even under perfect conditions it is impossible for the Secret Service to ensure the safety of the president 100 percent. In the running scenario this percentage dropped drastically.

If the president was intent on running, perhaps at least he could be persuaded to run in a safer, more controlled environment. One attempt to increase the president's safety was the construction of a running track around the perimeter of the lower roadway on the south grounds of the White House. It was exactly a quarter mile around, and it was hoped that would satisfy the president's needs. If he ran there, only one or two agents would be required to run with him. It would largely be a matter of posting a few agents in strategic locations—but President Clinton did not like the track and seldom used it.

After the running track idea failed, the next approach for providing better security was to try to steer President Clinton to venues such as nearby military bases. Half of his purpose in running, however, was to be out among the people and to escape the confines of the White House. While going to locations such as Fort McNair, a few miles from the White House, made sense and provided an excellent place for him to run, President Clinton would have none of it. He wanted to run in the streets and around the monuments, just like anyone else. The problem, of course, was that he was not like anyone else; he was the president of the United States, and, like all presidents, thousands around the world wished him ill.

The final plan devised by the Secret Service was to pre-stage large groups of agents borrowed form the various divisions in Washington around the morning's proposed running site, then surround the president with agents who could run with him while hoping for the best.

Many citizens wanted to run with President Clinton. To be selected as a guest runner was very prestigious and good for a significant amount of boasting at the next Georgetown cocktail party. These invited runners usually had some notoriety socially or had contributed enough money to the DNC to earn an invitation. Some of these politically motivated fitness enthusiasts had obviously spent more time shopping for running apparel than actually running. While most had spent a great deal of money on perfectly coordinated running attire and the latest in high-tech shoes, many finished the run inside the Secret Service follow-up or the tail car while being tended to by the White House physician for heat exhaustion or other ailments found in first-time runners. The Secret Service was always happy to see these guests, however—in fact, the more the better, as they presented excellent ballistic insulation around the president during these outings.

Each shift had some agents who could run three miles with equipment at President Clinton's usual nine-minute-per-mile pace. The problem was that this number was not sufficient. At a minimum, four shift agents and a supervisor were needed for each run, and all had to possess not just the endurance to finish but also enough reserve energy for responding to an emergency during or at the end of the run.

It was at this point that the mission of CAT expanded from being prepared to respond with speed, surprise, and violence of action against attacks on the president to also running with the president. While many PPD supervisors seemed to be at a loss about how to make the best use of CAT, there was one clear advantage to having buffed weapons experts around: Each could run forever while burdened with weapons and radios. Until each shift could field the sufficient number of runners, the decision was made that every morning CAT would provide runners to augment the shift.

Because CAT agents could run while simultaneously surveying the area for possible ambush sites, not merely keep up on the runs. CAT saved PPD and possibly the life of the president during the first year of the Clinton administration.

The utilization of CAT for the morning runs was, however, a stopgap measure only. The job of running with POTUS was really a shift responsibility. With a total of thirty to thirty-six agents in CAT during this period, pulling between two and four agents each morning for the run placed a strain on CAT operational readiness. Still, until enough shift agents were up to speed, CAT would continue to pull double duty.

On many mornings the CAT midnight shift that had already been up all night providing coverage at the White House was held over for another four hours to cover the run. Exhausted CAT staff watched their working shift colleagues depart the White House for home and sleep but soldiered on without complaint.

One day the SAIC of PPD called a meeting with all available PPD agents in an auditorium of the Old Executive Office Building. The purpose of the meeting was to lay down the law to agents that this president ran almost every morning, that it was the responsibility of agents to run with him, and that everyone, not just CAT and a few fit shift agents, was going to be required to help out by taking turns running.

Soon every agent who could run was training to help with this new PPD responsibility. As the weeks progressed, many agents joined the ranks. Others discovered that running on older knees and ankles was not a pleasant experience and were medically excused from the challenge.

There was no such thing as an uneventful run with President Clinton. It seemed that on almost every outing there was an incident of some sort that reinforced the opinion, held by most, that a public running POTUS was not the best of ideas. It was unsafe not only for him but, in some cases, for the public as well.

On one outing, we had begun the run at the reflecting pool in front of the Lincoln Memorial, dismounting the motorcade on Seventeenth Street in the middle of morning rush hour. This was a particularly memorable run for several reasons. The first thing that happened, even before the run began, was that a motorist driving south on Seventeenth Street looked to his right, where he was amazed to see the president of the United States in running apparel. Astounded, the motorist stared at the president until he rear-ended the car in front of him.

Our route that morning took us around the reflecting pool at the Lincoln Memorial. The run was going as it normally did, with the president plodding along at his usual nine- to ten-minute-per-mile pace. After one lap around the pool, President Clinton, to the surprise and horror of all, crossed Seventeenth Street without the benefit of the crosswalk and ran toward the Washington Monument. After crossing Seventeenth Street, he continued to run up the gradual but increasingly steep incline toward the Washington Monument and multitudes of tourists. At least he had not been run over crossing the street. This was not his usual routine of two or three times around the reflecting pool and then home.

I was one of two agents running trail that morning. As President Clinton ascended the hill toward the monument, the supervisor who was running next to him began to slow, then turned and signaled for me to take the off-shoulder position with the president. This required me to sprint uphill a good seventy-five yards to close the distance between my position and that of POTUS, who was now totally without agent coverage and seemingly unconcerned about it. I ran past the supervisor with a reserve energy born of adrenaline and extreme urgency as much as aerobic fitness, trying to catch up before POTUS disappeared over the top of the hill and into the unknown. Staff Sergeant McLean from my Quantico days was subliminally in my head at this point, reminding me that I could rest after I was dead and to get to the top of the god-damned hill now.

Just as POTUS reached the crest of the hill, I caught up with him, and we came face-to-face with about thirty unbelieving tourists standing at the base of the monument. Each began scrambling for what I hoped were cameras as I moved between them and POTUS while placing my right hand inside my running jacket around the grip of my pistol. As we descended the hill, with me now running while looking over my shoulder to keep an eye on the tourists at the monument, there was no other agent in sight.

Not long after topping the hill, President Clinton said to me, "Okay, Dan, let's go home."

"Yes, sir," I answered, trying not to appear as out of breath as I actually was. As he reversed course, heading back to the top of the hill toward the waiting tourists now aiming cameras, my biggest concern was that he would stop and work the crowd. On this day, however, he merely waved and continued down the side of the hill back toward Seventeenth Street and the waiting cars.

After arriving back at the motorcade, parked on Seventeenth Street, President Clinton performed his usual stretching exercises next to the limo. This was the most dangerous time of the run—we had been in this general area for about thirty-five minutes, and our presence was well known. The police had just finished working the accident that had occurred at the beginning of the run, and traffic on Seventeenth Street was beginning to back up. Many people were beginning to converge on the area as the president finally got back into the limo for the short trip back to the White House. This scenario was the norm three to four days per week.

Whether President Clinton intended to run on a given morning was always a matter of speculation. It seemed that no one on his staff ever had courage enough to ask him prior to his turning in for the evening if he planned to run the following morning or not. I never understood the reluctance to ask. The worst thing that could have happened was that President Clinton would have said he didn't know, or don't bother me now. By the end of each day most senior staff had gone home, leaving only young staffers still at the White House, and they were not going to ask the president if he intended to run the following day.

This lack of assertiveness by the staff made our work on PPD unnecessarily complicated, and we had to assume that each morning the president would run. Each morning we staged a motorcade on the south grounds of the White House outside the diplomatic entrance that led to the area where FDR once gave his "fireside chats" and were prepared to drive to one of President Clinton's designated running sites. This required the designated agent runners each morning to show up for shift change in running gear. That, in turn, required the runners to bring their business suits in a hanging bag along with everything else they would need to wear for the day: suit, shirt, belt, socks, shoes, tie, towel, toiletries, and so forth.

While the motorcade required for transporting President Clinton to his running sites was scaled down from the normal cavalcade, it was still large. In addition to Secret Service limo and follow-up, this motorcade required two marked units—one from Metro DC police and the other from Secret Service Uniformed Division—to serve as a lead car and tail car, respectively. Many mornings these officers and their vehicles sat and waited for hours not knowing whether they would be needed or not. Other vehicles needed for the procession were vehicles for the press, guest runners, and staff.

The usual running procedure was for the day shift, running outfits and all, to assume the posts in the White House. One post was on the main floor next to the front door of the White House. This was pre-9/11, when there were public tours most mornings. There the puzzled tourist would stare at some of the best agents in the Secret Service, wondering why each was dressed in workout attire. One particularly curious middle-aged woman asked me, as she leaned over the velvet rope barrier, why we were dressed in gym clothes? Not wanting to engage in conversation, I answered, "Sorry, the answer to that is classified." This seemed to satisfy her as her husband prodded her toward the North Portico and out of the building.

As the morning wore on, speculation would always begin as to whether President Clinton was going to run or not. Supervisors were put in a bind because they had to make the call after a certain point whether to keep agents in running gear or have them change into business attire for an upcoming move out of the White House.

When the elevator outside the family residence lit up, everyone knew that the president was on his way down. Upon the door opening the agent standing post there would immediately call out, "Eagle," the president was headed for the Oval Office or for the cars. If the call was to move to the Oval Office, we knew he was not running and we would sprint to our command post area, known as W-16, where we would change from running gear into our suits faster than supermodels changing outfits between runs down the catwalk. Running shorts and T-shirts flew as we tried to get into our work attire as quickly as possible. If the president emerged from the elevator in running gear, we all abandoned our posts and ran toward the motorcade, where we would get into the follow-up vehicle behind the limo and drive to the running site. Making the decision when to have the runners change into business suits was a matter of timing and luck, and on some occasions both were bad.

On one such morning, we were, as usual, standing our posts in running gear. It was getting late, almost nine o'clock, and still no President Clinton. The shift leader, feeling it was safe to do so, made the call for all runners to go ahead and change into our suits for a regular workday. We changed and had no sooner assumed our posts than the elevator delivered President Clinton, attired in running gear. He walked to the cars, as usual, but there was a problem: There were no cars. The motorcade cars had been cut loose and had returned to their off-site location and could not be recalled in a timely manner. Also, those of us who were runners were in the process of changing from business attire back into running gear. This time there were suit coats, pants, belts, and other masculine wardrobe items flying around the command post as if we were caught in a windstorm.

The president was not happy to find there were no cars waiting for him. He told the shift leader that he wanted to run off-site, and right now. The flustered agent suggested to the president that he run on the seldom-used track until we could put together some sort of motorcade package. With a look of frustration and without speaking, Clinton began running on the track. Using the emergency motorcade cars staged on the grounds and setting a record for changing outfits, we had cars and agents ready to go before Clinton had run two laps around the quarter-mile track. We proceeded to the reflecting pool, which was less than a quarter mile from the White House, and President Clinton got in his run.

After returning from a run, the running agents had but a few minutes to grab their suits and bags and get over to the showers, located in the Old Executive Office Building.

After running three and sometimes four miles in 90-degree heat and 100 percent Washington, DC, humidity, the body does not stop sweating immediately. Rather, it takes an hour or more. We would take cold showers, jump into our suits, and double-time back to the White House, where we would stand post still sweating, as if we had run the three miles in our suits. We were soaked and literally sweating through our clothes. It was miserable, but it was for the leader of the free world and we were getting paid, so what the hell. The rub was that the agents who did not run had to double up on their time on post while we runners were out of the rotation showering and getting dressed, so they received no downtime until we returned.

In the beginning we showered and got back on post as quickly as possible. After the nonrunners starting complaining that we were taking too long getting back to post, I began taking even longer to return. It became my personal policy and habit following a run to proceed into the White House, get a cup of ice water, and stand in the air-conditioned security room until I had cooled off enough to shower and get back on duty. This caused even more complaints from some of the shift members. I reminded some that while we were running our asses off with no complaints, they were merely standing around or sitting, and that they should stop bitching. Following this exchange, most of the complaining stopped.

President Clinton always enjoyed an end-of-the-summer trip to Martha's Vineyard, Massachusetts, where, for a couple of weeks, he played golf and hung out with friends and wealthy supporters,—such as Vernon Jordan, James Taylor, Carly Simon, and the beautiful people of show business. It was a nice place to visit and far more expensive than most agents could ever afford if they were to have gone on their own. I went on two occasions and enjoyed it. Clinton was relaxed and easy work at the Vineyard. He also loved to run while there.

I was on the afternoon shift, 4:00 p.m. to midnight, at Martha's Vineyard. On the afternoon shift it was always safe to run in the morning, because President Clinton seldom ran in the afternoon. The morning guys always handled it. Most days—not all, as it turned out.

One morning I had risen around nine o'clock after staying up a bit too late the night before. I got up, pounded back a lot of water to relieve my state of dehydration, and then went for a five-mile run. In the afternoon, I walked out of the hotel and into the waiting shift change van that would take us to POTUS's location to begin our shift. Inside, the shift leader was visibly upset. "What's wrong?" I asked. He nearly shouted, "POTUS did not run this morning; he is going to run this afternoon! Someone needs to go get running gear!" After an awkward moment of silence with no volunteers, I said, "Okay, what the hell. I'll go."

I had already run that morning, but if the president of the United

States needed an agent to run with, I estimated that in my current condition I would still do as well as anyone else who might be available. As I spilled out of the van to go back to my room for the right gear, another agent followed. He was also a former CAT agent. CAT once again mans up and saves the day while others whimper. We had fun with that one.

WAITING TO KILL THE PRESIDENT

Aside from not having enough running agents at times, the biggest problem with President Clinton's fitness program was that he liked to run in areas where any assassin could lurk, as could a random demented person with a gun. We ran through crowds, crossed city streets, and stood in the open for minutes at a time by the limo while Clinton stretched before and after the run, all of this with normal traffic flowing by. We also violated the most non-negotiable rules for security in such matters. We usually left the White House at the same time each day, using the same gate, and seldom varied our running sites or routes. We had four running venues and did not mix them up very well. We were an assassination waiting to happen. Were it not for an overseas trip, an attempted assassination in all probability would have happened.

During December 1993, President Clinton left Washington for two weeks and traveled to Russia. This was the trip from which I flew home on the backup plane after shaking hands with Lurch, the Russian security officer. Meanwhile, in Florida a man was threatening to kill the president. His basic plan was to drive from Orlando to Washington, where he would wait along one of our running routes and kill President Clinton as he ran by. There was speculation that he wished to die during the attack in a hail of Secret Service pistol lead.

One of the things the Secret Service has always benefited from is that potential assassins are largely unable to formulate and implement effective plans. Fortunately this man's plans were no different. The place where this man, having arrived in DC from Florida, is said to have sat day after day for over a week was indeed on a route we used regularly. The would-be assassin failed to realize, however, that POTUS was out of the country and would not be by anytime soon. Eventually he grew tired of waiting in the cold and returned to Florida, where he confided what he had done to a friend, who contacted authorities. The suspect was arrested, and in May 1994 he was convicted, in US District Court, of 18 USC 871, threatening the life of the president. He served four years in federal prison.

As a result of this incident and others not publicly revealed, the Service was finally successful in persuading President Clinton to stop the unwise practice of running in public. The president had pushed his luck long enough and had gotten away with it, but everyone knew that his luck would not hold out forever.

Not long after the threat from Orlando, the running issues were all resolved overnight when, at professional golfer Greg Norman's house in Florida, President Clinton caught his heel on a step and fell, tearing his knee. His running days were all but over, and he confined his fitness efforts to the White House, where he used a treadmill and stair-climber.

The next president, George W. Bush, was not a jogger but an honest-to-God runner. He ran at a six-minute-per-mile pace normally for three miles, and there were even fewer agents who could run with him than with President Clinton. Fortunately, President Bush never ran in public but rather at Camp David or the Secret Service training center in Beltsville, where it was much easier to protect him. There is, however, no such thing as a completely safe site, and although the use of more secure running sites meant that fewer agents were needed, the ones who accompanied President Bush still had to keep up with his six-minute pace. Most of those men were current or former CAT agents.

DRIVING THE PRESIDENT

In December 1993, President Clinton was vacationing for a few days in Hilton Head, South Carolina, where he spent most days playing golf and running on the beach. I had volunteered to do the advance because I was familiar with the layout of the island. My wife and I had spent our honeymoon at Hilton Head three years earlier, and I had vacationed there many times as a boy with my family. I had always loved the place, but it was strange how now all at once everything looked different from a security perspective. I discovered on this trip that work is work no matter where you are. Unlike all other visits to Hilton Head, this one did not afford me the opportunity to enjoy the island or its amenities.

I was doing the advance for the rented house on the beach where the president was staying and also managing the command post located at another rented house next door to his. These houses were located in a very affluent neighborhood on a short street with only one way in and one way out, making things easy to secure. The weather was beautiful and everything went according to plan, with the biggest nuisance being the people who lived on the street where the president's rental house was. Each seemed to feel he should have access to the president and First Lady since they were staying at a home on their street. Most were left disappointed.

On the final day of the assignment, I was sitting in the command post reading the following week's work schedule when my shift leader pulled me aside and said he wanted to talk to me in private. This type of thing was seldom good. We met in an empty room at the command post. Coming directly to the point, he asked which of the other sections of PPD I would like to go to, referring to the First Lady detail or the transportation section. Since CAT had been a section of PPD since 1992, I pointed out the obvious: that I had recently come from CAT and my section time had therefore been satisfied. He agreed with my logic but said that shift leaders had no say-so or control as to when someone on their shift came or went. It was simply their job to run the shift and call the formations around POTUS. He continued that the immediate directive was coming from the boss of manpower on PPD who was a GS-15, practically the highest level of Federal civil service professionals. A bit perplexed I told my shift leader to assign me wherever I could be best utilized.

After Hilton Head I had the weekend off and I reported for work at the White House on Monday. It was a normal day, and I was standing post in the main mansion when the supervisor of manpower approached. He informed me that, as a graduate of the Secret Service Protective Operations Driving Course (PODC), I was being moved from the shift to the transportation section the following Monday. There I would become one of a select few who would drive the president of the United States in an armored limousine, drive the working shift in the follow-up vehicle, and plan presidential motorcades.

The mission was twofold: One, of course, was to safely drive the president from point A to point B. The other was to do whatever was necessary, using skills perfected in PODC, to move the president out of a kill zone should the motorcade be attacked. We who drove the president were anything but chauffeurs. We were all highly trained agents, shifting our protective skills from walking and running alongside the president to a new dimension that included safely transporting him in a vehicle specifically designed to increase the chances of his survival in an attack.

The limousines we drove were very large and very heavy. In spite of their 450-cubic-inch engines, there was lag time between depressing the accelerator and the moment the car began to move. Conversely, one had to begin braking well before the car was expected to stop. Some of the ballistic glass of that era caused visual distortion, and it was hard to judge distance, even for a driver with perfect depth perception. Because President Clinton seldom wore a seat belt, a driver had to constantly think ahead of the car and the situation in order to avoid disaster.

Valentine's Day 1994 was a miserably cold, rain-soaked day in

Washington. It was one of my first days in the transportation section, and I was assigned the 2:00 p.m. to 10:00 p.m. shift, along with agent Mike Wilson, who had several months' experience in the transportation section. There was nothing on POTUS's schedule for the night, and it looked like it would be a quiet evening of paperwork and making telephone calls. It did not turn out that way.

At around eight o'clock, the phone rang in the transportation section office. On the other end was the shift leader of the president's detail. He announced that POTUS wanted to go to Andrews Air Force Base and surprise Hillary, whose airplane was scheduled to arrive in two hours. I was to drive the limo.

This should have been an easy assignment, only I would be driving a car as big as a medium-size boat with POTUS as my passenger. Because Mike Wilson was the senior agent, he did the advance work of making the notifications to the support authorities, such as Metro Police; I went downstairs to where the POTUS's operational vehicles were kept and prepped the limo, making sure it was ready.

Mike had driven this particular car on a number of occasions and offered some welcome advice prior to our departure for the White House. When we arrived at the White House, Mike disappeared to meet with his police counterpart. I was alone in the dark, sitting in the belly of the beast, which smelled like it had just come from the car wash, as all protective vehicles do.

As I sat, I pondered the fact that I was about to drive the president of the United States at night in some of the worst rain imaginable in an off-the-record motorcade with no intersection control—all so he could surprise his wife on Valentine's Day. He obviously had a great deal of confidence in us all.

The sound and movement of the right rear door being opened broke my trance. In stepped the president's daughter, Chelsea, and the president, who both greeted me by saying, simply, "Hi." President Clinton was familiar with me from our runs over the past year and my working with him for the past six months. He actually knew most of his agents by name, having a nearly if not totally photographic memory for faces. "Good evening, Mr. President," I said, and nodded at Chelsea. The thought now occurred to me that on the way back from Andrews, should we actually make it that far without me rear-ending the lead car, the First Lady would also be in the backseat.

The right rear door closed, and the detail leader opened the right front door, greeting me with, "Hi, Dan," as he settled into his seat. This particular supervisor could be a bear and was prone to reaming out unsuspecting agents with no notice. I had somehow avoided his attention until now, but the possibility always existed. I felt, given the circumstances this evening, that it was not only possible but also quite probable.

Over my earpiece, which was connected to the Secret Service car radio, I heard the voice of the shift leader calling the shift into the follow-up vehicle directly behind us. The marked police lead car began to move, and the detail leader looked at me and said, "Let's go." Off we went into the abyss.

The first obstacle to overcome leaving the south grounds of the White House was a set of serpentine barriers. Even with practice, of which I had none, I viewed it as a virtual impossibility to avoid the damned things, but somehow I managed. The idea was to not jostle POTUS any more than necessary, although I was more concerned about not crashing the limo containing the president of the United States. We left behind the security and lights of the White House and headed off into the ink-black night.

Driving less than a car length behind the lead car, staring at its taillights in the rain while looking through what appeared to be a fishbowl with windshield wipers, took every ounce of concentration I had. In addition to visual concentration, I also had to listen and pay attention to my friend Mike Wilson in the lead car requesting lane changes to the follow-up. When Mike saw that a lane shift was needed, he would call out his request to the follow-up. Once I heard "clear" from the follow-up, I would automatically make the lane change without ever taking my eyes off the taillights of the lead. The limo driver had to have complete trust and confidence in the follow-up, and I did.

With no intersection control, we were moving with the flow of traffic, and it was tense. Along the way to Andrews Air Force Base, which was about a thirty-minute drive in this weather, we saw several accidents; the flashing lights of the emergency vehicles on site refracted off the prisms of raindrops on the fishbowl, making things even more distorted. I had to keep my eyes constantly moving, from the taillights of the lead car to my panel (I had the rheostat turned almost all the way down) and then back up to avoid fixation on the lights and spatial disorientation. It was essential to keep this scan going, or you could easily crash into the lead, which was continually speeding up and slowing down with the traffic. After about thirty very exciting minutes, we arrived at Andrews and proceeded down an access road through a gate manned by an agent and out onto the tarmac to stage and await the C-9 aircraft bearing Hillary Rodham Clinton, First Lady of the United States.

The four of us sat in the limo—POTUS, Chelsea, the detail leader, and I. POTUS and the detail leader had a cordial conversation as we waited. POTUS had brought a bouquet of flowers for his wife and seemed happy and excited to surprise her. Ultimately, presidents are not much different from any other husband or father, I suppose.

Upon hearing on the radio that Hillary's aircraft had landed, we started our engines and prepared to move onto the tarmac. The blue-and-white Douglas C-9 with "United States of America" emblazoned on the fuselage taxied into the bright lights set up to illuminate the arrival for the media, who were standing by in their press pen.

The air force pilot in command applied brakes to this gorgeous product of the American aviation industry until he brought the aircraft to a full stop. We then moved the cars up to the plane, with the president's door on the right side facing the aircraft. As the door of the plane opened, a motorized ladder was placed alongside. Hillary emerged and descended the steps, waving to the press, not yet realizing the cars waiting for her were the president's. When she was about halfway down the steps, President Clinton and Chelsea exited the limo. POTUS stood there holding the flowers with a happy look on his face, much like any other husband hoping to pleasantly surprise his wife. It was apparent that Hillary was very surprised indeed at his appearance. The media snapped away. It all looked very nice: *Leave It to Beaver*, POTUS-style.

Mrs. Clinton and the president entered the rear of the limo with Chelsea between them, the door was closed, and we departed for the White House. Along the way, Hillary told her husband how surprised she was to see him. I tuned it out and concentrated on my sole purpose in life, which was delivering them all safely back to the White House.

The last major hurdle was guiding the limo around the barriers in reverse order and getting the massive vehicle back onto the south grounds of the White House without launching the president, the First Lady, and Chelsea into the front seat.

We arrived in front of the entrance to the South Portico, where I brought the beast to a stop so gently that the feeling of transitioning from motion to a stop was scarcely noticeable. The detail leader whispered, "Thanks, Dan," and exited the car, then opened the right rear door for the family to exit. I heard the president and Chelsea saying "thank you," as I discovered was always their habit. I replied, "My pleasure," and breathed a silent but heavy sigh of relief. With the leader of the free world and his family once again safely home, Mike and I cranked up the limo and follow-up and headed back to the garage. But first the limo had to be refueled.

If a limo's fuel supply fell to three quarters, it was standard procedure to get the tank topped off, as the possibility always existed that an emergency could occur during a motorcade that might force you to drive POTUS for a couple hundred miles. These armored limos only got about eight to ten miles a gallon as it was and were nearly fuel-critical from the time you pulled away from the pump. One could almost watch the fuel gauge drop when the accelerator was depressed.

When in Washington, we normally frequented a station on Fourteenth Street in a socioeconomically deprived area not far from where we stored the cars. It was always a show when we arrived. Everyone in this particular neighborhood knew who we were and who rode in the car we were fueling. So there I would be, standing at the self-service pump putting 93-octane gas into the president's limo at a station in the hood.

The local residents liked coming out to watch. I would not have chosen this particular station to fuel my family Volvo, but we always felt safe there. Everyone knew we were armed, undoubtedly dangerous, and would have no qualms about protecting the limo by any means necessary. In this case, I pumped fuel into the president's limo while Mike stood by and provided cover.

In those days, the president's operational cars were kept in a nondescript building located at 1310 L Street in Washington. The Service no longer leases space there, but for over forty years 1310 L Street was almost synonymous with the Secret Service. The address was where the office of training was located and where fully 80 percent of all academic training for agents, Uniformed Division officers, and administrative personnel took place.

There were also operational sections there, such as PPD transportation section and many others. Prior to the opening of FLETC in 1975, all Secret Service agents received most of their training there. There were a lot of ghosts there for those of us who had been in and out of the place for so long. When the Service abandoned the building, in 2000, it left all of its furniture behind for the General Services Administration to claim and use again. This furniture, however, looked nothing like the modern modular junk seen in the government offices of today. Some of the executive desks were oak monstrosities weighing hundreds of pounds, with gorgeous executive leather highback chairs and matching credenzas and bookcases—all sitting in empty offices formerly occupied by some of the most high-ranking men and women of the service. It was really beautiful stuff that had seen it all, including the JFK assassination, the Watergate fiasco, and the entire Vietnam War

The area outside the building was a normal-looking pedestrian zone during the daylight hours, with citizens going about their business. After nightfall, it became hooker alley. There were so many working girls standing around in front of the building, you sometimes had to wade through them to get inside the place.

When we would depart with the spare limo, limo, and follow-up, the girls would practically cheer as we passed on our way to the White House. They constantly asked if they could have a ride in POTUS's limo. We all said no to that one, as we valued our jobs far too much.

When new presidents enter the White House, they tend to travel little for the first few months. The early part of a new administration is spent learning the routine. Once things settle down a bit, new presidents discover the marvel known as Air Force One and begin to use it extensively, each seeming to feel the need to make more trips, foreign and domestic, than his predecessor. When Bill Clinton finally discovered he could travel anywhere he wished, anytime he wished, he began to exercise that privilege with total abandon.

During the early days of the Clinton administration, we did not have nearly enough agents to cover his almost impossible travel schedule. Most agents on PPD began working up to thirty days at a time, as I did, with no days off for months on end—in my case, for over five years, counting the Bush presidency. I finally began to feel the excitement of protecting the president lapse into a job performed at times while so fatigued I scarcely knew what day it was.

I had reported to CAT in 1989 with the mission of protecting the president of the United States. While presidential protection was one of the most important jobs in the world and I still received a great deal of satisfaction from the work, by 1994 it had begun to weigh on me more than anytime in the past. I had now reached the point at which, although still on my game, I was not as sharp as I had once been. This phenomenon is common among almost all PPD agents after about four years of continuous protection, and I was one year beyond that.

One morning I was home enjoying a rare day off when the phone rang. It was the operations agent directing me to leave immediately for a trip. I was to do the advance. For the first time in my career, I verbally removed the head of the messenger delivering bad news. After apologizing for my out-of-line comment, I hung up the phone and began to pack for yet another trip. I had been the operations agent in CAT for several months during my four years there and knew all too well the discomfort of calling an agent at home to inform him that he was going to have to leave unexpectedly for a trip.

In the life of a PPD agent, the interruption of one's routine to go on a trip is normal, and up until now, I would have merely acknowledged the instructions and begun preparing for the trip. This case was different, however, since in addition to being mentally and physically exhausted from five years of such phone calls, I had just returned from a long and particularly stressful foreign trip. My frustration was enhanced by the fact that this new excursion, which would cost the taxpayer a fortune, amounted to nothing more than a recreational trip for the president, in my opinion.

Everyone on the detail during this period was becoming irritable from the nonstop travel, and many were requesting transfer. Resentment was beginning to build toward management, who did not appear to feel that more people were needed on the detail and seemed unconcerned about the unrealistic work schedules. The Secret Service mantra of "just make it work" was wearing thin.

I had now been protecting presidents on a full-time basis for over five years. As my tour was coming to an end in the transportation section, thus signaling my return to the working shift, I asked for a transfer from PPD to the Atlanta field office. I had done everything I came to Washington to do and it was time to turn the page.

The following week I was told by the new ASAIC of manpower that I was being transferred, per my wishes, but to the Washington field office (WFO) rather than to the Atlanta office. I was to replace my wife, who was an agent there, and she would replace me on PPD. The Washington field office was the last place I wanted to be assigned, other than perhaps New York, and I preferred to remain on PPD until I could make the move to Atlanta.

I went home and telephoned the new SAIC of PPD to let him know that until I could secure a spot in Atlanta, I wanted to remain on PPD. He informed me that it was too late and that my transfer was final. I told him that if I had to leave the detail and could not move to Atlanta, I would prefer another assignment besides WFO. He said he could have me assigned to the training division as an instructor, and after some additional discussion, I accepted the assignment.

After being an agent for eleven years, I realized that, while protecting the president was still the most important thing the Secret Service did, it was not the only important thing. I also realized that presidential protection was something a person could not do indefinitely; even the strongest had their limits. There were many other vital jobs to be performed, and training the new group of young people who wished to become agents was critically important. I had enjoyed my years on CAT and PPD more than I can accurately describe, and although I was not going to Atlanta, I was going to a worthwhile assignment where I could perhaps pass on to others some of the knowledge I had acquired.

I checked out of PPD on a Friday, and my wife replaced me, checking in the following Monday. At the same time that she was putting her things in my old cubby inside White House Command Post W-16, I was checking into the Special Agent Training Education Division (SATED), then located at 1310 L Street. Over the following nine years, I would have a part in training over two thousand new Secret Service agents.

MY FAVORITE PRESIDENT?

Since retirement many, many people—friends, family, and the media—have asked, "Of the three presidents you protected while assigned to PPD, which was your favorite?" In this context they mean, Which one did you personally like the best?

The three presidents I directly protected—George Herbert Walker Bush, William Jefferson Clinton, and George W. Bush—had their own personalities, likes, dislikes, and habits. Professionally speaking, all were easy to work with, and each seemed to understand and appreciate the role of the Secret Service in their lives. Each was well aware that, without the Secret Service, neither they nor their families would live very long, and that we were prepared to give up our own lives if necessary to save theirs. I also believe they grasped the fact that most of us had families and that we spent a great deal of time away from those families on their behalf.

There have been stories written by others that portrayed various presidents as difficult to deal with and claimed that some were disliked by the Secret Service. This was not true during my career. In reality, most agents will never become close enough to presidents or their families to either like or dislike them, at least on a personal level.

The presidents I protected had both good and bad days at the office and in their personal lives. Even on their worst days, they did not treat any agent that I knew with anything other than courtesy and respect. If the president or a member of his family happened to walk by an agent without speaking or failed to thank one of us for our service, we did not feel insulted or offended. Quite to the contrary, we experienced no feelings at all one way or the other. Doing whatever was necessary to ensure their safety was our job, and we expected no thanks, although the three presidents and their families I protected frequently offered it. We were not there to be their best friends or their social equals; we were there to safeguard their lives and were thanked twice a month by the Secret Service when we received our pay.

I liked and admired each president I protected for his individual strengths. I recognized that each was a human being doing the best he could under extremely difficult circumstances. As one who has been privy to the inside operations of three administrations, I can say with certainty that being president of the United States is the most difficult job in the world.

★ CHAPTER 13 ★

Shaping the Next Generation

In the late fall of 1994, I left PPD and reported to the Special Agent Training Education Division, where I would become an instructor teaching special agent students, as well as offering refresher training for the major protective details.

SATED was divided into two basic sections: protection and investigations. Most of the investigations syllabus was taught by agents who had not served on PPD, while the protection syllabus was reserved for those who had either PPD or Vice Presidential Protective Division (VPPD) experience. Due to my having served on PPD, including the shift, CAT, and the transportation section, I was, logically, assigned to teach protection.

Most of the agents arriving in training from protection were, like me, very tired men and women who needed some downtime. Most of us had zero experience teaching anything, and there was no way to know if a person could or could not teach until it was too late to change things. As a result, many relied heavily on slides and PowerPoint and were boring instructors. That also described me at first.

Until I attended a one-week course known as Essentials of Instruction (EOI), I was not allowed to actually teach a class, so I spent the first few weeks monitoring my colleagues from the back of the room. Due to the small number of students it was a great chance for me to watch each class being taught and participate in several practical exercises. All was calm, and training was a good place to get back my health and sanity, both weakened by five years and three months of first-line protection. While I was initially bored due to being unable to teach, that soon changed. The Service had just received authorization to increase its agent population from two thousand to twenty-five hundred and we were about to go deep for the foreseeable future.

I finally attended EOI and was certified as a senior course instructor. I never understood the title because there was no such thing as a junior instructor. During EOI we were taught the basics of how to plan a class, teach a class, and attempt to keep students interested. Educational developmental specialists (EDSs) taught the course. An EDS was a non-agent—a professional educator who trained agents to teach as well as developing lesson plans and course curriculums. Most had been a part of the training division for years and were good at their work. It was no small task to take an agent with no teaching experience and turn him into an instructor in one week. The idea was that agents were experts in all areas related to being an agent and that they merely had to be trained in how to bring forth that experience and impart it to others.

The important thing about being an instructor was to be able to teach from a position of having done, in real time, what you were teaching. I found that the new students would automatically give you the attention and respect you deserved as long as you had actually performed the subject matter in a genuine setting. These were not children but adults, and many of them had vast law enforcement and military experience. If an instructor did not have the experience and was merely reading from the slides, the students picked up on it. I could always pull a story out of my pocket about driving President Clinton, the follow-up, or working a rope line or an advance. Most of the men wanted to know about CAT and how to get there.

I would begin each class by relating that they needed to listen to me for two reasons: One was that I only taught what they actually needed to know, with no bullshit thrown in, and the other was that they needed to pay attention or they would fail the course and be sent home. Today I teach college courses and still use the same introduction. Students have always seemed to appreciate this direct approach and usually respond accordingly.

Each class of twenty-four students was assigned two course coordinators, who stayed with the group for the entire ten weeks that the students were in Washington for the Special Agent Training Course. They also monitored the class while it was in the Federal Law Enforcement Training Center for ten weeks. These two instructors served as mentors, role models, and proctors. As with most things, it was a job that a person could put as much or as little into as he wanted. While some instructors took it seriously, others considered it a bother because it was so time-consuming.

The classes were only given to instructors who had been in training for some time. Although I wanted a class, I knew it would be a while before I had seniority. While waiting my turn at being a course coordinator, I taught all courses in the protection syllabus, but due to the numbers of classes arriving and too few instructors, I was to receive my own class much earlier than anticipated. I became a course coordinator in the spring of 1995, just a few months after my arrival in training.

My observation of other classes and their coordinators was that the classes were too laid-back, with almost no discipline. Instead of leaders and mentors, many coordinators wanted to be buddies with their charges. The result was loss of respect and discipline and a general feeling of disorganization. These students were sloppy, ill-kempt, and acted as if they had already graduated. My most notable observation was that there was no leadership by example during the mandatory PT sessions. That is, the coordinators were sitting in the office while the physical training instructors handled the class. Some coordinators canceled PT when the weather wasn't perfect.

All of this was about to change with my class. I would alienate some, but I won the respect of most students, and I also gained reluctant admiration from some colleagues, who came to realize that this was the way training should be conducted.

Contrary to the accusations and reminders of many in the training division, I knew I was in the Secret Service and not the Marine Corps—painfully aware, on most days. Few days went by without some wizard training genius saying, "Dan, this is not the Marine Corps." I would thank them for their keen insight, acknowledge that I was aware of this fact, and drive on. I believed, however, that many of the same principles used to produce marine officers could also be used to produce outstanding Secret Service agents. There was an acceptable median between the world of extreme military training and the Secret Service, and I would find it.

The principles and traits of leadership were the same no matter if one was talking about the marines, IBM, or the Secret Service. It was all pretty simple and straightforward, as far as I was concerned. As the Marine Corps does, I believed in initially breaking down the students physically and taking away as much of their personality and ego as possible. Then at the proper moment, begin to rebuild them into a cohesive, disciplined unit, with the end result being one damned fine group of special agents capable of handling anything that came their way. I saw it as my responsibility to the Service, the students, and the American taxpayer, who had a right to expect the best from the Secret Service.

I was assigned to be the course coordinator for SATC 138, which would arrive in the late spring of 1995. My assistant coordinator, John Mrha, was a good friend and my former assistant team leader in CAT when I was new there. Like me, he was a military veteran, and unlike me, he was a great athlete.

We were a good team and agreed that our class would be made intelligent, disciplined, and fit, and that we would run the class along the same lines as police academies and the military. We also were in firm agreement that we would not require our class to participate in any physical training unless we were leading them.

SATC 138

The new class that would become SATC 138 arrived in June 1995 for the Special Agent Introductory Training Course (SAITC). SAITC was a one-week course of instruction offering the new class initial indoctrination and weapons familiarization prior to their ten-week stay at FLETC. They would then return to Washington, where John and I would have them for ten weeks prior to graduation.

SAITC was a chance for John and me to introduce ourselves to our new class and lay out what we expected of them. It was also a chance for us to conduct some preliminary evaluations of what we had to work with. I made it very clear what we expected: total effort at all times no matter what the endeavor was. Anything less than 100 percent in any area would be rewarded with a ticket home. We also promised to lead them in all physical activities.

At the end of the first day, John and I gave the fitness test to our new class. The test consisted of pull-ups, sit-ups, push-ups, flexibility, and the 1.5-mile run. Most did okay, and at the end of the run, they thought they were finished. Not! After the run, John and I formed up the class and ran them another several miles.

At the end of the additional running, we informed the class to expect the unexpected, that this was the easiest day they would have, and that if anyone did not think he or she could hack it, now would be a good time to be man or woman enough to say so and go home. There were no takers

Following one week of SAITC, the class left for FLETC, where they would undergo the criminal investigators training program (CITP). They probably thought they had seen the last of us for a while.

John and I flew down to Brunswick, Georgia, one day to surprise them, let them know we were always close at hand, check on their welfare, make sure FLETC was not unfairly harassing any of them, and take them for an impromptu fitness session.

While at FLETC, Secret Service students are under the control of FLETC, not the Secret Service, so upon arriving John and I had to make contact with the FLETC fitness coordinator who was responsible for the class our students were in. John and I found him having a smoke outside the PT building before class. John and I informed him who we were and told him that we intended to take the Secret Service part of his class for a freelance session. We did not really ask if it would be okay; we just said we were going to do it. He was hesitant as he smoked his cigarette, but we prevailed.

After his class of forty-eight, including our twenty-four Secret Service students, formed up, John and I appeared and took the Secret Service students for a "tour of the complex." We began the run at approximately 3:30 p.m. At 4:30, we were still going.

After over one hour of running in 90-degree heat, we stopped at the main fitness building to allow the class a water break. John and I abstained from drinking any water. They were proud that they had run a solid hour without stopping. Many, never having run that far, had not believed they could. There was only one problem: To everyone's disbelief, the run was not over.

The class returned to the parking lot from the comfort of the air-conditioned fitness building and the cold-water dispenser and formed up. We spoke to the class briefly about the importance of mental hardness and told them that the body could take a hell of a lot more than most thought. We then informed them that now that we were warmed up, we could begin the PT session. You could hear the panic erupt from most of them. I invited anyone who did not want to continue the session to pack for the trip home. All elected to continue.

We did not run much longer. The second session was really an attitude check to see if anyone would balk or quit. No one did, but an incident did occur that today remains the topic of humorous discussion anytime I have the honor of talking to a former member of 138.

We had gone about ten more minutes after the water break when a student began to moan and cry. I asked the distressed young man what the problem was. He shouted back at me, "I am tired and it hurts!" That was, as you might imagine, not the correct response.

Actually any response other than "nothing is wrong" would have been incorrect. I informed him and the rest of the class that we would practice being tired for a little while longer, until the young man stopped his disgusting display of emotion and began to act like an agent.

Concerned that we might be on the verge of permanently damaging someone, John and I returned the class to the parking lot, where we gave them another water break, with John and I once again abstaining. Upon returning to formation, we told them that we were going for yet another run and offered again that anyone not wishing to continue could quit the program now. This was a critical moment, because we knew that they were as physically done as we dared make them without putting people in the hospital. The class stared at us with the blank looks of prison camp survivors, but none would quit. Satisfied that we had a pretty decent group, we dismissed the class with no further running, much to their delight and relief.

John and I handed out no compliments that day, however. We let the class know that their job had been to run until John and I decided the run was over, and that no one was going to thank them for doing their job.

It was on this day that the class began to show signs of pulling together as a team and take pride in the fact that together they had survived what many would have not. They also began to form a bond that can only be formed when a group is subjected to common hardship. That had been the purpose of this brutal session. It was not that we liked to run for miles in the heat; we wanted to build confidence and a team.

The exercise also proved to the class that John and I were true to our word and would always lead them, and that whatever we made them do physically we would always join them in. And for the moment, John and I gave them something to dislike (the two of us), which made them an even tighter group.

A few weeks later, 138 returned from FLETC to begin their ten weeks of special agent training in Washington and Beltsville. John and I greeted them upon their return with another sixty-minute run around the complex. This session included running up and down the stairs of the hundred-foot rappelling tower until someone became physically ill.

This became a class joke and also the indicator of when we had run the tower enough times. After a few trips to the tower, the class caught on that we would stop running the tower after someone lost lunch. At that point, they decided ahead of time who it would be for each run, and the student would gag himself or herself, thereby reducing the number of trips up the tower. It was all good fun, and the class had a great time with it.

While it may sound strange to some, this type of training helps build camaraderie and aids in the development of dark humor, which is essential to people in dangerous professions. It is the part of training that teaches a person that, while being concerned with the welfare of others is important, laughter at misfortune and hardship while continuing onward can partially relieve the pain and stress of the situation.

We reminded the class for the first week of SATC that the pain could stop at any time just by saying, "I quit." It was apparent at this point no one was going to quit and that the class was now really ready mentally and physically to begin their training to be Secret Service agents.

The class would travel by van from their hotel in Georgetown to 1310 L Street, where the students would proceed to their classroom on the tenth floor. There was of course an elevator, the same one I had been deposited in twelve years earlier handcuffed with my shorts to my knees, but for our students as well as John and me it did not exist for the ten weeks of their training. We required them to run up the ten flights of stairs with all their gear. John and I would be waiting for them there—to make sure they were all accounted for. Then we briefed them on the running route of the day. These stairs were also effective tools for addressing bad or forgetful behavior.

If, for example, a male student neglected to shave in the morning, he would be running those ten flights of stairs until I was satisfied that his attention to grooming standards set by me were remembered.

While it was clear to the students that John and I were in charge and were not there to be their best buddies, the feeling began to develop that we were all in this adventure together, student and coordinator alike, not unlike Marine Corps officers and their men. We were leading this class, not managing it, and the difference was apparent. This class began to enjoy the reputation of being the most physically fit and academically bright class anyone could remember. They were also the most respectful of authority, sincerely addressing all staff as "sir" or "ma'am." In short, they proved to be by far the best class ever to have done the training. It was not magic but quite simple: Lead by example, set the example, demand accountability, accept no excuses for anything, and people will rise to the occasion. It was really nothing more than leadership 101. I learned it in the marines and John had learned in the army, but it seemed a mystery to many.

We began each day with a six o'clock morning run down to the Washington Mall, the Capitol, the Lincoln Memorial, and back, which took about one hour. The sight of the sun rising over the Capitol and the monuments was always moving, and the students seemed to enjoy it. At least they never complained, but then again, complaining was not allowed.

Since John and I lived about thirty miles from downtown Washington, we had to get up earlier than the class, and we did not leave until the class had departed for the day. The class knew this, and leadership by example stopped any complaining before it started, at least from the class. Complaining from other instructors was a different story.

Some instructors complained to John and me that our class was having trouble staying awake during their lectures; they wanted us to ease up and give the students more rest. I told these instructors that if their classes were interesting, the students would not have a problem staying awake. Some complained to management about it, but, much to our surprise, management backed us up. It was a sign that at least some of the boys on mahogany row were starting to buy into the program. Many, however, were still watching in quiet disapproval.

John and I were purposely putting the class into sleep deprivation, because Secret Service agents are usually sleep-deprived, whether it is on protection or in the field. We were training them to become familiar with fatigue, to overcome it mentally and physically, and then to drive on with the mission.

In the real world, an agent could not tell the president of the United States he was tired and needed some rest. He could not say to him that it was too hot or too cold to run. John and I told our class that we had run with President Clinton in 100-degree weather and in close to 0-degree weather and that there was a purpose to everything we were subjecting them to.

It was now November. On many morning runs the temperature was below freezing in Washington and the sun was an hour from rising. One morning it snowed but we ran anyway, and if a run was planned it was never canceled for any reason.

In spite of our demanding approach, John and I still kept a close watch on the class for signs of injuries. We knew when to back off and give the class a little more rest at times, as needed. When we saw the students were reaching the end of their rope we would give them a Friday off from PT so that they could rest up for three days. If they had done exceptionally well in a certain area we would reward them with a day off from formal PT or allow them to do whatever they wanted during PT time. Without handing out awards or saying, "Good job, good job," we were rewarding good behavior in our own way, and it was working. The class was beginning to buy into the fact that in the world of the Secret Service everyone did not get a trophy just for showing up. They were learning that the true reward for hard work was the satisfaction of having done a good job, not from someone patting you on the back.

The class was doing well in all areas, especially fitness, but we were beginning to bore them and ourselves to death with standard workouts. It was time to raise the bar.

THE OBSTACLE COURSE

During the 1980s and until 1997, when the James J. Rowley Training Center built its own obstacle course, part of CAT training involved running the obstacle course at Fort Meade, Maryland, located about ten miles north of the JJRTC. This ugly assembly of concrete and pipe was built sometime during World War II. It was several hundred yards long but seemed to go on forever and was laid out in the shape of a horseshoe. Although it was not a part of the SATC syllabus, John and I decided it would be a great morale booster for 138 as well as a hell of a good workout. It had nearly killed me during CAT school in 1988, while John sometimes ran it just for fun. After obtaining permission to conduct the obstacle course training from the ASAIC of training, a former marine and recipient of the Silver Star and Purple Heart, both awarded for service in Vietnam, we proceeded to Fort Meade and the awaiting obstacle course.

On a cool November afternoon in 1995, with the leaves on the trees bordering the Baltimore–Washington Parkway showing their brilliant colors of red and gold, John and I took 138 to Fort Meade. We began by explaining to the class the purpose of this training. We emphasized that, in addition to fitness, there was a job-related, practical reason for it. As criminal investigators in field offices, agents might very well find themselves in a foot chase with a criminal suspect, and failure to apprehend a suspect due to lack of fitness or the inability to negotiate a wall or fence was unacceptable. John and I then ran the course together as a team, demonstrating the best, most efficient way to negotiate each obstacle. Then it was the students' turn.

We started them off two at a time and directed them to finish the course with their partner. After surviving the ordeal, we then sent them through again, this time individually. Some did well, and others looked, as we pointed out, like monkeys trying to mate with a football, but the exercise was a huge success. So much so, in fact, that our boss directed that all future classes undergo the Fort Meade obstacle course.

The problem with this order was that, other than John and me, few instructors would subject themselves to being checked out on the course. Many felt it beneath them to get dirty with a class, and many were afraid to try because of the risk of being embarrassed in front of a class if they could not negotiate an obstacle. This, in spite of never-ending offers by John and me to show each instructor all the tricks necessary in order to complete each obstacle.

As time went on, I took all SATC classes to the course and did demonstrations. Some course directors watched in sheepish discomfort, arms folded. Fatigue makes cowards of us all, and yet due to the true believers—among them John, Mike Carbone, Scott Marble, Todd Bagby, and a few others—no class failed to be introduced to the obstacle course during my tenure as an instructor.

As the week before graduation approached, it was apparent that all were going to make it. Our students would soon be agents. After our last official PT session together—as always, we ran the tower until someone threw up—I informed the class that they could now call us by our first names. There was stone silence as each student looked shocked and suspicious. Even after this offer, no one wanted to be the first to call us Dan and John. Training was almost over, and the Secret Service was about to receive a great group of new agents.

SATC 138 finally graduated, and at the ceremony, our students resembled recruiting poster models in their suits, with lean, chiseled faces created from the loss of any unnecessary fat. Awards were presented to students who had distinguished themselves in the areas of academics, firearms, and fitness. When the scores were read for the top fitness award, there was an audible response from the audience. All were amazed at the fitness level of this individual and of the class as a whole.

After the ceremony, our charges shook our hands and thanked us for the training, leadership, and guidance we had provided. John and I told them that no thanks were needed and that our final order to them was to be the best agents in Service history. I am proud to say that now, nineteen years later, most in the class lived up to that order.

The experience of being a course coordinator had been very rewarding but had practically consumed me, and I was ready to begin teaching the standard curriculum once more. After everyone had left the area following graduation, my boss took me aside and said that he wanted me to run another class, SATC 141, which would be arriving in the next few months. He said that he wanted 141 run exactly the same as 138 and expected another stellar class. I replied, "Yes, sir." It would be done.

That afternoon, I had a few beers at home and fell into a deep sleep, totally satisfied that I had done the best job possible with the class. I never wanted another class. My goal had been to take one class, give it everything I had to produce the best possible group, then go back to my regular teaching in the Protection Squad. It was not to be so, as no good deed goes unpunished.

SATC 141

In that all classes were selected from the same basic applicant pool, I had always believed that most classes were more or less the same, with the only difference in class quality and performance being the people who led them. I firmly believed undisciplined coordinators produced undisciplined classes, while disciplined, demanding coordinators produced the best classes. While I continued to believe that throughout my years as an instructor, I came to realize that each class had its own distinct personality. I was also about to learn that, due to the new and yet unknown political sensitivity of Secret Service management at the headquarters level, it would only take one student's groundless complaints of alleged mistreatment to damage careers and diminish most of what had been accomplished in changing the philosophy of training over the past year.

Unbeknownst to everyone outside of headquarters, the Service, like the US government, was in the process of moving into a new chapter of gender-related sensitivity. In this chapter, a vacuum was created between the old Service, where few complaints from any student would have been entertained, and the new Service, where one student making hollow accusations would result in an immediate rush to judgment against those accused. I was pulled into that vacuum along with my new assistant, Scott, and then we were both dropped into the perfect storm of the emerging political correctness mania of the 1990s, which, with the infamous navy Tailhook scandal, had overtaken the entire government.

Close to 141's graduation, one of our female students failed to return to training on time after irresponsibly missing a flight from a city she had visited over the weekend. She was disciplined accordingly, as any other student would have been. The punishment did not sit well with her, and she made the accusation against Scott and me that we had singled her out for punishment and had imposed unreasonable physical fitness demands on her and the rest of the class.

While our student had merely alleged that she had been singled out for punishment, everyone who was aware of the situation assumed, because a female had lodged the complaint, that we were being accused of sexual harassment, which was never the case. The fact she had failed to return to training on time or at the earliest possible time after missing her flight seemed to go selectively unnoticed. It was also apparent that she either sensed or was informed of the change in the social paradigm of the Service as she continued to perfect her role of victim.

Although initially too naïve to realize it, she was a victim, but not of any action by my assistant or me. In the end, she was a victim of her own frivolous complaint, after which certain high-level managers used her as a pawn to demonstrate the new world order of the Secret Service.

INSPECTION

As a result of our student's accusations, the assistant director of training ordered a formal investigation of the verbal allegations against Scott and me. After numerous interviews conducted by agents from the Office of Inspection with all students in the class, as well as with Scott and me, the investigation finally ended with the submission of a final report to the assistant director of training. The official findings of the six-month inquisition by the Office of Inspection were: "No evidence was found to support the accusations of individual harassment or the imposing of excessive physical training." The matter was closed. Meanwhile, SATC 141, complete with the student who had complained, graduated and moved on to their careers.

This entire six-month debacle was much to do over nothing but was significant in that it marked the beginning of a new era for the Secret Service in terms of political correctness and acquiescing to certain groups that complained of being singled out when going along with the program like everyone else did not suit them.

During the course of the inspection and subsequent to 141's graduation, I continued to teach physical training and the protection syllabus to all SATC classes. As always, I did my best to prepare these young men and women to survive in a world that is not politically correct, and where there is no gender norming. In that world, there are those who would kill a person because that person carries a badge, and none of these predators care if the carrier of the badge is a man or a woman. I remained determined that no student under my instruction and leadership would ever meet such a fate because I had not done enough to prepare them.

AMERICA AT WAR

On Tuesday, September 11, 2001, I was teaching a practical exercise when an instructor told me that an airliner had flown into the World Trade Center. I had a bad feeling that it was not an accident, although no details were yet available. While assigned to New York and living in New Jersey, I had on many occasions rented a plane and flown up the Hudson corridor past the Trade Center. There was no way even a half-assed pilot could accidentally fly into either tower in the perfect weather experienced on the East Coast that day.

As I continued with my instruction, another instructor brought news that another plane had flown into the other tower of the Trade Center. Now I knew that we were at war, and I correctly guessed that Osama bin Laden and al-Qaeda were behind it.

America was catching hell on 9/11, and I knew that training division was about to catch hell as a result. The automatic response of the US government in times of violent crisis is to hire more people. The Secret Service began hiring agents in record numbers to fill the newly authorized slots. It meant that we would be training classes six days per week for the foreseeable future.

I realized that due to the numbers involved and the shortage of instructors, I would probably be made course coordinator yet again, although I hoped it would be otherwise. In the time since the inspection, per my request I had not been given another class as a coordinator, and I was quite satisfied to teach the normal syllabus.

One day in 2002, my concern was realized. I returned from taking a class for a run to find my boss waiting for me in my office. He told me that, due to the number of classes under way, it was necessary for me to be assigned as the course coordinator for the next class coming aboard. He also informed me that the son of the director of the United States Secret Service would be a member of this group. Training legacies was nothing new, and most were decent students, although this would be the first son of a director to pass through the academy. Fortunately, things turned out well.

With nineteen years on the job and one year to go before I would be eligible for retirement, I proceeded to run this class with the usual reckless abandon, director's son and all, with no concern about anything other than not killing a student.

There were some weak sisters in the class, and I don't mean women. Several of the men had to be repeatedly counseled due to their lack of motivation and effort. The admission of many students with motivational issues was a result of mistakes in the hiring process that were prevalent for about one year following 9/11. Any time a small, elite organization expands too quickly, standards falter and quality can suffer.

In one particularly horrid case, an SAIC was summoned from his office to headquarters for the purpose of explaining in person to the director why he had hired a particularly problematic agent trainee. Following this appearance, the assistant director of training asked me for a retention or dismissal recommendation regarding this student. I recommended dismissal, explaining that this was the worst student I had seen during my eight years as an instructor and producing irrefutable documentation in support of my claim. The student graduated nonetheless.

From 2002 to 2003, about one third of the students in each class—eight students—were fireballs who loved training and would develop into fine agents; one third were average Caspar Milquetoast types; and one third essentially had no business being in armed law enforcement at any level. As the other instructors and I did our best to straighten out some of these mistakes, my boss said to me one day, "Dan, you can't make chicken salad out of chicken shit." I continued to don my magician hat and try, as I was being paid twice a month. Fortunately, due to strong leadership from the director, by the time I left training in 2003 this unfortunate episode in Secret Service history had largely reversed itself.

The class that would be my last as a course director finished their training with no major incidents other than the usual complaints from some about the perceived severity of the fitness program. After their graduation, I went about my regular instructor duties and forgot about them. With eight years in training and nearly two thousand students under or over the bridge, it was easy to forget a class the minute they walked out the door, and all students were beginning to look exactly the same to me.

HAVE SOME BALLS, AGENT

The indispensable trait of courage is a large part of the Secret Service culture and has been demonstrated by its agents countless times over the years. Many of these examples of courage are well documented, such as Tim McCarthy taking a bullet meant for President Reagan, while many others that occur each day will never be known by anyone outside the Secret Service.

Agents need high levels of both moral and physical courage to face the numerous challenges and dangers that arise over the course of a career. The necessity for this trait in an agent was perhaps summed up best one day at a Secret Service agent graduation in very black-and-white terms.

The keynote speaker at Secret Service agent graduations is usually a retired agent. Many of them still live in the DC area, which makes them easily available. The speeches are usually too long, hard to follow, too much about the accomplishments of the speaker, and boring. The students, soon to be real agents, have been in training for six months and care little for the keynote speaker's words. They really just want to go home for some well-earned R & R.

I attended many such graduations as an instructor. There was one I will never forget; nor will anyone else who attended. The guest speaker was Red Auerbach, now deceased, former coaching great of the Boston Celtics.

As we instructors sat in our seats looking forward to hearing this icon of American sports speak, we could not help but notice the aromatic scent of a cigar somewhere in the area. Of course, this was not possible, as there was no smoking allowed any longer in government buildings. To light any tobacco product in a government facility could result in death by lecture from some offended, by-the-book type who could recite the regulation forbidding such conduct.

When Red took the podium, it became clear where the aroma was coming from. Red stood there halfway slumping over the podium and microphone, ready to begin his remarks with a lit cigar. He began his speech with some amusing anecdotes about coaching the Celtics and kept his audience highly entertained. As he began to wind down, he suddenly became dead serious, paused for effect, stared at the graduates, and proclaimed in a low bulldog voice to all the newly commissioned agents that throughout their careers they should above all else "have some balls." For those not familiar with the phrase, it is a metaphor for having physical and moral courage—the willingness to face danger and stand for what one believes, no matter the price.

As I listened, I thought that no truer words had ever been spoken. As Red gave this, the most memorable speech I ever heard at an agent graduation, he smoked that giant, wonderfully offensive cigar, blue smoke drifting up past the No Smoking signs in the auditorium. He cared nothing about offending anyone or about some sign proclaiming "No Smoking." He had been the invited guest speaker and was going to do and say what he damn well pleased. Red Auerbach came from a time in American history when men drank whiskey and beer with their giant hamburgers and steaks, not daiquiris and white wine with their salads. They also smoked cigars in public places if they wished.

One could almost hear the politically correct upper management from headquarters squirming in their seats on the stage. They worried that, with so many civilians in attendance, the Service image would suffer. As far as I know, no one complained, and Red Auerbach's words were a good reminder to all in attendance to get back to the basics. To Red, balls mattered, and all should have them, especially in a profession such as the Secret Service. "Have some balls"; damned good advice, Coach. By the way, no one had the balls to tell or ask Red to put out the cigar.

PROMOTION AND RETURN TO PPD

One uneventful day in 2002, I was teaching a class when my boss walked into the classroom and announced that I had been promoted to GS-14, assistant to the special agent in charge (ATSAIC) in the training division. He then walked out and left me with my class. While I was happy to finally be promoted, I had not really been expecting this good news and was a bit in shock over the matter for the remainder of the class, as well as the remainder of the day.

The following afternoon I received a telephone call from the director of the Secret Service, Brian Stafford, congratulating me on the promotion. I appreciated his taking the time to call and thanked him for his personal involvement in the matter. Afterward I sat at my desk and, in spite of the No Smoking signs, opened a window and lit a cigar.

Eligible for retirement in one more year, I decided to try to get back to PPD for one last operational assignment. I had spent far too long as an instructor and, like an actor too long in one role, had been typecast. Many believed that I had been away from the operational side of the house for so long that teaching was all I was capable of. Perhaps they were right, but I wanted the chance to find out.

In August 2003, I requested and was selected for reassignment back to PPD as one of two supervisors in charge of CAT. After a nine-year absence, I was returning to protection.

★ CHAPTER 14 ★

Retirement and the CIA

November 2003 found me reporting back to PPD and CAT after a prolonged absence from operational life. For the past nine years, I had taught others how to protect presidents and get and stay in shape. Now I was back helping to accomplish the most important mission in the Secret Service, which, of course, is protecting the president of the United States.

On my first day back, a supervisors' meeting was held by the SAIC of PPD. As I walked into the meeting, I was greeted by legions of old friends now in charge of the detail. In spite of having less hair on their heads and more lines on their faces, they were all in great shape. All but two or three were former CAT agents. It was, in my opinion, a Who's Who of the best agents in protection and in the Secret Service. These were the men I had started the job with in 1983, traveled the world with, and respected greatly. Most were former CAT teammates and PPD shift mates, and I could see that the Secret Service was selecting the best people to protect the president. It was great to be back.

A few months after arriving back on PPD, however, I was presented with a major decision that would have long-range effects on both my family and me. One year earlier, in 2003, when I had reached the twenty-year mark of service, thus making me eligible for retirement, I began looking for a post–Secret Service retirement position within the federal government. Obtaining a new job within the government can be a long process, and although I was not yet ready to retire, it was time to at least begin looking.

While many retired Secret Service agents were heading over to the newly formed Transportation Security Administration (TSA) or the Treasury Department, these jobs held no interest for me. Friends had gone to these agencies and reported that the jobs presented no real challenge or interest but merely represented a paycheck and another retirement. I could not accept the idea of going to work just for the money and easy lifestyle most retirement jobs represented. Always the hopeless idealist, I was only happy if what I was doing seemed relevant to me. What now seemed relevant to me was contributing directly to the war effort.

Since 9/11 I had wanted to contribute in an active manner to the war on terror. Age was a problem, however, or so I first thought. Even though I was in good physical condition, by 2001 I was still forty-six, which is a bit long in the tooth for any meaningful fieldwork. Still with the goal in mind of somehow playing a direct part in the war, my thoughts turned to America's main intelligence service, the Central Intelligence Agency, which from all reports was very active in this war that had been forced upon us. This is where I felt I could best serve.

While the CIA was in many respects a gigantic bureaucracy like all other government agencies, its heritage, which dates back to World War II, is quite colorful. Thankfully, some of that color can still be seen in many of its young operatives.

Prior to World War II the United States had no intelligence service per se. The FBI and the Department of State were the only entities that handled such matters as espionage and counterespionage, and then only as needed. With the onset of the war, these agencies had no presence in areas held by the Axis powers, and it was decided that America needed an agency devoted fully to the espionage business.

In order to fill this void, President Franklin Delano Roosevelt in 1942 authorized the creation of the Office of Strategic Services

(OSS), the predecessor to the CIA. He appointed his old Colombia law school friend William "Wild Bill" Donovan as its director. Donovan had been a recipient of the Congressional Medal of Honor in World War I and had been a successful attorney prior to his appointment as head of OSS. In his role as director of the OSS, Donovan answered only to the president and had his full backing, which insulated the OSS from the prying eyes of J. Edgar Hoover, who had lobbied aggressively yet unsuccessfully for the FBI to be given complete autonomy over both foreign and domestic counterespionage.

The OSS would operate largely under military cover, with its agents wearing the uniforms of the three branches of service. In this way they could operate without attracting notice from the many enemy agents who operated in and around US military facilities.

The first American spies would train in the United States at what is now Congressional Country Club, in Potomac, Maryland, as well as areas in Thurmont, Maryland, and overseas in Great Britain. Today, few realize that the now pristine fairways of Congressional Country Club, which each year hosts the PGA, were once occupied by firing ranges, obstacle courses, demolitions training areas, and parachute drop zones. The clubhouse, bar, and dining areas were converted into barracks, and one wing was devoted to creating devices and hardware for the graduates to employ against Hitler and Hirohito's forces.

The main function of the OSS was to train, equip, and aid resistance fighters in enemy-occupied territories throughout Europe and the Pacific. In addition they worked to disrupt Axis communications, assassinated top-level enemy officers, and hindered the enemy's ability to make war in general. Agents of the OSS were a bold lot, known for their intelligence, bravery, and willingness to take risks. Many were Ivy League–educated, hailing from universities such as Harvard, Yale, and Princeton. This was due in part to the fact that Donovan was a Harvard man and selected his people from that pool. In turn, they selected their subordinates from those institutions.

Only the best and brightest were selected for the OSS, and one did not apply to become a member. The OSS targeted and selected the people it wanted, and they were a very eclectic lot. The great actor Sterling Hayden, for example, was recruited by the OSS straight from Marine OCS in Quantico. His OSS exploits included parachuting into occupied Croatia where he blew up German railroads and aided the Resistance in its covert war against the Germans. Had he been caught, he would have been tortured and then executed by the Gestapo, a fate that was met by many brave members of the OSS, men and women alike.

The OSS, while colorful, was very short-lived. After World War II had ended, and following the death of President Roosevelt, the new president, Harry Truman, was not comfortable having a spy agency within his government and abolished the OSS. Wild Bill and his OSS agents were thanked for their service, presented with OSS lapel pins, and sent home. For decades they discussed their exploits with no one except each other.

With the onset of the cold war against America's old ally the Soviet Union, Truman reconsidered the need for a spy agency. In his view, it would be much like the OSS, yet more sophisticated—this was a cold, not a shooting, war with Russia. In order to keep it from becoming a shooting war, intelligence gathering was needed in order to better prepare America against any aggression by the Soviets.

On July 26, 1947, President Truman, seated in his presidential aircraft at National Airport, signed the National Security Act of 1947. Part of this act created the Central Intelligence Agency, which was the object of my new career ambitions.

CIA, THE APPLICATION PROCESS

In my home office on a Saturday evening in 2003, scanning the CIA website, I completed my initial online application. Hours later I sent the application hurtling through cyberspace. I felt it would probably never be seen by a human. Joining the CIA seemed so improbable that I felt that my life's last career ambition would remain just a wish.

Because the CIA is part of the intelligence service, not the law enforcement community, earning a slot there would require going through a full application process, not simply retiring from the Secret Service on a Friday and beginning at TSA or at the Department of the Treasury on a Monday. It would essentially require starting over in almost every respect.

While I was forty-eight years old when I applied, I was to discover that the CIA had no age limits for practically any job. Their only concern was attracting the best people for a myriad of jobs. As long as a person was physically qualified for the position he was were applying for, all was good to go. 9/11 had occurred two years earlier, and the CIA was in full hiring mode, attracting a large group of people with wide and varied backgrounds. In appearance the applicants ran the gamut from biker to Wall Street executive. Each applicant had his or her own set of skills, talents, and specialties.

Three weeks after I submitted my application, I had a message on my answering machine from a CIA recruiting officer. The following week I was sitting in a nondescript CIA building somewhere in Virginia taking a written examination designed to determine my suitability to serve as an intelligence officer. Over the course of the next several months I underwent a battery of additional testing, as well as interviews, psychological examinations, and a very brutal full-scope polygraph exam.

The CIA vetting process for new employees and the continuing security process maintained throughout an officer's career are both crucial to keeping the CIA safe from the penetration of hostile intelligence services. For this and other reasons the process is by necessity long and painful. If one is to join the agency, however, it is a pain that must be endured.

From the first day on the job, almost everyone at the CIA has access to classified information that, if compromised, could damage national security. Anyone who has access to the CIA information systems, which is almost everyone in the CIA, has the keys to the kingdom, as the office of security constantly points out. Even the cleaning crews who vacuum CIA office spaces have to undergo a thorough background investigation, as they are frequently in close proximity to classified information and privy to conversations that should not be repeated.

Of all the steps in the vetting process, the polygraph is the most daunting for almost everyone. The CIA is concerned that people with questionable motives will try to infiltrate the agency. One set of questions asked during the polygraph deals with counterespionage issues. The other set deals with lifestyle issues. The CIA believes so completely in the polygraph that all officers are subject to random retesting over their entire careers.

The fact that I was an active Secret Service agent assigned to the president was of no help in getting me through the process. I was treated as a twenty-two-year-old straight out of college would have been.

On a Monday morning in March 2004, I sat in the polygraph waiting room. I had every expectation that this obstacle would be cleared in short order. For the past twenty-one years I had held the highest security clearance the government could bestow, with updates conducted every five years. Other than enjoying good scotch and an occasional cigar, my life was pretty boring, and my only concern was simply getting the test over with. The young examiner who was assigned my case, around twenty-three years old and fresh from polygraph school, had other ideas.

I suppose we got off on the wrong foot when the young man approached me in the waiting room, introduced himself, and—asked by what name I wished to be addressed. Apparently he was asking about my first name—was it to be Danny or Dan? He looked so much like my former SATC students that I told him that people his age normally addressed me as Mr. Emmett. He took this as an affront to his authority and position and was noticeably unhappy; from this point on, things went largely downhill.

For the next four hours this young man ran several series of polygraph tests. He raked me over the coals, practically accusing me of being a Russian spy attempting to infiltrate the CIA. He was obviously going by the polygraph school playbook, hoping to obtain some reportable information. At one point he rolled his chair inside my personal space and asked, "Are you Dan, or are you Ivan?" I laughed out loud, convinced he could not possibly be serious, but the look on his reddening young face told me that he was. He then asked what I would do if I failed the test and did not get into the CIA. I answered that I would remain at the Secret Service as a supervisor in the Presidential Protective Division. A bit flustered over this response, he terminated the session and directed me to return the following day for more polygraph adventures.

In all likelihood he had been given my case because it should have been easy and provided good experience, as my adult history was a matter of record he had in front of him. I already held a Top Secret clearance. He was probably instructed that I be given no special consideration because of my position at the Secret Service. Overcompensating, he came on as a hardass. I understood the necessity for a thorough vetting, although it was difficult to take seriously someone twenty-six years my junior who was only five years old when I entered the Secret Service and not yet born when I became a marine officer. I felt that I at least rated an experienced examiner closer to my own age, of which the CIA had many. Nonetheless, I tried to straighten up and do my best to respect the position he held. I reminded myself that I was starting over in this new world of intelligence and had to play the game if I wanted in.

After two aspirin and a beer at home, I contemplated not going back for the second session, but my wife talked me into returning. "What do you have to lose?" she asked. She was correct, as usual, and the next morning I returned to the polygraph arena ready for another marathon round of questions designed to lay bare a man's soul and determine his trustworthiness to safeguard classified information, something I had already been doing for over twenty-five years, including my Marine Corps time.

The calamity of the first session had apparently persuaded the CIA that I needed a more experienced polygraph officer to handle my case. The following day I had a different examiner, in his midthirties, mature, and, as it turned out, a former street cop. I was in and out of the seat in less than an hour. I passed the polygraph from hell with no issues and had proven myself to be worthy of trust and confidence, at least on paper.

The same day I took the second polygraph, I was given a thorough mental exam by an agency psychiatrist whose job it was to determine if I was sane, or perhaps insane enough to be a CIA officer. The doctor was at least in his late eighties. He had been with the agency in one capacity or another since 1947. Among other legendary stories attributed to him, he had once played a round of golf with some other US personnel while serving in an overseas station. That is not unusual. What is unusual was the doctor's method of arriving at the golf course. As the remainder of his foursome awaited their colleague, they heard the drone of an airplane engine over the golf course. They looked up to see the doctor—dressed in golfing attire, complete with the proper shoes, and with golf clubs packed in a weapons container—slowly descending under a parachute canopy. At the time of my application, the agency still had a number of geriatric legends within its ranks some still from the days of the OSS during World War II. One had to love a culture that rewarded risk taking and coloring outside of the lines.

One afternoon as I was sitting in my office, the phone rang. It was the CIA recruiting officer who had been assigned my case months ago, calling to inform me that I had been accepted for the position. It was déjà vu all over again. He informed me that I had up to six months to either accept or decline the appointment. I thanked him and sat at my desk with much the same feeling of anticipation I'd had two decades earlier when the SAIC of Atlanta had called to inform me I had been accepted into the Secret Service.

Now, with twenty-one years as a Secret Service agent, and a career poised for further advancement, I had a very big decision to make. Stay with the Secret Service and enjoy the soft life of management, taking long lunches while underlings did much of the work? Or retire and move to the CIA, where I would be back in the game, albeit as the world's oldest rookie?

A large part of the decision was what my wife thought about the venture. After all, my leaving the Secret Service for the CIA was not only a career risk but a real one as well. The first American killed in Afghanistan was a CIA officer and former Marine Corps captain, Johnny Spann. As a husband and father I was not certain I had the right to take this kind of risk so late in life. Donnelle's attitude, however, was the same as it had always been throughout my career. If becoming a part of the CIA was what I wanted, she would support it. If she was against it, she never said so.

In my den late that evening, attired in a Marine Corps sweatshirt and PT shorts, the last fire of the season burned as I sat with my thoughts and, yes, a twelve-year-old scotch. Staring into the flames, I played back my entire career, from when I first dreamed of becoming a Secret Service agent through to the present. I thought also of the fact that a Secret Service agent was what I had been for the past twenty-one years, and that once I pulled the pin to retire, there was no putting it back in. I thought about these and many other things until very late, then went to bed. Sleep did not come easily, but when morning arrived, the feeling from the night before was still very firmly in place. As illogical as it all seemed, I was going to retire from the Secret Service as soon as practical and join the CIA.

Through the years, I had heard others say that when it is time to retire, an agent just knows. I always wondered if it were true, and on this morning in late April 2004, as the old sages said it would be, I just knew. With the winds of social change inside the Secret Service now raging at full force and this wonderful, almost too-good-to-be-true offer from the CIA on the table, it was time to move on.

I had acquired a skill set some at the Central Intelligence Agency thought could be useful, and the possibility of contributing even a small part to the war effort as a CIA officer was very enticing. My feeling was that I had been given certain talents and aptitude for this type of work, honed into skills with a sharp edge by the marines and the Secret Service. If America could now use my skills against our enemies, I felt it was my duty to step up. I called my recruiter and accepted the position.

The toughest part of retiring was breaking the news to the SAIC of PPD, a good friend of many years. As I walked across the waxed tiles of the Old Executive Office Building through the corridors of the PPD offices on my way to meet with him, I saw many old colleagues. I was a bit sad that this was perhaps one of the last times I would see some of them. (In fact, I would see more than one former Secret Service agent in the halls of CIA headquarters. It seems that I was not the only Secret Service agent who wanted to play a more active role in the war.)

I came to a door with a sign reading SAIC/PPD and walked into the waiting area, where the boss immediately greeted me. I sat down and told him of my plans to retire and where I was going. Although this was against CIA regulations regarding cover, I felt I owed him an explanation as to my departure, and I knew he could be trusted to keep the secret. He said he was sorry to see me retire, asked if I was sure this was what I wanted to do, and added that he and the Service would miss me. Although he outranked me by two grades I always considered him a friend first and a boss second. He was understanding and wished me luck at the CIA. We shook hands and I went home.

I later learned that my SAIC did in fact reveal the secret of my new employer. He informed President George W. Bush, who was reportedly happy to hear that upon retirement, I was going to the CIA.

I was initially brought into the CIA under cover. This meant that

I was to tell virtually no one of my CIA affiliation. Being brought into the CIA under cover made leaving the Secret Service a bit touchy—when an agent announces retirement, all wish to know where he is going.

Living under CIA cover is a very slippery endeavor until one gets the hang of it. CIA officers under cover must be able to discuss with a degree of convincing detail a job that in some instances does not actually exist. The CIA in effect takes very honest people of the highest integrity and by necessity teaches them in certain cases to lie and lie convincingly. Living under CIA cover is the most prevalent example of this, and a great deal of a CIA officer's life is a lie. For the past twenty-five years I had been able to truthfully answer what I did for a living; now I had to lie to friends, family, and strangers alike.

Just prior to my retirement I was having lunch one day with another agent and his wife, who wanted to know what my new job was going to be. I had yet to receive a detailed cover briefing from the CIA and stumbled through her questions as best I could but probably did not fool her. I later learned that she had worked with her share of spooks, and, while she had been able to guess where I was headed, out of professional courtesy she had dropped her line of questioning.

LAST NIGHT AT THE WHITE HOUSE

My final two weeks in the Secret Service were spent as an acting shift leader on the midnight shift at the White House and on weekends at the presidential retreat at Camp David, Maryland. It was the perfect way to bring my Secret Service career to a close.

I had first entered the White House as a CAT agent fifteen years earlier. Now I was responsible for the safety of the president and First Lady, who slept upstairs in the second-floor residence. Should anything, from an attack on the White House to a medical emergency, occur between the hours of 10:00 p.m. and 6:00 a.m., I would be responsible for directing the immediate action of getting the president and First Lady to safety.

On the last night of my operational existence as a Secret Service agent, after things had settled into their usual midnight routine, I walked about the quiet dimness of the mansion, thinking about all the years I had spent there. In many ways, the White House felt like home. During various periods of my career I had spent more time there than at home. I thought of the three presidents I had directly protected there, my years in CAT, the working shift, running with and driving President Clinton, and the Christmas parties Donnelle and I had attended. And I thought of all the friends I had made there, some no longer living. When the morning came, it was difficult to imagine that I was walking out for the last time. I had known it would be difficult.

THE OLD EBBITT AND SAYING GOOD-BYE

My retirement party was held a few days later at the Old Ebbitt Grill. The Old Ebbitt was the place to drink and have dinner in Washington if you were anywhere close to the White House. It was and still is a classy place, where most of the men wear suits and the women dresses, with pantsuits being in noticeably short supply. It features a long mahogany bar in the main area. My party was held to the left, in a newer addition. The Old Ebbitt in a sense was as much a part of my career in Washington as the White House had been. It had been the unofficial HQ and gathering place for all Washington-area agents, especially those on PPD.

I took a cab to the party and back home because I knew that there would be a lot of old friends to see and the night would run late. There were, and it did. There were at least a hundred or so agents in attendance, most of whom had passed in and out of my life and career for the past twenty-one years. Others I did not know; they were there simply because Secret Service retirement parties were usually a lot of fun.

There were many former students I had helped train. They seemed to enjoy telling stories of how hard the fitness sessions were and how much they had appreciated what they had been subjected to. With each story told and each drink knocked back, the run distances increased by miles and the heat increased or decreased to levels unendurable by humans, until I had trouble recognizing truth from fantasy.

At about 2:00 a.m., as I moved through the almost empty bar en route to the front door, my cab, and my departure from the Secret Service, I thought of all the fun I'd had there over the years. I walked past the bar stool where I had pre-proposed to my wife fourteen years earlier and the table my parents and I had shared one evening for dinner. I took one last look around the place and walked out to my waiting ride.

The following day, in a small ceremony at the Old Executive Office Building, with my wife and son present, I officially retired from the Secret Service. It was May 16, 2004, twenty-one years to the day I took the oath of office in Charlotte, North Carolina. Many of my friends from PPD were there, as well as some young agents from CAT whom I had supervised and helped train. My good friend John Mrha was also there and presented each award and plaque due an agent at retirement. The main retirement plaque, which is the Secret Service equivalent of a gold watch, reads, in part:

> Your 21 years of dedication and contributions to the missions and goals of the United States Secret Service are hereby gratefully acknowledged and affirm you to be worthy of trust and confidence.

My family and I left the proceedings and walked to our car outside the White House, parked on West Executive Avenue. The Secret Service was behind me, and new adventures and challenges awaited me at the CIA. It was an exciting time.

TAKING THE OATH AT THE CIA

On June 27, 2004, I stood in a room just off the food court at CIA headquarters in Langley with a group of new officers. A deputy director told us to raise our right hand, and we repeated back to him the oath of office. It was the same oath I had taken in 1977, to become a Marine Corps officer, and in 1983, to become a Secret Service agent.

During my first twenty months at the CIA, most of my time was spent assigned to the Directorate of Operations, first within the Counterintelligence Center (CIC) helping to ferret out those whose motives for being in the CIA and gaining entrance into the CIA were questionable, then in the Counterterrorism Center (CTC), where my work was exclusively focused on the current war.

A CIA education in the ungentlemanly art of espionage is unique, and while I would never become a master spy, I had during those twenty months learned at minimum the rudiments of espionage, tradecraft, CIA weaponry, and how to incapacitate the enemy in any number of ways.

In the Secret Service, a law enforcement agency, agents are trained in what are known as defensive tactics, or the use of minimum force in order to subdue an opponent. At the CIA, an intelligence service, we were trained in offensive tactics, or how to kill quickly and efficiently using any object at our disposal. We learned that there were no rules of engagement or concerns over legal issues to be faced for killing an enemy in a foreign land. After twenty-one years of being held accountable to the escalation of force model that has cost more than one law enforcement officer his life, this new doctrine of kill rather than subdue was quite refreshing.

OFF TO WAR

After training and learning some of the basics of the business, I was made a deputy branch chief in the Counterterrorism Center. The group in which I worked was very active in the war, and I knew it was only a matter of time now before I would be, as the agency likes to say, "on the tip of the spear." This is what I had asked for.

One quiet morning in Potomac, Maryland, after Donnelle had gone to her job at Secret Service headquarters and I had taken our son to day care, I watched as all of my neighbors went about their lives doing whatever people who are not in the Secret Service or CIA do. Sitting in the same chair I had sat in when making the decision to retire from the Secret Service and join the CIA, I listened as the grandfather clock ticked away in the hall. I wrote a letter to my wife and son and became so engrossed in my thoughts that I failed to notice a taxi as it pulled into my driveway. The sound of the taxi driver blowing his horn snapped me back into the moment. I walked over to the front door, picked up my bag, and headed for Afghanistan and the CIA's war there.

AFGHANISTAN 2006
The Tip of the Spear

Uncomfortably cold on a dreary morning in late winter of 2006, I stood drinking the world's worst coffee with two other members of the CIA's National Clandestine Service, formerly the Directorate of Operations, at a CIA base camp somewhere in the seemingly infinite expanse of Afghanistan.

As a deputy branch chief, I was in Afghanistan to aid in the mission of my branch while assessing its needs. In order to do this I needed to get dirty and function as a working member of the group. Not long in country and still suffering from the mother of all jet lags (we were 9.5 hours later than Washington, DC, time), I shook the cobwebs out of my head and prepared myself for what was not exactly your normal day at the office.

While temperatures were beginning to rise as spring approached in this primitive land, there was still much snow on the mountain peaks surrounding the northeastern part of the country that divided

Afghanistan and Pakistan. The mountains were of a rugged beauty not found in other parts of the world, and I marveled at their majestic appearance while continuing to prepare for the day's work. With their jagged peaks covered in snow and shaped by the winds of millions of years, their beauty was deceiving. These ancient mountains were the home of the Taliban and al-Qaeda. All throughout this terrain existed countless caves and sites seemingly custom-made for these terrorists, enabling them to ambush their enemies by small-arms fire, rocket attack, and the IED. Then they would disappear back into the holes from where they had emerged.

Today, the enemy was America and the CIA, which had aided some of these same people in their war against the Soviets from 1979 until 1989. But that was then and this was now. It was the classic example of how certain events can cause old friends to become enemies and how loyalties fade with time. Twenty-five years earlier in their struggle against the Soviets, these people would have welcomed my colleagues and me. Now they would cut our heads off with rusty blades if given the chance.

This was not the gentleman's CIA of cocktail parties, martinis, and tuxedos. In that CIA, if an officer was apprehended by the opposition he would simply be sent back to the United States. Afghanistan was the workingman's CIA, where dirt, cold, heat, bad food, and never-ending danger were the officer's constant companions. If captured, my group and I would be tortured, used for propaganda purposes, and slaughtered like goats and sheep.

After dumping the last of my cold coffee on the cold Afghan ground, I slipped into body armor and shrugged on the load-bearing vest containing spare ammunition magazines, knife, radios, and a Glock pistol. Joints and ligaments made stiff from decades of abuse in the name of physical fitness protested as I pulled on my equipment in the cold Near East dawn. Making sure I also had my all-important Snickers bars in one pouch, I placed my Colt M4 carbine—loaded with a magazine of thirty rounds, stock collapsed and muzzle down—between the driver's seat and the right front seat of our lightly armored SUV. Climbing into the driver's seat, I started the engine of the vehicle that would carry our group on a potentially lethal assignment. A silent prayer and off we went into the breach.

After leaving the relative safety of our covert base and avoiding the many mortar impact craters on the road, some dating back to the Soviet occupation, I scanned the terrain for potential ambush sites as well as performing the prescribed procedures for the detection of anyone who might have followed us from base. This was important, as the only thing keeping us alive on a daily basis was the secrecy of our location. I recalled our group chief's final predeployment mission briefing, delivered in the safety of CIA headquarters.

Prior to departing for the most dangerous country in the world, we had been reminded that our primary mission was not to seek out the enemy for a fight but to gather intelligence that would prevent another 9/11. We were further reminded that our secondary mission was to capture or kill any top-level members of al-Qaeda should the proper set of circumstances present themselves. During the time of its existence, our group was very successful in those stated missions both primary and secondary.

As the boss was walking out of the briefing, he looked back over his right shoulder and said, "One final thing, never get caught by this enemy." Having seen video and still photos of others who had been captured, I thought it was excellent advice.

Al-Qaeda had of late begun to use the age-old tactic of placing spurious checkpoints along routes traveled by Americans and their allies in the region. Once a vehicle had stopped, it was then either lit up with automatic weapons fire or the occupants abducted and later executed. While legitimate members of the Afghan security forces manned some of the area checkpoints, there was no way to tell if certain checkpoints were a trap. Consequently we never stopped at any checkpoint unless it was clearly manned by Americans or UN forces.

A few hours later, with our mission of the day complete and

darkness falling, we began the trip back to base. It was never advisable to be driving the back roads of Afghanistan even in the daytime, much less after sunset, so we were in a hurry. As always, we were also careful to note if we were being followed. As we rounded a curve we saw an upcoming checkpoint less than a hundred yards away; it was definitely not manned by Americans.

As I began to accelerate the SUV, I quickly assessed whether it would be best to drive straight through the threat or risk hitting a mine by going off road to avoid the possible ambush. The area to both the left and right of the checkpoint dropped off into a drainage ditch, which made the decision for me. We were going through. As I continued to accelerate toward the flimsy temporary barricade, an Afghan in battle dress uniform with a Kalashnikov rifle slung across his chest squared off at the checkpoint and held up one hand like a traffic cop. I had made my decision as to our course of action; he now had one to make. His decision would be whether to live or die on this late afternoon in Afghanistan.

Back at base that evening I considered the events of the day, our mission for the next day, and my current situation. Meanwhile, back in Washington at the CAT office, a close friend I had recommended as my replacement was sitting in my old comfortable chair signing paperwork and watching the war on Fox News. I was reminded of the old saying: Be careful what you wish for, you just might get it.

★

Epilogue

By the time of my retirement from the Secret Service in 2004, twenty years had passed since that day in November 1984 when I stood alone in President Kennedy's house in Hyannis Port contemplating his cuff links. Many great things had happened in my life and career during those two decades: I had fulfilled my childhood dream of protecting not one but three presidents and had the unexpected good fortune of having found the perfect wife. I am constantly reminded that I was phenomenally lucky to have been a Secret Service agent.

I attained my career goals through a determination to succeed hardwired into my DNA at birth and a work ethic instilled by my parents and welded into place by the Marine Corps. Any disappointments over career goals not accomplished were erased by a feeling of gratefulness by those that did come to pass. By taking the road less traveled, I had eliminated the need for regret.

At the age of forty-nine I was given the opportunity to be a part of the CIA. Alongside some of the most intelligent and courageous men and women to be found anywhere in the world, I was able to contribute in a small way to keeping America safe from terrorist attack.

As I now enjoy retirement from government service and the many blessings of freedom this still great country has to offer, I often think of the Secret Service agents and CIA officers I served with both at home and half a world away. Some have been regrettably lost in the fight, while many are still poised on the tip of the spear. Godspeed, my brothers and sisters in arms.

REGRETS AND WISHES

Almost everyone has some regrets at the end of a long career or in the autumn of his or her years. Some question career decisions or lament the fact that more promotions did not come their way. Others perhaps wish that they had chosen a different course altogether. I have only one wish regarding my choice of career and the experiences that came as part and parcel of it. I wish I could do it all again.

★ APPENDIX 1 ★

A Brief History of the Secret Service

The Secret Service is not the Federal Bureau of Investigation or the Central Intelligence Agency. Too many times to count, I have mentioned to someone at a social function that I worked for the Secret Service, only to have them introduce me to someone else as an FBI agent or a CIA agent.

The Federal Bureau of Investigation is the largest federal law enforcement agency in the United States and falls under the Department of Justice, tracing its modern history to the appointment of J. Edgar Hoover as director in 1924. The FBI has a very broad scope of investigative activities, far wider than that of the Secret Service, but the FBI has nothing to do with presidential protection and is in no way officially associated with the Secret Service. It is interesting to note that several Secret Service agents were tasked with helping start up the new FBI and that prior to Hoover, William J. Flynn, the director of the Secret Service, was appointed FBI director.

The Central Intelligence Agency is the premier intelligence service of the United States but has no authority to make arrests and no law enforcement function. Its primary duty is to gather intelligence in foreign countries and present that intelligence to the president so that he can make better-informed decisions regarding foreign policy. Like the FBI, it has no direct association with the Secret Service in terms of mission. When referring to an American employed by the CIA, it is incorrect to use the term "CIA agent." Americans who are members of the CIA are officers, not agents. CIA agents are citizens of other nations who spy against their own countries on behalf of the CIA; they are also called assets. They are also obviously traitors, and if they are caught spying for the CIA, they and their families can be tortured, executed, or imprisoned indefinitely, depending upon the country they come from. This is why the CIA so fiercely defends its sources and methods.

The Secret Service is an independent law enforcement agency with full power to make arrests. From its beginning in 1865 until 2002, it fell under the Department of the Treasury. After the attacks on 9/11 and a reorganization of American law enforcement, the Service was placed under the Department of Homeland Security, where it remains; it is unique among federal agencies in its dual mission of investigations and protection. The majority of people think of the Secret Service as the agency that protects the president of the United States. While this is certainly true, the Secret Service is also an investigative agency that helps protect the financial infrastructure of the United States.

Today all US paper currency is printed at the Bureau of Engraving and Printing, in Washington, DC. In 1865, at the conclusion of the Civil War, individual banks produced the country's paper currency, and much of the paper currency in circulation was counterfeit. It was determined that the creation of a federal agency to fight this plague was needed, and this agency was the United States Secret Service.

On April 14, 1865, the day he was assassinated, President Abraham Lincoln signed the bill that brought the Secret Service into existence, thereby creating the agency that would one day protect the president. Even if the Service had already existed, however, it would have done President Lincoln no good. The Service did not begin protecting presidents until thirty-seven years later, in 1901, after President McKinley was assassinated in Buffalo, New York.

The Secret Service was thus originally created for the purpose of combating counterfeiting. This mission of counterfeit suppression remains one of the Secret Service's main investigative missions today and is carried out by field offices that cover all fifty states and most of the world. In addition to counterfeit investigations, the Secret Service has the main federal jurisdiction over the statutes regarding credit card fraud and various types of financial crimes, as well as government check forgery. The Service also investigates threats against anyone it provides protection for, most notably the president of the United States.

When a person is hired as a new special agent in the Secret Service, he or she begins his or her career in a field office, which could be located anywhere in the United States. A new agent investigates the above-mentioned violations and does not serve on a permanent protective detail. While these investigations have little media appeal, they are extremely dangerous, and one can unexpectedly be killed.

After an agent serves approximately six years in a field office conducting investigations, he or she may then move on to a full-time protective assignment, such as the presidential detail. This time in the field is really an agent's tryout for protection. If an agent does not prove to be trustworthy, intelligent, proficient with weapons, and hardworking, it is unlikely he or she will ever see the Presidential Protective Division.

It is mandated by law that the following receive protection: the president of the United States and his immediate family, the vice president and his immediate family, the president-elect and vice president-elect and their immediate families, former presidents and their spouses as well as children under age twelve, major presidential candidates, visiting foreign heads of state in the United States on an official state visit, and anyone else the president so dictates. The Secret Service does not protect members of Congress or the Senate, as is widely believed. That task is performed by the US Capitol Police.

Only the president and vice president must accept Secret Service protection. All others mentioned may decline protection if they so desire, and many do, most notably foreign heads of state who do not want Secret Service agents around them.

Richard Nixon is the only former president to have refused protection. In 1985, eleven years after leaving office and feeling he no longer needed the Secret Service, he hired his own private security detail, saving the taxpayer millions of dollars.

Never confuse the Secret Service with any other government agency, and, please, never introduce a Secret Service agent to anyone as an employee of the FBI or CIA. You have been sufficiently educated.

★ APPENDIX 2 ★

Glossary of Terms and Acronyms

ASAIC: assistant special agent in charge
ATSAIC: assistant to the special agent in charge
CAT: Counter Assault Team
CP: command post
DSAIC: deputy special agent in charge
FLETC: Federal Law Enforcement Training Center
FLOTUS: First Lady of the United States
Hawkeye: call sign for CAT
Halfback: follow-up vehicle
JJRTC: James J. Rowley Training Center
NYFO: New York field office
POTUS: President of the United States
PPD: Presidential Protective Division
SAIC: special agent in charge
VPOTUS: Vice President of the United States

★

About the Author

From May 1983 until retirement in May 2004, Dan Emmett was a special agent in the United States Secret Service.

During those twenty-one years, some of his more high-profile assignments included the Presidential Protective Division (PPD) and the Counter Assault Team (CAT), where he provided direct protection worldwide for Presidents George Herbert Walker Bush, William Jefferson Clinton, and George W. Bush. Mr. Emmett's final assignment in the Secret Service was as assistant to the special agent in charge of the Presidential Protective Division.

Subsequent to retirement from the Secret Service, the author joined the Central Intelligence Agency, where he served six years both at home and in the war zone as an officer in the National Clandestine Service.

A former captain in the US Marine Corps, the author holds a BS degree in criminal justice from North Georgia College and a master of science degree in education from Troy University.

Now residing in the southeastern United States, he is an adjunct professor at two universities as well as a security consultant to both private corporations and the US government.

Index